QUALITATIVE RESEARCH IN EDUCATION

Research Methods in Education

Each book in this series maps the territory of a key research approach or topic in order to help readers progress from beginner to advanced researcher.

Each book aims to provide a definitive, market-leading overview and to present a blend of theory and practice with a critical edge. All titles in the series are written for Masters-level students anywhere and are intended to be useful to the many diverse constituencies interested in research on education and related areas.

Titles in the series:

Atkins and Wallace	*Qualitative Research in Education*
Hamilton and Corbett-Whittier	*Using Case Study in Education Research*
McAteer	*Action Research in Education*
Mills and Morton	*Ethnography in Education*

BERA
BRITISH EDUCATIONAL RESEARCH ASSOCIATION

QUALITATIVE RESEARCH IN EDUCATION

Liz Atkins and Susan Wallace

Los Angeles | London | New Delhi
Singapore | Washington DC

SAGE Publications Ltd
1 Oliver's Yard
55 City Road
London EC1Y 1SP

SAGE Publications Inc.
2455 Teller Road
Thousand Oaks, California 91320

SAGE Publications India Pvt Ltd
B 1/I 1 Mohan Cooperative Industrial Area
Mathura Road
New Delhi 110 044

SAGE Publications Asia-Pacific Pte Ltd
3 Church Street
#10-04 Samsung Hub
Singapore 049483

Editor: Marianne Lagrange
Assistant Editor: Kathryn Bromwich
Production Editor: Jeanette Graham
Assistant Production Editor: Nicola Marshall
Copyeditor: Carol Lucas
Proofreader: Isabel Kirkwood
Marketing Manager: Catherine Slinn
Cover design: Wendy Scott

Typeset by Dorwyn, Wells, Somerset
Printed and bound by CPI Group (UK) Ltd,
Croydon, CR0 4YY
Printed on paper from sustainable resources

**Library of Congress Control Number:
2011944978**

**British Library Cataloguing in Publication
data**

A catalogue record for this book is available
from the British Library

ISBN 978-1-4462-0806-9
ISBN 978-1-4462-0807-6 (pbk)

CONTENTS

ABOUT THE AUTHORS

Dr Liz Atkins is a lecturer and researcher in education at the University of Huddersfield. She originally trained as a psychiatric nurse, moving to education in 1992. Since then she has worked in schools, further education (FE) colleges, universities and as an LEA Advisor. She is an active member of the British Educational Research Association SIG Post-compulsory and Lifelong Learning, for which she was co-convenor 2007–10.

Liz's research is concerned with in/equalities in education; she has particular interests in the formation of learning identities among marginalised students and policy contextualisation of the FE sector. Her work in this area has been widely published and she has also produced a number of practitioner texts drawing on her teaching experience with students undertaking a broad range of education programmes including teacher training, MA, EdD and PhD.

Lydia Spenceley is the Coordinator for Teacher Education Programmes at Grantham College where she manages and contributes to a range of initial teacher education programmes. Her main areas of research interest are the development of teacher identity, special educational needs and visual research methodology. She has published papers on the development of identity, autoethnography, and the problems encountered by 'beginning' teachers in an FE setting. She has a broad experience in education and training, having previously worked in settings ranging from commercial training to prison education and most recently further and higher education.

Susan Wallace is Professor of Continuing Education at Nottingham Trent University, where much of her teaching involves supporting the professional development of teachers and other education professionals. She has two particular areas of research interest: the behaviour and motivation of 16- to 19-year-old learners in FE colleges; and the purposes and processes of mentoring in education.

Susan is the author of several books for teachers, including *Teaching, Tutoring and Training in the Lifelong Learning Sector* and *Getting the Buggers Motivated*, and is co-author of two recent books on mentoring, including *Dial M for Mentor: Reflections on Mentoring in Film, Television and Literature*. She has also taught for ten years in the further education sector, and has worked in a local authority advisory role for post-16 education.

ACKNOWLEDGEMENTS

We would like to thank friends and colleagues for sharing with us, and with our readers, the stories of how their research was disseminated. They are, in alphabetical order:

Joanne Cassar, University of Malta
Paul Drury, Nottingham Trent University
Helen Sage, Board of Education, Diocese of Blackburn
Caroline Tomlinson, Rushcliffe School, Nottingham
Jonathan Tummons, Teesside University.

In addition we would like to thank William Barry for his kind permission to quote from his PhD thesis in Chapter 7 and Jon Melville for his kind permission to quote from his MA research in Chapter 4.

INTRODUCTION

The theme of this book is the interdependence of teaching and research. It takes as its starting point the importance of practitioner research as a means of informing teachers' professional practice. We place considerable emphasis on the notion of the professional educator throughout the book, and in doing so interpret professionalism as a willingness on the part of the educator to explore and reflect on their work in a critical and systematic manner and to use this to inform their own practice and that of others. This is not a new concept: writing in 1975, Lawrence Stenhouse called for a research-based model of teaching, arguing that 'curriculum research and development ought to belong to the teacher' (Stenhouse, 1975 p. 142): he also asserted that 'it is not enough that teachers' work should be studied: they need to study it themselves' (p.143). This book aims to facilitate education professionals to do this, by developing their understanding of and skills in educational research. It has five main objectives, which are to:

- equip teachers, student-teachers and other education professionals with the skills and understanding necessary to carry out small-scale qualitative research;
- highlight and discuss some of the issues, debates and dilemmas specific to educational research;
- explore the application of a range of qualitative methods to practitioner research;
- encourage engagement with ethical issues arising from research in an educational context;
- build practitioner confidence and encourage the concept of the practitioner-researcher.

Throughout this book, you will find questions. Some of these will relate to the 'vignettes' or real-life illustrations we have used to provide you with opportunities to consider how you would respond if a similar issue arose in your own research. Other questions are posed in the narrative of the book. Like those relating to the vignettes, these are intended to get you thinking about some of the 'big issues' in qualitative research. There are, all too often, no right or wrong answers. However, there are two key imperatives in the conduct of your research. The first is that the study is rigorous, and the claims you make are grounded in data which arise from well constructed instruments. The second, more important still, is that your research is *ethical*. By this, we mean not only that you give consideration to potential ethical issues arising from the study, though this is obviously very important (see Chapter 2), but also that the research is conducted in a moral and reflexive manner so that, at all times, the research has integrity. The need to undertake research which is moral in both its execution and in its outcomes forms themes which recur in each of the chapters in this book, as does our belief that a critical and analytical exploration of policies and practices is a necessary part of what we mean by being a 'professional' in education. Chapter 2, which explores ethical issues in educational research, draws particular parallels between the values of the professional teacher and the values of the professional researcher, with particular reference to the ethic of respect for others.

Educational research for positive change

All educational research is grounded in values; these may be personal, institutional, professional or corporate but, none the less, those values will determine the focus of a study, the methodological approach and the conceptual framework used. We cannot, therefore, separate our values from our research, so the important thing is to acknowledge those values – which include our attitudes, principles, beliefs and prejudices, and which may be acknowledged by us or invisible to us – as influencing aspects of our research and to be self-reflexive in our research. Being self-reflexive simply means to reflect on those values and attitudes and consider how they might influence not only our own behaviour, but the other actors in the research as well as aspects such as methodology, data analysis and interpretation.

We have both spent many years reflecting on our educational values and integrating them into our work. Many of those values are shared, and include things such as a commitment to honesty and morality in our personal lives and professional practice, and a shared understanding of social justice. We believe that stating these values is critical, not only in taking a self-reflexive approach to our own research, but as a means of 'walking the walk' towards social justice, a concept that Griffiths (2003: 55) describes as a verb, emphasising that our personal and professional actions should reflect a commitment to social justice. Similarly, Walker (see Griffiths, 2003: 125) argues that 'only through doing justice can we make justice'. Such concepts form part of the theoretical frameworks we use in our own research, and influence the way we write and think about educational research.

Confusion and misconception

There are many common misconceptions and areas of confusion in educational research. In this book we have tried to address some of those that are most common among students undertaking educational research for the first time. This confusion can be around some of the terminology used – words such as epistemology, ontology and paradigm can be bewildering at first, as can some of the philosophical aspects of research and concepts such as theoretical framework. Language and concepts such as these are introduced in Chapter 1 and developed through subsequent chapters. There are, however, more fundamental areas which are commonly misunderstood. For example, many students confuse case study and action research. Therefore, in the chapters on Action Research and Case Study, as well as explaining what they *are* we have also explained what they are *not* and how they differ from one another. We have also tried to explain concepts that some students find challenging in more concrete terms to avoid confusion. For this reason, in Chapter 4 ('Writing a literature review') for example, we have explained what critical engagement with the literature means, and given examples of what it might look like.

Developing skills in critique and analysis

Each chapter of this book is introduced with a summary of its content and concludes with the key points of the chapter and suggested additional reading, including useful websites which can provide resources and guidance for undertaking different stages and approaches to educational research. Each chapter also contains a range of learning activities designed to support you to develop practical skills and theoretical understanding of educational research. The learning activities fall into two broad categories which we have called 'Building critical research skills' and 'Reflective activities'. The reflective activities are intended to support you to reflect on your own practice, and on situations which might occur in your own practice, as a means of developing reflexivity and deepening your understanding around some of the dilemmas which can be posed in qualitative research. The other group of activities, 'Building critical research skills', draws on real-life situations to help you develop your understanding of the more practical aspects of undertaking research, and of extending the academic skills which are necessary to achieve this.

There are few 'right' answers: the activities are about provoking thought, rather than 'testing' you in any way. Your response to the activities will differ according to where you are now on your academic and research journey. However, they can be used by students at all levels as a means of developing and enhancing the skills and understanding necessary to carry out effective and rigorous educational research.

The level of critique required will differ according to the level at which you are studying. Broadly speaking, if you are working at first degree (BA) level, you will be able to demonstrate familiarity with a field of knowledge and current developments in that field, at Master's level you will have understanding of, and the ability to critically discuss, current knowledge in a field, while at Doctoral level, you will be making claims for new knowledge and demonstrating its significance in your field.

Structure of the book

You will find broad similarities between all the chapters in this book: all include learning activities, for example, which are designed to develop your understanding of issues and concepts associated with educational research. However, there are also some differences. Some of the chapters are more practical, focusing on how to undertake a particular aspect of your study (for example, Chapter 5 gives guidance on interviewing) while others are slightly more theoretical. In general, those chapters concerned with different methodological approaches, such as those on case study and ethnography, tend to focus slightly more on the theoretical basis to the approach. The content of each chapter is summarised below: where they relate to and draw upon one another, we have signposted this. However, we have also tried to make them independent of one another so that if, for example, you were planning an action research study you could read Chapter 7 in isolation without the content being dependent on what has gone before.

Chapter 1, 'Research in education' introduces the concept of educational research, and explores its purposes and processes. Drawing on the theme of undertaking research as an aspect of a consistently ethical approach to professional practice in education, the chapter presents research as an integral and essential part of professional practice. It also introduces some of the terminology associated with educational research in an exploration of some of the key issues which need consideration during the planning of a research project. This is done through a discussion of issues such as questions of subjectivity and scope, positivist and interpretivist approaches, and the distinction between assumptions and hypotheses. By the end of this chapter you should be able to formulate your own answers to the questions: 'Why do we do educational research?' and, 'How do we articulate and pursue our research questions?' and be ready to move on to a consideration of other issues in educational research, such as understanding the concept of ethical research, and applying that understanding to your research. These issues are explored in Chapter 2, 'Ethical research in education'.

It has been argued that 'ethical considerations outweigh all others' (Wellington, 2000: 54), and the importance of undertaking research as just one aspect of a consistently ethical approach to professional practice in education forms a major theme of this book. Chapter 2 looks at the concept of ethics more specifically. It begins with a discussion of the ethical principles underpinning educational research, and introduces the reader to existing ethical guidelines, including national guidelines such as those provided by the British Educational Research Association (BERA, 2011) as well as those developed by their own institution. Drawing on a range of real-life scenarios, it encourages consideration of how such codes of practice might apply in a variety of contexts, and explores the reasons why ethical considerations are of particular importance to researchers in the field of education. These considerations have a particular resonance in Chapter 3, 'Insider research'. Many novice researchers undertake their study as an 'insider' – that is, within their own institution – and this chapter explores the tensions as well as the advantages associated with researching in this context. In doing this, it provides example scenarios and draws on real-life examples to illustrate key issues.

Chapter 3 discusses a wide range of issues related to insider research, including confidentiality, rights, responsibilities, impartiality and power relations, and the methodological and ethical considerations surrounding these. Many of these issues relate to tensions between, for example, being able to write up your study, drawing on key data, while maintaining the confidentiality of individuals or being able to publish your study while maintaining the integrity and confidentiality of the organisation, something which is particularly significant in the competitive educational markets of further and higher education.

Many of the issues which arise in insider research have parallels with those in ethnographic research; consequently this chapter draws on the content of Chapter 8, 'Ethnographic research', as well as on that of Chapter 2. It is also closely related to Chapter 6, 'Case study', as well as to Chapter 7, 'Action research', since many insider studies, particularly those undertaken by novice researchers, utilise either an action research or case study approach to their research project. Irrespective of the approach taken to your research, one of the things we emphasise throughout the book is the importance of having a clear theoretical framework and engaging critically with existing understandings in your field in the form of the literature review.

How to achieve this is explored in Chapter 4, 'Writing a literature review'. This chapter contextualises the literature review in terms of both the empirical study being undertaken and the theoretical framework in which a study is situated, and discusses its role in familiarising the researcher with current knowledge in their field of interest. Undertaking a literature review for the first time can be daunting, and we go on in this chapter to explore ways in which a literature search can be conducted, and, drawing on the questions most frequently raised by students, discuss how the literature should be analysed, synthesised and finally structured into a critical review. The chapter includes guidance on referencing and citation, which, done correctly, is a critical part of a good literature review and also suggests strategies for critiquing the literature more effectively, such as exploring the extent to which it is supported by evidence and questioning what it might be saying or implying about particular groups.

We move from theory to method, in this case the use of the interview, in Chapter 5, 'Interviewing in educational research'. While one of the most common forms of data gathering in qualitative research, interviewing is also possibly one of the most challenging. In this chapter we discuss the stages of the interview process, including the choice of interviewees, the drawing up of questions, the conduct of the interview and subsequent considerations of ethics and interpretation. In this, the chapter draws on the earlier content of Chapter 2. Interviewing presents many advantages to the researcher, but also has a number of challenges and pitfalls: we draw attention to these using a series of examples to illustrate and explore the various practical epistemological issues which the use of interviews may raise. Towards the end of the chapter the reader is presented with an extract from a postgraduate assignment for critical comment, in which the use of interviews is described and discussed. We then move on to the chapters discussing the most common methodological approaches taken to qualitative research in education.

In Chapter 6 we introduce the reader to a range of ways in which case study research can be applied in an educational context in order to illuminate particular issues and phenomena within a particular setting. The chapter explores the diversity of case study and discusses the different stages of this approach to research, from design and preparation, through the collection and analysis of data, to the drawing of conclusions or the framing of further questions. It draws attention both to the strengths and to the risks associated with this method of research, and, similar to the other chapters, uses a series of examples to illustrate and explore the epistemological questions which the use of case studies may raise. Case study is often confused by students with action research, so in Chapter 7, 'Action research' we make clear how action research is defined and how it differs from case study.

In addition, we discuss the principles and practices of action enquiry and consider, with the use of real examples, how these might be applied as part of practitioner research in an educational context. The chapter also briefly covers the history and practice of action research: this is used to contextualise the theoretical and philosophical basis for traditional action research as well as more contemporary approaches such as participatory action research (PAR) and transformational action research. We then go on to provide practical guidance on undertaking an action research project, from early consideration of the identification of an issue or problem through to planning the project; framing the research questions and determining the nature of the data which might be collected. We emphasise the importance of rigour throughout these processes and the subsequent analysis and documentation or writing up of the project. This section of the chapter is supported by Chapter 11, 'Analysing and reporting qualitative data'. Finally, we conclude this chapter with suggestions about changing practice in the light of the project or evaluation.

We move on to discuss ethnographic research in Chapter 8. A limited amount of educational research may be defined as 'an ethnography' but much, including examples of both case study research and action research, draws on ethnographic principles and approaches while not meeting the criteria for true ethnography. We begin the chapter by clarifying the difference between true ethnography and the use of an ethnographic approach. The chapter also outlines the origins of the ethnographic approach and highlights some more contemporary forms of ethnographic research, such as netnography, providing real-life illustrations of situations in which these may be used. It discusses ways in which an ethnographic approach can be used to illuminate, among others, cultural, communication and relationship issues. As ethnographic methods are often used to illuminate issues in organisations, the chapter also draws on some of the content of Chapter 3 in highlighting some of the implications of 'insider ethnography', and also has close parallels with Chapter 2 ('Ethical research in education') particularly given the human relationship issues which arise in ethnographic research.

Chapter 8 goes on to discuss some of the practicalities of data collection, analysis and presentation, again drawing on real-life examples to provide suggestions for overcoming some of the difficulties associated with ethnographic research. The chapter includes a section on conducting observation, a key data-gathering method in ethnography, and also draws on Chapter 5, 'Interviewing in educational research' and on Chapter 11, 'Analysing and reporting qualitative data' in discussing how to respond to the large quantities of data generated by ethnographic research.

From the study of people in Chapter 8 we move on to explore the written word in a discussion of discourse analysis in Chapter 9. In addition to discussing the principles of discourse analysis and demonstrating ways in which it can provide a useful tool in analysing national, local and institutional policy documents and discourses, the chapter also considers ways in which it can contribute to exploring issues such as the convergence or divergence of policy and practice in all sectors of education. In doing this, the chapter also highlights the ways in which the impact of policy and policy discourse on educational provision and practice have been substantial and unrelenting over the past two decades. It begins with an exploration of what discourse actually means in the context of educational research, and goes on to explore its application in the analysis of policy documents, something which is touched on earlier in Chapter 2, 'Writing a literature review'. Chapter 9 focuses very much on the written word, and ways in which the written word can become part of our spoken discourses, influencing practice and attitudes to others, for example by the 'othering' or homogenisation of groups.

Chapter 10, 'Text and image in qualitative research', develops this theme in an exploration of developing relationships between text and image, the image maker and the image, the viewer and the image, and considers how meaning and interpretations can be drawn from this. This chapter also examines some of the challenges associated with using images as a research tool and explores the possibilities which they present when used in conjunction with other research tools as part of a unified strategy.

Chapter 11, 'Analysing and reporting qualitative data', addresses the difficulties this can present, and makes practical suggestions that can be applied to your own study. The chapter begins with the process of selecting data for presentation. To illustrate this, the researcher's role is compared with that of a detective faced with an abundance of information who must embark on the demanding task of drawing likely conclusions about relevance and meaning. The chapter goes on to explore some of the difficulties and ambiguities that can be encountered in the interpretation and analysis of qualitative data, and discusses some of the strategies that can be used to overcome these. Finally, it examines a range of approaches which can be used for the analysis of qualitative data gathered by interview. This discussion is based largely around the interview transcripts from Chapter 5, 'Interviewing in educational research', with which you will already be familiar. The analysis of data also draws on the literature, as the researcher seeks to position their findings in the context of existing knowledge. Therefore, the analysis stage depends not only on systematic and rigorous analysis, but also on an effective and thorough critique of the literature in the field.

Finally, Chapter 12 looks at what happens after the analysis and the writing up are completed. Drawing on contributions from colleagues across the field of education who have disseminated their research in a wide variety of ways, influencing thinking and practice in their fields, it provides advice and guidance on dissemination in both professional and academic journals, conference presentations and workshops. However, applying research findings can be challenging, so this chapter also discusses some of the opportunities and obstacles which this can present. The final chapter then summarises the key themes of this book, the interdependence of teaching and research, and educational research for positive change in a conclusion to the text.

Additional online resources can be found at http://www.uk.sagepub.com/beraseries.sp

References

British Educational Research Association (BERA) (2011) *Ethical Guidelines for Educational Research*. Available at: www.bera.ac.uk/publications/guidelines/.

Griffiths, M. (2003) *Action Research for Social Justice in Education: Fairly Different*. Buckingham: Open University Press.

Stenhouse, L. (1975) *An Introduction to Curriculum Research and Development*. London: Heinemann.

Wellington, J. (2000) *Educational Research: Contemporary Issues and Practical Approaches*. London: Continuum.

CHAPTER 1

RESEARCH IN EDUCATION

Summary

The aim of this chapter is to explore the concept of educational research, its purposes and processes. It presents research as an integral and essential part of professional practice, and it explores some of the key issues which researchers need to consider when planning their research, such as questions of subjectivity and scope; positivist and interpretivist approaches; and the distinction between assumptions and hypotheses. In the process, it introduces some vocabulary that will be useful to you as a researcher. By the end of this chapter you should be able to formulate your own answers to the questions: 'Why do we do educational research?' and, 'How do we articulate and pursue our research questions?'

Key words used in this chapter: *qualitative, quantitative, subjectivity, interpretivist, positivist.*

Educational research – why do we do it?

If someone asked us why we do educational research, we would probably come up with an answer along the lines of: 'We carry out research into education in order to help us – and others – to a better understanding of what constitutes effective teaching and learning.' The focus of the research may be about issues as disparate as funding, student behaviour, inclusion, teacher education or social justice; but in the end the purpose of the enquiry – the use to which its discoveries are put – will normally be to improve the effectiveness of our professional practice and the systems within which we operate to support learners in their learning. We shall be arguing throughout this book that research, both into our own professional practice and into the impact which policies have upon its context and content, is central to the concept of teaching as a *profession*.

Gender and the geography teacher

Mo teaches Geography to 11- to 16-year-olds. He has noticed over the past three years that the girls consistently perform better than the boys, both in their homework and in classroom activities. This pattern is apparent across all year groups. Mo is undertaking a Master's degree in education as part of his continuing professional development, and decides that he would like to focus on this issue as part of his research project. As a first step he must formulate his research question. After some thought, he comes up with the following:

• Why do the boys in my classes achieve less well overall than the girls?

Building critical research skills: activity

We shall return to the wording of Mo's question shortly, but first take a moment to think of a question about your own teaching, or the way your institution operates, or the functioning of the education system as a whole – the question you would most of all like to discover an answer to at this moment. For example, it might be:

• To what extent do my head teacher's (or principal's) beliefs and priorities affect my classroom practice?
Or it might be:

- Would my students be better behaved if I changed the seating arrangement in my classroom?

Or perhaps it would be:

- If national standards of achievement for post-16 learners are continuing to rise, why does classroom behaviour seem to be deteriorating?

Take some time to think of your own particular question, and then write it down before reading on.

Now let's look again at Mo's question – 'Why do the boys in my classes achieve less well overall than the girls?' – and consider it in more detail. Why, for example, might he need the answer, and what use could he make of it?

An obvious reason for wishing to answer this question is that it might help him to arrive at strategies which would enable him to help the boys improve their attainment levels and work to their full potential as the girls already appear to be doing. Even as he formulates the question, he might well have some possible answers in mind. For example, he might suspect that the subject matter, or the teaching resources, or even his own style of teaching are likely to engage the girls more easily than the boys. The answer that he might have in mind we can call his **hypothesis**. It might be a conclusion which he's come to as a result of his own observation and experience; or it might be an idea which has been proposed by another researcher whose work he's read in an academic journal, and which he wants to test out for himself. On the other hand, he may have no preconceived idea of the answer at all. In that case, his research will not be testing a hypothesis, but will be a case of collecting data in order to form a possible answer or set of answers – answers which may in some cases take him by surprise.

Having formulated his question, his next step will be to look at what has been published on this topic by other teachers and academics. He may find that some possible answers or theories have already been suggested, tested and even 'proved'. If this is the case he may feel that his curiosity is satisfied. On the other hand, he may decide to see whether these answers really do work when applied to his own professional practice. In other words, he will continue to pursue the research question. The steps he will have taken to this point can be summarised like this:

1. Reflection on his professional practice in order to identify a question.
2. Formulation of the question.

3. Review of the literature which already exists on this topic.
4. Design of a research process to answer the question, or to test existing theories, for himself.

His next task will be to collect the necessary evidence; analyse it to discover what it tells him; compare what he finds with what was claimed in the literature; and draw some conclusions. If we summarise this process, the steps in his research journey now look like this:

Step 1. Reflection on his professional practice in order to identify a question. Mo has been thinking about his teaching and the main issue which concerns him is the achievement level of boys, compared to girls.

Step 2. Formulation of the question. He decides to formulate this as a research question in order to explore possible ways in which the issue could be addressed: 'Why do the boys in my classes achieve less well overall than the girls?' One advantage of phrasing the research title as a question is that it will help him to keep his focus when he is exploring the literature and planning the collection and analysis of his data.

Step 3. Review of the literature which already exists on this topic. He uses the key words, 'boys' achievement' to find articles in academic journals which throw some light on this question. He uses the same key words to search specialist publications such as the *Times Education Supplement* (TES) for recent, relevant reports. He discovers a number of theories relating to boys' achievement. One of these suggests that boys respond less well than girls to continuous assessment, and tend to perform better in time-constrained tests and examinations.

Step 4. Design of a research process to answer the question, or to test existing theories, for yourself. In the light of the literature, he decides to rephrase and refine his research question, giving it a sharper focus. It becomes: 'Do the boys in my class perform better on timed tests and less well on coursework than girls?' Now he will test this theory by introducing some timed tests as supplements to the students' coursework.

Step 5. Collection of data. He assesses the class using both timed tests and coursework.

Step 6. Analysis of data. He analyses the results of the timed tests and the coursework according to student gender, and also compares the results of individual students in both assessment methods. He finds that, overall, boys score better in the tests than girls, and that the majority of individual boys' scores in the tests are higher than their scores in the coursework.

Step 7. Conclusion. He finds that his own research appears to confirm the claim that boys achieve better in time-constrained tests than in continuous assessment, and resolves that he will look at ways in which a greater element of timed testing could be introduced into school-based coursework.

He may – and we hope he will – want to add a further step, which is:

*Step 8. The **dissemination** of his findings* so that other educational professionals can learn and benefit from them.

Activity

Mo's was a fairly straightforward example of practitioner research. Now let's look again at the other examples that we listed:

To what extent do my head teacher's (or principal's) beliefs and priorities affect my classroom practice?
Would my students be better behaved if I changed the seating arrangement in my classroom?
If national standards of achievement of post-16 learners are continuing to rise, why does classroom behaviour seem to be deteriorating?

And consider the following questions:

- To what extent would each of these three research questions fit neatly into the model of the research process we've just looked at?
- Which of these three research questions do you think would be easiest to answer, and why?

You should give yourself some time to think carefully about this and make some notes. When you have some ideas that you would be happy to share, you might find it useful to discuss them with someone else, such as a colleague, a fellow student or a mentor.

Why some research is less straightforward than others

So, is there anything about each of these research questions which might make it difficult to fit them neatly into our first model of the research process? We suggest that you compare the notes you've made with what follows.

1. To what extent do my head teacher's (or principal's) beliefs and priorities affect my classroom practice?

This question poses a number of problems. First, how will you reliably identify your head teacher's beliefs and priorities? Are you going to assume they are implicit in his or her policies or actions or conversation? Won't this raise problems of interpretation? How would you know that your understanding of the head teacher's beliefs was the same as your colleagues' understanding of them? Whose would be 'true'? Perhaps you could interview the head teacher as part of your research, and ask him or her to describe their values, priorities and beliefs. Ah, but then how would you know they were telling you what they genuinely believed, and not what they thought you thought they ought to say? Or what the local authority or government thought they ought to say? How could you ever really reliably identify those 'beliefs and priorities'?

Then, how could you measure how they affect your own classroom practice? How could you know? What would your evidence be? In what sense would it have any **reliability**? Could it ever have any status as a 'fact' or a 'truth'?

Here we see that this type of research question, that sets out to enquire about personal values, motives and beliefs, is of a different order to one which compares student achievement under different types of assessment. It is the sort of question that might need rephrasing or reframing before we can attempt to answer it. You might like to think of ways in which this question could be adapted in order to make it more accessible to research.

Now let's consider this question:

2. Would my students be better behaved if I changed the seating arrangement in my classroom?

This question fits rather better into our initial model of the research process. Nevertheless, there are two things about it which distinguish it from the 'boys' achievement' type of question First, there is the fact that it will probably lead us to try a number of different strategies. We can keep changing the seating arrangement until we've tried every possible pattern. If there's no improvement in behaviour, the answer to our question is probably 'no'; but if one particular configuration coincides with an improvement in behaviour and does so every time we try it, we have arrived at a 'yes' answer. And it is exactly that element of 'trial and error' which is the first distinguishing feature of this question. It encourages us to try out strategies to find one that works. The second feature which distinguishes it from the 'boys' achievement' type of question is that whatever answer we find is probably particular to that class of ours at that time. We're not trying to explore or answer a wider question about 'all students and all classes' which we've found in the literature. We're looking to see whether an **intervention** or **action** which we take will have a desired effect on that class. It may not work with other classes, or for other teachers, but we are looking at our own teaching, here and now. This type of question falls into the category of **action research**, and we shall come back to it in a later chapter.

In terms of which would be the easiest of those three questions to answer, this investigation about room layout would probably be the one. And it is easiest to answer because it involves trying actions or strategies to see what 'works'. It doesn't rely on subjective assessments and value judgements which may call its results into question.

Activity

- *Or does it?* Can you see how and where this question might well involve some degree of subjectivity?
- And if you've spotted the potential difficulty, have you also spotted a way to reduce the potential for unreliable, subjective judgements in this research?

Take some time to think carefully about these two questions and make some notes. When you have some ideas that you would be happy to share, you might find it useful to discuss them with someone else, such as a colleague, a fellow student or a mentor.

Let's look now at the third question in our list. It was this:

3. If national standards of achievement at post-16 are continuing to rise, why does classroom behaviour seem to be deteriorating?

You will probably have noticed straight away that this question is different from the others in terms of scope. It is asking a question which refers to trends on a national scale: trends in post-16 achievement and student behaviour. As the question stands, it is not one which you could address within the parameters of, for example, an MA research skills module. If you wanted to explore this issue as part of a postgraduate programme you would be advised to scale it down to your own institution or group of schools. The question then might become: 'Why are standards of student behaviour in the school deteriorating even though standards of achievement at post-16 within the school are continuing to rise?' This limits the scope of the enquiry to within manageable parameters. It provides you with a question to which you have some possibility of finding an answer, if you can design your research in a way that enables you to collect relevant data.

Activity

- What data would you need to collect here, and why?
- Can you see anything which is still problematic about the revised version of the question?

When you have some ideas that you would be happy to share, you might find it useful to discuss them with someone else, before reading on to compare your ideas with what we have to say.

You probably noticed very quickly that our revised question – 'Why are standards of student behaviour in the school deteriorating even though standards of achievement at post-16 within the school are continuing to rise?' – still makes an assumption which may not be easy to substantiate. While it should be straightforward to find and present documentary evidence that post-16 achievement at the school has shown a steady improvement (if it has), it is another matter entirely to substantiate the assumption that standards of behaviour have declined.

Activity

- What evidence could you find and present for this?
- How reliable would it be?
- To what extent are judgements about standards of behaviour subjective?
- What problems does this raise for a researcher?

If you did not identify this issue as a problem, take your time to think it through now, until you feel confident that you understand why it could present difficulties for a researcher. Discuss it with a colleague, mentor or fellow student if you wish.

Your own research question

Let's go back now, at last, to the research question we asked you to write down for yourself earlier in this chapter – the question relating to your own professional practice for which you'd most like to find an answer.

Activity

- Consider whether your question fits within the model of the research process which we drew up around the 'boys' achievement' question.
- If it does, fill in the steps as we did for that question earlier. Here they are again:

1. **Reflection on your professional practice in order to identify a question**
2. **Formulation of the question**
3. **Review of the literature which already exists on this topic**
(You won't be able to discuss what the literature suggests about the topic until you've had a chance to do a literature search in the library or online.)
4. **Design of a research process to answer the question, or to test existing theories, for yourself**
5. **Collection of data**
6. **Analysis of data**
7. **Conclusion.**

If your question doesn't fit the model process very well, or raises some of the questions or problems we identified earlier, such as issues about:

- subjectivity;
- reliability;
- unquestioned assumptions;
- lack of opportunity for evidence collection;
- scope or scale,

then the best way to start on this task is to identify where your question does and does not fit the model we've been looking at in this chapter, and to reflect on alternative ways of collecting data which help you to throw some light on possible answers. This will make a useful reference point for some of the theories and approaches we'll be covering in the chapters which follow.

Qualitative and quantitative approaches to research

This is a book about **qualitative** research. To explore what is meant by this term, let's take as our starting point a short extract from one of the books listed in the recommended reading for this chapter:

> It remains a mystery to me why those who work in education should attempt to aspire towards science when scientific methods, processes and codes of conduct at best are unclear and at worst lack the objectivity, certainty, logicality and predictability which are falsely ascribed to them. Surely educational research would do better to aspire to being systematic, credible, verifiable, justifiable, useful, valuable and 'trustworthy' (Lincoln and Guba, 1985).
> (Wellington, 2000: 14)

There is a lot of argument packed into this one short paragraph. For one thing, Wellington is suggesting that even 'scientific' research – often held up as a model of factual and disinterested objectivity – is not necessarily as objective as it is claimed to be. He then goes on to argue that 'objectivity' is anyway not necessarily the best test of good research, and that other characteristics and qualities may be more important. The qualities he mentions here are:

- systematic (carefully planned and carried out);
- credible (realistic and believable);
- verifiable (based on evidence that can be checked and verified);
- justifiable (a convincing case can be made for undertaking it);
- useful (its findings can be applied in practice);
- valuable (will enhance current practice);
- trustworthy (honest, genuine and based on sound research ethics).

The point Wellington is making is an important one, because qualitative educational research, like research in the other social sciences and the humanities, is sometimes subjected to criticism from those who favour a quantitative or scientific model of research for being 'too subjective' or too much based on feelings and personal responses. Feelings and personal responses are not accepted by such critics as being reliable data in the same sense that numbers or percentages or anything else measurable in figures are. And of course there's very little educational researchers can do about this, since by its very nature education is concerned with human beings; and human beings are not predictable or static in the same way that inert materials or fixed numbers are. So what Wellington is arguing is that we shouldn't feel we have to apologise for the fact that our research in education is not often conducted like a laboratory experiment with measurements and control groups, or the fact that our findings are not often reducible to repeatable formulae; but that we should set ourselves standards (such as those listed above) which are appropriate to the more people-centred approach which our research often takes.

Can educational research be 'objective'?

Although the notion of objectivity in educational research is sometimes problematic, this is not to say that educational research is never about numbers and percentages, nor that it should be. When we undertake research which measures something – responses, numbers of students, examination results – in finite terms, and in which we present our findings in terms of numerical data, we call this **quantitative** research. An easy way to remember this is that **quantitative** research measures **quantity** (although of course this is rather an oversimplification).

Activity

Have a look again at Mo's research question and decide whether or not we could class this as quantitative research.

Do the boys in my class perform better on timed tests and less well on coursework than girls?

Of course, the answer to that last question is: *'It depends what data you decide to gather and how you gather it'.*
  The way we planned to investigate this research question earlier in the chapter made it a straightforward quantitative enquiry. We planned to measure and compare results of tests and coursework, and to present our data as numerical scores and comparisons. So if you answered on those grounds that, 'Yes. It's quantitative research' you were right.

But what if we had decided to collect the data in a different way? What if we had asked the boys and girls which means of assessment they preferred, or which they thought they performed best at, or whether they thought they performed better than the opposite gender? What then? We might still have come out with some sets of figures for our results: 'so many boys said this'; 'so many girls said that'. So would this still make it quantitative research? And what if, instead of presenting the findings in terms of figures, we had chosen instead to quote the sort of things that the students had told us about their assessment preferences?

Activity

Now look again at your own research question which you formulated earlier. You may have revised or refined it since then. You may find it useful now to identify what sort of data is going to help you to answer it: quantitative or qualitative? And why? The simplified table (see Table 1.1) may help you to arrive at an answer.

Table 1.1 Qualitative and quantitative data

Qualitative data	Quantitative data
Stories, accounts, observations presented in the form of: • Quotes from interviews and questionnaire responses • Personal reflection • Pictures	Numbers, percentages, scores presented in the form of: • Graphs • Charts • Tables

Positivist and interpretivist approaches to research

So, how do we use those terms, quantitative and qualitative? Well, we've seen that a quantitative approach to research is often regarded as more 'objective' than a qualitative, people-focused approach. And we've seen that data gathered in the process of research may be described as quantitative if it deals with finite measurements and numbers, and qualitative if it focuses on presenting or interpreting people's views, interactions or values. We must be careful, however, not to assume that 'quantitative' means the same thing as 'positivist'. The **positivist** stance is usually typified by a relatively objective style and approach, and searches for 'facts' which can be generalised; whereas a more typical approach in small-scale educational research would be an **interpretivist** one which acknowledges some degree of subjectivity in the researcher and other participants, may be written in the first person, and seeks to throw light on a particular case or situation. *But it may involve the collection of qualitative or quantitative data, or both.*

Table 1.2 is another simple table and summarises the main contrasts between the positivist and the interpretivist approach. It will help you to identify which sort of research you are dealing with when reading journal articles, and it will help you to identify your standpoint in the research which you plan to undertake.

Table 1.2 Interpretivist vs positivist paradigms

Interpretivist	Positivist
Investigates by focusing on case studies and people as individuals and groups, their histories, their personal accounts, their interactions	Investigates using the model of the natural sciences
Often uses the first person – I, me – when writing up the research (e.g. I conducted an interview ...)	Writes in the passive tense (e.g. An interview was conducted ...)
Researcher acknowledges their own viewpoint, values and preconceptions and explains the measures they have taken to prevent these from contaminating the data	Researcher claims the research has been conducted with maximum objectivity
Its purpose is to throw some light on and develop understanding of particular cases and situations	Its purpose is to discover 'facts' which can be applied to all cases in the relevant category
The researcher may treat others involved as participants in rather than subjects of research	The researcher treats those involved as subjects

Activity

Now think back to Mo's research question:

'Do the boys in my class perform better on timed tests and less well on coursework than girls?'

Using Table 1.2 above, you might find it useful to reflect on how (a) a positivist and (b) an interpretivist researcher might approach this research and what claims they might make for the findings.

Reliability, subjectivity, transferability, generalisability and epistemology

Let's look more closely now at some of the specialised vocabulary we've encountered so far, and some that may be new to you. In research, the terminology we use is an important set of tools, and – as with any skilled job – those tools have to be used with precision. In the dialogue below, Mo and his research tutor, Alia, discuss Mo's **methodology** – that is, his rationale for the data collection methods he plans to use.

Mo   So when I'm planning to write this up, I need to write about method *and* **methodology**? I'm not sure I quite understand what the distinction is.

Alia OK. Method is a description of what you do, in practical terms, to collect your data. So in your case you're going to be explaining about introducing timed tests and comparing the results by gender with coursework results, and so on. The **methodology** section is where you provide a theoretical and philosophical justification for this choice. In other words, having described the WHAT, you explain the WHY. Why you've designed the research in this way; why you've chosen these participants and this number of participants; why you've opted for this method of data collection. And you can draw on three main sources for this explanation. One source would be literature about research: works such as Opie (2004), Wellington (2000), Cohen, et al. (2011) and so on, where the advantages and disadvantages of various procedures and methods are discussed. Another would be published research which you've found in the research journals – and, of course, in your case this has already played a large part in influencing your research design. A third source of argument or justification is philosophical considerations about the nature of truth and knowledge – the area of philosophy we refer to as **epistemology**.

Mo   So are you saying I need to write a watertight justification for the method I've used?

Alia No. Because no method is 'watertight'. There are always potential flaws and doubts. But what you do need to do is to demonstrate, as far as possible, that you're aware of these. So, for example, when you write about trying out the timed tests you should acknowledge the possibility that any improvement in the boys' performance might be coincidental, or might be due to the novelty of the activity rather than the nature of the test itself. You should acknowledge the potential for unreliability in your method and explain the steps you've taken to minimise this. In your case, you're going to repeat the tests to see whether the data is replicated – in other words that the first time wasn't a fluke.

Mo   Right. I think I've got that now. Method is what and how, and methodology is why. But can we just go back to **epistemology** for a minute?

Alia Yes, of course. **Epistemology** is the term we use for the study or the theory of what constitutes knowledge. For example, if you were to measure this room with an accurate tape measure you would have a firm basis on which to make a claim about knowledge of its dimensions. But if you had never been inside the room and you simply asked someone who had been inside to tell you how big they thought it was, your claim to knowledge about its measurements would be on much shakier ground. Similarly, if you were to look for evidence about boys' achievement in tests and coursework by simply asking the boys' opinions about it, the epistemological questions there would be: 'How can you know what they say is true? How can you justify the opinions they express as a basis for a claim to knowledge?'

Mo   So doesn't this call into question all data that's collected by means of interviews and open-ended questionnaires?

Alia   Well, yes, in a way it does. This is one of the difficulties the qualitative researcher faces. In education our research naturally focuses on learning and teaching, which in themselves are lived experiences. The sort of data we need is often only obtained by listening to people or observing them or asking them questions. If we could get the answers by simply measuring or weighing people, life would be much simpler! But the questions we explore are often complicated ones requiring data which draws on people's accounts of themselves and their experiences. So we have to think hard and write clearly about how we justify the claim that our findings constitute 'knowledge'.

Mo   So how does the concept of **reliability** fit into this?

Alia   It fits in very neatly. When we talk about research outcomes being '**reliable**' we mean that the same data would have emerged from the enquiry if it had been conducted by a different researcher, or by the same researcher using different data collecting methods. With your research, for example, you will be making a comparison of test scores and assignment grades and looking at correlations with gender. It should be the case that any other teacher or researcher scrutinising your data will draw the same results or conclusions from it. So you're on fairly safe ground. Your evidence should be pretty reliable. But if you were obtaining data by using interviews, for example, your analysis of the data might be more open to influence by your own preconceived ideas, and a different researcher might draw alternative conclusions or arguments from the same data.

Mo   But the boys in my sample might perform differently in tests on different days. So the results might not be reliably consistent. If I'd tested them the week before or the week afterwards, for example, the data could have been different.

Alia   Yes, that's a possibility. You've tried to address that, though, by doing the tests more than once. And that's good. The important thing is that you write all this up accurately in your **methodology** section, so that you demonstrate that you're aware of the need for **reliability** and that you've taken steps to improve it as far as possible.

Mo   OK, so what about **bias**? Is that the same thing as **unreliability**?

Alia Yes and no. It depends on the context. For example, if you were using questionnaires, and out of 100 only 15 were completed and returned, you would have to consider the possibility that your data will be biased.

Mo Why?

Alia Well, because it's possible – even probable – that the respondents who bothered to complete and return them were people with more interest in the topic of your enquiry than those who didn't bother. And this would mean that they might hold views in common which wouldn't have been apparent in the other 85 responses, had you had them. So that would be an instance in which your data might be biased. It could be like trying to find out people's opinion of cats by only asking cat owners.

And then there's researcher bias. That would be where you only see in the data what you're looking for and ignore anything else. Or where you choose only to question cat owners because you like cats yourself. Or where you have a policy axe to grind and only present those aspects of your data which support your view.

Mo Got it. Thanks. So there was one other thing I wanted to ask you about and that's to do with the sort of claims I can make about my research when I write it up. If I do demonstrate that boys at my school do better in tests than in coursework, am I allowed to make a point from that about male pupils in general?

Alia The short answer to that is 'No'. But I need to qualify that a little bit. The thing about doing small-scale research as part of your professional development is that it's often conducted within one institution – your own. So at every stage of your research paper or assignment you need to be absolutely explicit about that, all the way through from the title to the conclusions you draw at the end. That way, you're being up front about the **scale** of your enquiry. And this doesn't only mean explaining that the context is one school, but also that it's a particular year group and a particular subject. It may be, for example, that boys perform well in maths tests, but not in English tests. In other words, results of research done with a maths group will not necessarily have **transferability** to the context of other subjects in the curriculum. And, in the same way, we may find that conclusions drawn from work with a Year 9 group aren't transferable when we look to apply them to Year 10. So, findings may be specific to a particular group at a particular stage in their education at a particular school. But that doesn't make the research any the less valid and useful for you and your institution. And although your results may not be **generalisable** to other schools or situations, your research may prove to be illuminative to a wider range of practitioners, because it may help shed light on issues in their own institutions and provide them with a point of comparison. That's what you found, after all, didn't you, when you were reading other people's research about boys' and girls' attainment? You read what they had discovered in their own schools and decided to investigate whether the same applied in your own.

Mo   So their results *may be* **generalisable**?

Alia That may still be too strong a claim. But you do hope to test whether they are **replicable** and, if they are, that would speak strongly for the reliability of that research and of your own.

Mo   And all of these issues we've talked about need to be mentioned in my **methodology**?

Alia Not just mentioned, but discussed in an informed way. Just chucking in the terminology won't cut the mustard!

Research and professionalism: reflective activity

We began this chapter by looking at the question of why we undertake educational research. Our answer so far has been that we can use it to inform and enhance our practice. But it serves another purpose, too. By involving us in reflection upon our own practice and how we can monitor, regulate and improve it, it marks us out as professionals. Carr and Kemmis (1986: 9–10) argue that:

> if teaching is to become a more genuinely professional activity, three sorts of development will be necessary. First, the attitudes and practices of teachers must become more firmly grounded in educational theory and research. Secondly, the professional autonomy of teachers must be extended to include the opportunity to participate in the decisions that are made about the broader educational context within which they operate; that is, professional autonomy must be regarded as a collective as well as an individual matter. Thirdly, the professional responsibilities of the teacher must be extended so as to include a professional obligation to interested parties in the community at large.

1. Which three key features do the authors identify as distinguishing what we mean by a 'profession'?
2. To what extent do you agree with this analysis?
3. How would you apply their argument to the context or sector in which you yourself teach?

(Continues)

(Continued)

Although this was written over a quarter of a century ago, we believe it is as relevant now as it has ever been. The status of the professional working in the field of education and training is enhanced by engagement in research and by the dissemination of good practice to the wider community. And we would add to this a belief, which we shall return to in the chapters which follow, that qualitative research in education is valuable above all for its potential to change lives for the better, both those of teachers and of learners, and of the community at large.

Key points 🔑

- The purposes of educational research.
- Key steps in the research process.
- The importance of dissemination in educational research.
- Epistemology: what can we 'know' for sure?
- What is qualitative research?
- Positivist and interpretivist approaches.
- Problems of subjectivity and scope.
- Assumptions and hypotheses.
- Reliability, transferability and generalisability.
- Why we should see research as a defining aspect of professional engagement with practice.

References and further reading 📖

Carr, W. and Kemmis, S. (1986) *Becoming Critical: Education, Knowledge and Action Research.* Lewes: Falmer Press.

Cohen, L., Manion, L. and Morrison, K. (2011) *Research Methods in Education.* 7th edn. London: Routledge.

Kay, E., Tisdall, M., Davis, J.M. and Gallagher, M. (2009) *Researching with Children and Young People.* London: Sage.

McNiff, J. and Whitehead, J. (2009) *Doing and Writing Action Research.* London: Sage.

Opie, C. (2004) *Doing Educational Research.* London: Sage.

Wellington, J. (2000) *Educational Research: Contemporary Issues and Practical Approaches.* London: Continuum.

Wilson, E. (2009) *School-based Research: A Guide for Education Students.* London: Sage.

CHAPTER 2

ETHICAL RESEARCH IN EDUCATION

Summary

This chapter introduces the concept of research ethics and provides opportunities for the reader to familiarise themselves with existing ethical
guidelines, both those developed by their own institution where relevant,
and with national guidelines such as those provided by BERA (2011). It
encourages consideration of how such codes of practice might apply in a
variety of contexts and scenarios, and explores the reasons why ethical
considerations are of particular importance to researchers in the field of
education. A recurring emphasis in this chapter is on research activity as
just one aspect of a consistently ethical approach to professional practice
in education.

Key words used in this chapter: *ethics, values, morality, (in)formed consent,
privacy, power, deception, honesty, harm.*

Taking an ethical approach to educational research

An ethical approach should pervade the whole of your study. It is *not* merely a recognition of the need for anonymity or consent, but should inform every aspect of your study from the initial planning stages, through the data collection and analysis to the final reporting. By this we mean that at each stage you should be asking yourself: is this action ethical? Is it honest and moral? Is it respectful of others and of key values? This type of approach goes far beyond a brief discussion of the actions you have taken to preserve anonymity and reference to the guidance you have followed. This means giving consideration to issues such as 'How will I respond to any unexpected ethical issues?' – and there are almost always unexpected ethical issues, some of which can be life-changing for the individuals concerned and which thus places you in a position of great moral responsibility.

Wellington (2000: 54) argues that all educational research should be 'ETHICAL', using capitalisation to emphasise the significance of ethics. We believe that an ethical approach to educational research is essential not *only* in the context of undertaking ethical research, but because it is part of being an educator, which demands a similar moral approach. Practice as a teacher is grounded in a particular code of professionalism and ethics – much of it unwritten – that demands certain standards of behaviour and is founded on principles of care and respect for individuals. The similarities between the two may be seen in the five principles underpinning educational research identified by BERA (2011: 4). These are that:

> all educational research should be conducted within an ethic of respect for:
> * The person
> * Knowledge
> * Democratic values
> * The quality of educational research
> * Academic freedom.

If the word *education* is substituted for *educational research* in this quote, then the statement comes to provide an underpinning ethic which most teachers aspire to in their practice, and which is consistent with the various codes of conduct for teachers in all phases of education. This might include, for example, the Institute for Learning (IfL) *Code of Professional Practice* for teachers in the lifelong learning sector, which is founded on values including integrity, respect, care and responsibility (IfL, 2011) or the General Teaching Council (2009) *Code of Conduct and Practice for Registered Teachers*, which relates to those teaching in the compulsory (5–16+) phases of education and which includes responsibility, care, honesty and integrity among its core principles.

One of the reasons that an ethical framework needs to be reflexive is the potential for conflict among the principles as illustrated in the following activity.

Reflective activity

Consider the implications of informed consent where a person is deemed to be vulnerable – for example, a child or young person, or perhaps a student with a mental health problem or a learning disability. In this case, asking a responsible adult such as a parent, carer or advocate to consent on their behalf may seem to be the right thing to do. However, asking another to consent on their behalf in this way may also be seen as an infringement of the vulnerable person's autonomy and right to make decisions.

When you have had time to think about this scenario make a brief list of the ethical issues it raises followed by brief notes on what might be an appropriate and ethical response to this dilemma.

Tensions such as these illustrate that it is not possible to take a mechanistic approach to ethical issues – for example, I have applied the university guidance and anonymised my data, so that's OK – and emphasise the importance of considering all the possible implications of your study not just at the planning stage but, as the research progresses, with an awareness of the five principles discussed at the beginning of this chapter. One response to such a dilemma would be to deal with it in a *situated* and *reflexive* manner. This means that where, for example, an unanticipated ethical issue arises, you would respond to it in a thoughtful and reflective way, and try to ensure that your response is moral and in the best interests of all concerned; in other words, to construct, apply and practise ethics in the context of your research.

A range of potential dilemmas may call for such a response. Key among these are issues such as informed consent, power relationships, deception and honesty, protection from harm and value judgements, autonomy, privacy and reciprocity; these are addressed individually in the following sections. It is important to be aware, however, that this list is not exhaustive and that you may come across an ethical issue in your study which is not directly addressed here. If that is the case, you should take the opportunity to discuss it with a tutor or supervisor and explore it in writing and with reference to texts on these issues (see, for example, Simons and Usher, 2000; Sikes et al., 2003). At a practical level, you should make the situated and reflexive response mentioned above.

Informed Consent

What exactly is 'informed' consent? How informed are the participants? How aware can they be of the possible implications of participating in educational research? Most research assignments state glibly that participants gave informed consent. Usually, this means that the participants signed a consent form which outlined their right to privacy or to withdraw, and which described the purpose and planned process of the study. However, informed consent is a much more significant issue than it appears on the surface. It is important to be clear in any research report exactly what you understand by informed consent and how you have addressed this issue, and its implications (some of which are discussed at more length later in this chapter). A key aspect of this is that very few participants have the same level of understanding of research as the researcher. This makes it absolutely morally incumbent on the researcher to anticipate any possible harm, distress or change which might be experienced by the participant since the participant cannot be expected either to anticipate these, or to be aware of their possible implications. This is explored in more detail later in this chapter.

Consent also raises issues around respect and autonomy. Making consent as informed as possible demonstrates respect for individuals' autonomy since they are able to make a more objective personal decision about the implications of participating and also, in some cases, about withdrawing from the study if they come to feel that they no longer wish to participate.

Vignette 1

Nigel was a secondary teacher whose study involved his pupils and their parents as participants. He gave careful consideration to the ethical implications of his study and produced a very comprehensive ethical framework document to issue to all his participants, which outlined everybody's rights and responsibilities, the purpose of the study, the way in which confidentiality would be assured and data stored and so on. Nigel believed – with some justification – that he had given as much consideration as he possibly could to potential ethical issues. However, there was a major flaw in his framework; written in what might be called 'PhDese', the language was not readily accessible to the audience. If they did not understand it, the document and process could not be considered to demonstrate respect for them as individuals and they could not be regarded as giving informed consent if they did not fully understand the process and its implications.

Privacy

How can you reconcile an individual's right to privacy with the fact that your research report will be a public document? Most researchers address this issue by anonymising individuals and institutions. But what do you do if individuals cannot easily be anonymised? Or if they do not wish to be anonymised? And does anonymisation in itself fully address issues of privacy? In order to answer these questions it is necessary to consider some of the issues which may arise in educational research, and to look at some examples.

Josh's PhD study explored the training experiences of young surgeons in England in their immediate post-qualification phase. This was a participant group who, by virtue of the small size of the potential group of participants, the number of organisations who elected to, or not to, participate could be identified easily. If age and gender were included, then many of the participants were identifiable within their field. Josh addressed this by not identifying age or gender. Instead, he gave his participants non-gendered pseudonyms, using major world cities (Berlin and Rio for example) as participants' names. He also avoided mention of the size of organisations or their geographical location. This provided an effective strategy for maintaining individuals' privacy. However, Liz's study of the aspirations and learning identities of young people on level 1 vocational programmes presented a different challenge. The young people participating in her study wanted to be recognised: they regarded their participation as important and felt that it conferred value and celebrity on them. Liz was conscious that some had made disclosures which should be anonymised – illegal drug use and termination of pregnancy for example – but wanted to respect their wishes. In the end, a compromise was achieved – the young people were anonymised, but chose their own pseudonyms. These disclosures raise a more thorny issue around privacy which is the focus for the next reflective activity.

Reflective activity

In interviewing people, and investigating aspects of their lives, are we committing an invasion of privacy? If so, can it be justified in the context of the need for understanding that is the purpose of educational research? How might it be justified?

Power relationships

To what extent does your power relationship influence an individual's willingness to participate? Could it amount to coercion? Similarly, what are the issues if you want to involve individuals in your organisation – a headteacher or a principal for example – in a study? This has methodological as well as ethical implications, in that if a researcher feels that they cannot fully critique a situation, or that data has to be reported in a particular way in view of the position of some or all of the participants, then this not only produces a bias in the research, but it raises ethical questions about the honesty and integrity of the study. Victoria's MA study of assessment for learning (AfL) in a large comprehensive school was funded by her school as it was an area the school management was trying to develop. As well as issues around her role identity, this created two levels of tension in power relations. The first was between Victoria and her seniors, who wanted to use AfL as a means to improve pupil outcomes and so the school's position in the national league tables. The second was between Victoria and the other teachers, who were acting as participants at the request of school management, and many of whom were not implementing AfL in the classroom, or were paying lip-service to the concept. Issues such as this are common in small-scale educational research, much of which is 'insider' research and thus involves undertaking research with participants who stand to you in varying degrees of power relationship and with whom you have particular professional relationships. Taking on a researcher role can blur the boundaries between these roles or identities.

These are not always straightforward: you may, for example, interview members of the senior management team (SMT) or observe your students. In these situations, the power relationships and hierarchies are obvious. However, even if your participants are colleagues at the same grade, there will be myriad small hierarchies within that single grade. For example, someone may have a particularly close relationship with a more senior staff member, such as the head of department; someone else may be a natural leader, or a natural follower. Such differences in relationships and personalities contribute to sometimes tiny but often significant fractional positionings in the context of power differentials, and these should always be given serious consideration, especially where you are undertaking research in an 'insider' role. Such relationships can also undergo change (with further implications for your research), particularly if there is confusion about when you are a professional and when you are a researcher, and the relationship between those roles.

Deception

Is it always morally wrong to deceive even where this is the only way to elicit necessary data? This question has vexed researchers for many years, and two of the most famous research studies involving deception are still the subject of debate today. Neither of these was an educational study: one was an ethnographic, social sciences study and the second a psychological experiment. However, it is possible to draw lessons from these studies in terms of ethical practice where this is related to deception and indeed, to potential harm to the participants.

The first of these studies was conducted by Laud Humphreys in the USA during the 1960s and published in 1970 under the title *Tearoom Trade: Impersonal Sex in Public Places* (the term tea-rooming in American slang has the same meaning as cottaging in English slang). This ethnographic study explored anonymous male/male sexual encounters which took place in public lavatories, during which the researcher masqueraded as a voyeur and did not gain consent from the individuals involved. He later tracked down some of these men – many of whom were married – using their vehicle licence-plate numbers and interviewed them in their homes, in disguise and under false pretences. This study was open to criticism at many levels on ethical grounds.

The second study formed part of psychologist Stanley Milgram's research into obedience and authority. It was intended to explore whether the war criminal Adolf Eichmann and his contemporaries had a shared sense of morality and was conducted at the time of Eichmann's trial in Jerusalem. The experiment involved volunteer participants being given the role of 'teacher' who had to teach a 'learner' a series of word pairs. The teachers and learners could communicate but not see each other. The 'teacher' was required to administer an electric shock to the learner whenever they gave an incorrect answer. The voltage would increase incrementally for each incorrect response. Some of the 'teachers' were told that the 'learner' had a heart condition. In reality, there were no shocks and the 'learners' were all actors. As the experiment progressed, many of the 'teachers' expressed concern about the 'learner' and asked to stop. Some exhibited symptoms of severe stress but all were told that they would not be held responsible and must continue. Participants were given four verbal prods to continue: if they still wished to stop they were allowed to do so, otherwise the experiment was halted after they had 'given' the 'learner' three 450-volt shocks in succession. Like Humphreys' work, Milgram's study can be criticised in ethical terms at a number of different levels.

Both studies took place during the 1960s and it would not be possible today, in a time of ethics committees and human rights legislation, to replicate them. However, Humphreys in particular addressed the ethical issues arising from his study, and the debates these studies generated are still pertinent today, since they provide lessons for us on issues such as honesty and harm in research. In terms of honesty, participants were deceived in both studies, and yet it is probable that neither could have achieved the findings they did, and made the contribution to knowledge that they did, without that deception. Similarly, participants were exposed to potentially harmful situations in both studies, yet again, the results of both studies may not have been possible had this not been the case.

Building critical research skills: activity

In a small group, discuss Humphreys' and Milgram's studies separately, considering

- deception used;
- strategies for gathering data used;
- potential for harm to the participants;
- value of contribution to human knowledge.

Then debate the following for each:

1. Are the deception and data-gathering strategy used in this study outweighed by the findings and the contribution it has made to human knowledge?
2. Is the potential harm suffered by participants in these studies outweighed by the findings and the contribution each has made to human knowledge?

Now choose *one* of the studies and answer the following question:

What are the possibilities for an alternative methodology which could have avoided deception and harm *and* generated similar results?

Honesty

Is honesty the same as or different from the absence of deception? However you respond to this question, it is certainly clear that being honest in educational research and conducting that research with integrity, raises profound philosophical questions and debates. Obvious cases of dishonesty in a research context would include those cited above, in which the participants were deceived about the nature of the research or not told that they were being observed for purposes of research; another form of dishonesty would be to falsify your data. Yet even here, there may be a complex moral dimension. Questions of truth and morality in this context formed the whole premise of C.P. Snow's 1934 novel, *The Search,* which is about a scientist who makes an error in his data, loses his career as a consequence but who later does not mention the deliberate falsification of data by a younger scientist, as this other man has a wife and family to support. Snow was a scientist as well as an author and government adviser. He was very concerned about the search for truth in research, and about the responsibility of the researcher, as illustrated in a statement attributed to him which argues that 'A scientist has to be neutral in his search for the truth, but he cannot be neutral as to the use of that truth when found. If you know more than other people, you have more responsibility, rather than less.' (cited in Moskin, 1966: 61). Snow's concern with some of the 'big' ethical issues in research, such as honesty, was very much ahead of his time, and may reflect his interests in education and the humanities as well as his work and training as a physicist.

It is unlikely that a study conducted, for example, as part of an MA, would raise the significant issues discussed above. However, issues around honesty, integrity and deception can occur on a smaller scale and some of these are associated with the tensions of researching in an educational context. It is important, from an ethical perspective, to be aware that honesty and integrity are core values, and as such, they can be argued to elevate seemingly minor issues around honesty and integrity to the same level of importance as those in Milgram's and Humphreys' studies or those discussed by Snow in his novel. By this, I mean that if there is an issue around truth and integrity, it does not become of less importance because the study is smaller/less important; the moral dimension remains unchanged. It is also necessary to be aware that upholding values of truth and integrity can have negative consequences.

Vignette 2

Sarah was undertaking an MA dissertation evaluating the use of a nurture room in her primary school. Her MA was paid for by the school, which had an interest in the results of the study. Data suggested that there was inconsistency among SMT and teaching staff with regard to the use of the nurture room. An SMT policy on the purpose and use of the room lacked clarity and was implemented differently across the school. Effectively, this meant that children were referred to the resource for reasons as diverse as rewards for good work, to exclude them from the classroom, and when they were in need of social or physical support, such as clean clothes. One teacher stated that she refused to use it unless directed to do so as she considered that children should be in the classroom, learning. These data had the potential to bring Sarah into conflict with both SMT and her colleagues.

Reflective activity

In Sarah's position, what would you have done? How would you have presented the data? What potential is there for dishonesty (either misrepresenting or suppressing data) in circumstances such as these?

Billy used action research (AR) to improve relationships and teaching and learning in an American High School. While he was successful in doing this, the imperative for honesty at all levels and in all situations led him into conflict with the local area schools management board, and as a consequence he had to leave his post. Thus, for Billy, honesty and integrity in his study may be seen to have contributed to the loss of his livelihood.

Reflective activity

In Billy's position, what would you have done? Discuss this with a colleague and make notes.

Another aspect of this may be seen in the way we manipulate, rather than intentionally misrepresent data. This is a particular issue in the context of interviews, which are used heavily in qualitative research, and in the way individuals are represented. This is because all data is mediated, so whatever a participant says, and however honestly you try to reflect that, some of what you say will reflect your own interpretation, and thus your values and positionality, rather than those of the participant. Because of this, ethically, a researcher cannot 'lift the results of interviews out of the contexts in which they were gathered and claim them as objective data with no strings attached' (Fontana and Frey, 2000: 663). Such an approach not only fails to acknowledge the different situations of the researcher and the researched, but also, which is perhaps more morally questionable, raises the possibility that the participants might be represented in ways which they would not recognise. Issues such as this might be particularly apparent in research exploring areas such as behaviour and motivation, for example.

Harm

What constitutes harm? How can you quantify harm? Is there any way in which harm can ever be justified? Fontana and Frey (2000: 662) argue that protection from harm forms one of the three traditional ethical concerns in qualitative research (the other two are informed consent and the right to privacy). There are obvious examples of potential harm to individuals in some research studies. In the context of the examples used in this chapter, Milgram's research caused harm to the participants in terms of the distress they experienced at the time, and possibly in the future when they reflected on the implications of what they had done. Sarah's nurture-room study raised the possibility of harm to individual teachers who might have been recognisable and faced particular consequences as a result of their interpretation of a school strategy. In this context, Sarah herself was at risk of harm in terms of the potential effect on her relationships with others in the school as a result of the way she interpreted and presented her data and the conclusions she drew from it. These examples illustrate an important point. Harm may not just include the immediate consequences for participants, but future consequences both for them, for others involved in the study (such as the researcher or co-researchers) or even, possibly, for others doing similar work or researching the same setting at some point in the future. Dan, for example, in attempting to gain views from a truly random sample of the population, determined to stop every tenth person in the street and ask them to complete a short questionnaire. The questionnaire included demographic information, and a complaint was subsequently received by his institution from a woman who objected to being asked her date of birth. As a consequence, very rigid policies on research and supervision were introduced which severely restricted the scope of future studies in his institution.

Other dilemmas related to protection from harm may include the disclosure of certain information to the researcher, which is given 'in confidence' and related to issues of individual harm, such as criminality or abuse. Disclosures such as these are less uncommon than you may think. They are, perhaps, more likely to occur in studies which explore issues such as identity or those which use approaches such as life history research. Joanne Casser's study provides a good example of educational research which had the potential to cause harm to individuals as a consequence of disclosure. Joanne explored emerging sexuality among Years 12 and 13 girls. Her study took place in Malta, a society which maintains very traditional Catholic morality and values, and which meant that she had to address significant ethical issues in terms of disclosure of sexual activity and the potential identification of participants, particularly at the point of dissemination of the study, within a very small and 'village like' community. The strategies Joanne used to disseminate her study are explored further in Chapter 12, 'Disseminating your research'.

Concerns about harm also raise issues of reciprocity. Every research project depends upon the goodwill of those who act as participants. Think back to the last time you filled in a questionnaire or completed an interview or survey and work out how long it took you. In co-operating with the study, you had to give up valuable time. As a researcher, you depend upon similar co-operation from participants in order to generate the data you need for your study. Because of this, and the potential for research to be disruptive to individuals, there is a question around 'payment' for participation. Is it reasonable for a participant to expect payment and should this always be in a monetary form? Costs to cover some token payment are often calculated into budgets for funded research, and this raises methodological as well as ethical issues. Would participants be as willing if they were not paid? And if not, does that mean that the data generated is different to the data that might have been generated without payment? Does this matter? In a small-scale study, such as for a Master's degree or even a PhD, monetary payment is unlikely. However, you may wish to provide tokens such as packs of sweets for young participants, which raises the same ethical and methodological questions. If a study involves colleagues, you may not do this, but the exchange of 'favours' in giving up time may lead you to ask similar questions.

Value judgements

Ethical issues can also arise from the value judgements that we and others make. These cannot be avoided – such judgements and beliefs are part of our identity – but they must be recognised within the context of any educational research project, given their possible implications. For example, consider Joanne's study, and think how this might have been influenced had she had particular values regarding the advisability or otherwise of sexual experimentation among young people. The potential for value judgements in Joanne's work is obvious, However, a brief consideration of your educational values will also raise areas for potential judgements or even conflict. In relation to the curriculum, how would you respond if asked to implement a strategy with which you disagreed? For example, this might include the inclusion/exclusion of vocational subjects or the use of specific strategies to teach reading and may draw into conflict values around professionalism, social justice or the value of particular types of learning. Although all educational research is conducted with the aim of making positive change, negative outcomes can occur and this makes the acknowledgement of values and the potential for value judgements an important ethical issue.

Reflective activity

Reflect on and write down your own values. These might include values such as honesty, integrity, respect or social justice. What value judgements do you make on others – particularly students and colleagues? (Try to be honest about this.) Finally, reflect on how these judgements could influence the research you are planning or undertaking.

Ethical guidelines

It is essential to draw on ethical guidance, such as that provided by BERA, applying the spirit as well as the letter of the guidance. By this we mean that it is possible to interpret guidance quite literally, and to respond to it in an instrumental way, rather than giving consideration to that guidance and asking yourself not just 'How does this apply to my study?' but 'What are the implications of this guidance for my participants?' 'How can I use it to develop a more moral and rigorous approach to my research?' 'How can I embed that ethics and morality in the research process?' Perhaps the best example of this is the guidance on informed consent. According to the BERA guidelines (2011):

The Association takes voluntary informed consent to be the condition in which participants understand and agree to their participation without any duress, prior to the research getting underway.

11 Researchers must take the steps necessary to ensure that all participants in the research understand the process in which they are to be engaged, including why their participation is necessary, how it will be used and how and to whom it will be reported. Social networking and other on-line activities, including their video-based environments, present challenges for consideration of consent issues and the participants must be clearly informed that their participation and interactions are being monitored and analysed for research.

12 Researchers engaged in action research must consider the extent to which their own reflective research impinges on others, for example in the case of the dual role of teacher and researcher and the impact on students and colleagues. Dual roles may also introduce explicit tensions in areas such as confidentiality and must be addressed accordingly.

13 Educational research undertaken by UK researchers outside of the UK must adhere to the same ethical standards as research in the UK. ... Especially sensitive ethical issues arise when researching particular communities which are marginalised because of their age, culture, race, gender, sexuality, socio-economic standing or religion. Ethical issues also arise when researching in sensitive situations influenced by contexts of cultural difference and which impact on educational experiences.

Openness and Disclosure

14 The securing of participants' voluntary informed consent, before research gets underway, is considered the norm for the conduct of research.

Despite the guidance being explicit about conducting research within 'an ethic of respect' (BERA, 2011: 5), which implies a considered and reflexive approach to ethical issues, many new (and some more experienced) researchers tend to use a rather instrumental approach. Many times, we have read both students' (and other) work in which the author has identified, for example, informed consent as an ethical issue, then reported that the participants were asked to sign a consent form and told they could withdraw at any

point. Such an approach does not really address the implications of the concept of informed consent in a meaningful way. For example, Fine et al. (2000:
107–28) pose the question 'Inform(ing) and Consent: who's informed and
who's consenting?' in a discussion which raises issues about the validity of
informed consent and this, perhaps, gets to the heart of the issue. Who is
informed? To what extent are they really informed? And if they are not really
informed (particularly of the power and relationship implications of participating in educational research), how can they give informed consent? Many
of these questions revolve around understanding – it is unwise to assume that
participants have the same level of understanding of educational research
and its possible implications as the researcher, who, by definition, is going
through, or has gone through, some degree of research training.

Many educational research projects involve students or children as participants, for whom consent will have been obtained from the young person and
possibly also from a parent or guardian. However, for the most part, this
audience will be unaware of the human relationship issues arising from
ethnographic studies, and will, by definition therefore, be giving consent but
not informed consent. While this may satisfy some ethical guidelines, in
terms of conducting educational research as moral practice Sikes and
Goodson (2003: 48) have suggested that 'this view reduces moral concerns
to the procedural: a convenient form of methodological reductionism'. So,
how is it possible to address an issue such as informed consent, without
resorting to the type of approach criticised by Sikes and Goodson?

This was a dilemma that Liz faced in her study, which involved level 1[1]
16–19 students. The young people were very keen to be involved in the
study, and to appear in the book which would arise from it. They had no
real understanding of the possible implications of participating – such as the
acute distress which was caused to one young woman by the apparently
innocuous question 'Does your family support your wish to return to college
next year?' – so, bearing this in mind, how could it be addressed? At a practical level, Liz addressed this by keeping participants involved and informed
throughout, using both verbal and written forms of communication, and
attempting to establish an ongoing dialogue with them through the medium
of email as well as face to face during visits to the colleges. However, after
the study was completed she reflected that:

> I remain concerned that the consent given was not truly 'informed', although I
> also remain convinced that I used every strategy available to me to try and
> ensure that it was. This does not absolve me of responsibility but leaves me
> with an ongoing debate about the ethics of consent. Would it have been more
> or less ethical to discontinue the study in acknowledgement of this dilemma?

More ethical possibly, in not exploiting a lack of understanding, but also possibly less ethical in denying these young people the opportunity to speak for themselves.

Ethical requirements in different settings

It is also important to take into account the ethical requirements of your institution. These vary widely. For example, in many primary schools staff and children are often the subject of observations and case studies by trainee teachers and nursery nurses, and staff often undertake research as part of ongoing continuing professional development (CPD). Therefore, many schools issue a consent form at the beginning of each academic year asking parents to agree to their children participating in research activities in school and to having their photographs taken when engaged in school activities, for use in displays and marketing. This approach is also common in many secondary schools. This means that the principle of gaining consent is not usually problematic, and that the organisation is likely to support a project, particularly where they can perceive a benefit to you, the student group it serves or the institution as a whole. In some alternative settings, the position is very different.

Vignette 3

Mac is a basic skills and music teacher. While undertaking a Master's module he wanted to explore staff perceptions of the purpose of education in his institution. For most organisations, this would not have been a problem. However, Mac is employed in the education department of a high security prison. The institution and wider service requirements in terms of gaining permission for his study were enormous, despite his clear and comprehensive ethical framework and the fact that only staff, such as teachers and prison officers, rather than prisoners, were intended to participate in the study. When permission was eventually granted – after applications to multiple layers of management and consideration by committee – Mac was given permission to involve prison teachers, but no other staff group, in his study. This had a methodological impact in terms of the original focus of the study and the amount of data that was then available.

Finally, there are circumstances in which the ethical guidance, when followed, will provide methodological challenges for the study and these will have to be reconciled. For example, most institutional ethical frameworks, as well as the BERA guidance, identify research involving vulnerable people – including children, those with learning disabilities or mental health problems, and so on – as needing additional ethical consideration. Often, this can mean applying to an ethics committee, with a proposal for the study and an ethical framework which illustrates how the dignity of participants is to be supported, anticipated ethical issues and strategies in place to address them. This can take a considerable period of time, so if you are undertaking a small-scale, time-bound study, such as a Master's module, you may wish to consider alternative sources of data which present fewer ethical challenges. However, you will also have to consider whether such data will provide the answers you are seeking. This is a common tension in educational research and often, like Mac, it is necessary to compromise.

Building critical research skills: activity

Rebekah is a Year 6 teacher in a primary school in an area of significant economic and social disadvantage. Many of her children have parents with chaotic lifestyles. As part of her MA studies, she is planning to involve the children and their parents in an evaluation of a weekly nurture and homework club she is running.

- What potential ethical issues arise from this study?
- What would be the key aspects of an ethical framework for such a study?
- Aim to respond to these questions in some detail.

Key points

- Ethical and moral debates have no clear answers; this means that we are placed under a considerable moral responsibility to conduct educational research in the best possible interests of everyone concerned.
- Ethically, educational research must be underpinned by respect for others and the intention to achieve positive change.
- Every phase of a research study has potential ethical implications, from planning through to data collection and interpretation to writing up and representing the data, and these implications should be considered, reconsidered and addressed at every stage.
- Instrumental activities such as getting participants to sign a consent form are *not enough* for you to make the claim that your study is ethical.

Websites ⌐₀

Resources on ethics are available at:
- www.bera.ac.uk/publications/guidelines/
- www.bera.ac.uk/beraresources/ethics/

The guidelines will provide the framework for you to develop an ethical approach to your study. The resources provide a number of discussion documents which explore ethical debates, issues and dilemmas and which can be used to inform your approach. Further guidance and suggested reading on informed consent is available on the Teaching and Learning Research Project website at: http://www.tlrp.org/capacity/rm/wt/bridges/bridges6.html. Other pages on the same site provide a broader consideration of the philosophical issues around ethics, and provide suggestions for further reading.

Note

1. Level 1 is the approximate standard expected by the average 14-year-old in the UK, and is the lowest level at which mainstream (rather than special education) programmes are offered post-16.

References and further reading ▢

British Educational Research Association (BERA) (2011) *Ethical Guidelines for Educational Research*. Available at: www.bera.ac.uk/publications/guidelines/.

Fine, M., Weis, L., Weseen, S. and Wong, L. (2000) 'For whom? Qualitative research, representations, and social responsibilities', in N. Denzin and Y. Lincoln (eds), *Handbook of Qualitative Research* 2nd edn. London: Sage Publications.

Fontana, A. and Frey, J. (2000) 'The interview: from structured questions to negotiated text', in N. Denzin and Y. Lincoln (eds), *Handbook of Qualitative Research*. 2nd edn. London: Sage Publications.

General Teaching Council (GTC) (2009) *Code of Conduct and Practice for Registered Teachers*. Birmingham: GTC.

Humphreys, L. (1970) *Tearoom Trade: Impersonal Sex in Public Places*. London: Gerald Duckworth.

Institute for Learning (IfL) (2011) *Code of Professional Practice*. London: IfL.

Moskin, J.R. (1966) *Morality in America*. New York: Random House.

Sikes, P., Nixon, J. and Carr, W. (eds) (2003) *The Moral Foundations of Educational Research: Knowledge, Inquiry and Values*. Maidenhead: Open University Press. See especially Sikes and Goodson, chapter 3 'Living research: thoughts on educational research as moral practice'.

Simons, H. and Usher, R. (2000) *Situated Ethics in Educational Research*. London: RoutledgeFalmer.

Snow, C.P. (1934/2011) *The Search*. Looe: Stratus Books.

Wellington, J. (2000) *Educational Research: Contemporary Issues and Practical Approaches*. London: Continuum.

CHAPTER 3

INSIDER RESEARCH

Summary

This chapter explores some of the advantages and pitfalls associated with insider research in education. It illustrates these with example scenarios drawn from the authors' own practice and points the reader towards current debates and useful literature. The chapter explores some of the issues around confidentiality, rights, responsibilities, impartiality and power relations in insider research, and the methodological and ethical considerations surrounding these. It discusses the innate tensions involved in insider research, such as writing up and disseminating a study, drawing on key data, while maintaining the confidentiality of individuals and organisations, something which is particularly significant in the competitive educational markets of further and higher education.

The content of this chapter relates closely to that in Chapter 8 ('Ethnographic research') and to that in Chapter 2 ('Ethical research in education') where the example of Victoria illustrates the way in which the power relationships in insider research can pose profound ethical and methodological challenges. Other practical examples used in this chapter include that of Richard, who, despite his personal views about the issue he was researching, was able to undertake a rigorous and reflexive study supported by methodological triangulation.

Key words used in this chapter: *insider/outsider, role identity, boundary conflict, confidentiality, relationships, power relations, impartiality.*

Introduction

Much educational research, particularly that which is undertaken as part of postgraduate study, occurs inside the researchers' own institution and is conducted by a 'researching professional' rather than a 'professional researcher' (Wellington and Sikes, 2006: 725). Undertaking research as an insider has many advantages, such as ease of access, the opportunity to make positive change in one's own setting, and so on. However, it also raises complex ethical and methodological issues arising from undertaking the study from an 'insider' perspective and generates debates about the insider/outsider relationship in educational research, all of which need to be considered as the project progresses. Of particular note are the tensions and dilemmas which can arise as a consequence of the study. For example, it may not be possible to anonymise some key informants, or a situation may arise in which the outcomes of the study, particularly if they are critical of practice, may bring you into conflict with colleagues or senior managers within your institution. There is also particular difficulty around role definition in insider research – to what extent are you a professional and to what extent are you a researcher in each situation that you find yourself in? This theme recurs throughout this chapter. You will also have difficulty if you are planning to claim *objectivity* in your study, since an insider will naturally be *subjective* about the organisation and the focus of the study.

These challenges make it particularly important that the wider implications of undertaking insider research, and the specific implications of undertaking your own study, are considered in detail, in both practical and theoretical terms, before you begin your research. As a starting point, it can be helpful to think of insider/outsider research as a continuum and place yourself, and the study you are doing, on that continuum. There are 'for' and 'against' arguments in relation to insider/outsider research (that only insiders have sufficient insight into the organisation to do 'proper' research and only outsiders are sufficiently impartial to do 'proper' research), However, as Trowler (2011) has argued, these arguments are a fallacy since it is rare for anyone to be a complete insider or a complete outsider. An example of someone who became both insider and outsider is Jaskaren, a teacher who undertook insider research during which colleagues came to perceive him as a researcher (outsider) as well as a colleague, something which had implications for his relationships with others and for the data that colleagues provided. Locating yourself and your research on a continuum will help you to determine the extent to which you are an insider/outsider and the possible implications that this has for *your* research.

The continuum produced by the Teaching and Learning Research Programme (TLRP, 2011) is helpful here. Are you:

- a researcher who undertakes action research within his or her own classroom?
- a researcher who undertakes research within his or her own school, university or education department?
- an external researcher who is invited in to help a school by conducting some research on its behalf?
- a researcher who is conducting research on behalf of, eg a local education authority with which a school is obliged to co-operate?
- a researcher pursuing his or her own research interests and seeks the agreement of a school to participate?
- a researcher travelling overseas to conduct some research in a community in which he or she is a complete stranger for an alien culture?

Reflective activity

Place yourself and your study on the continuum above, then ask yourself how your positioning on that continuum affects: your relationships with others (both participants and non-participants) and what the possible implications are for your research and for future working relationships. Try to consider these questions in some depth. Make notes and keep them to return to later.

Advantages of insider research

Most novice researchers choose to undertake insider research for purely pragmatic reasons: gaining access to organisations and the people within them is critical to any research study, and often one of the most time-consuming aspects of the research process. By undertaking a study within your own workplace you bypass these difficulties and achieve instant access to both the organisation and to your colleagues/students as potential participants. Further, the colleagues, students and others you hope to involve will be people with whom you already have established interpersonal relationships, meaning that they are far more likely to be prevailed upon to participate than complete strangers might be and your interactions with them will be far more natural. As well as being more likely to participate, colleagues may well disclose more to you because a pre-existing relationship means that they have greater trust in you than they might have done had you been an outsider researcher. This offers the potential for gathering different, perhaps more illuminative, data which can tell a more informed story – or generate 'thick(er) description' (Geertz, 1973: 3) – than might have been possible to an outsider researcher. These existing relationships, and your membership of a particular world, also have the benefit of giving you insights and understandings into the culture of the organisation and into practices which might be invisible or incomprehensible to someone from outside.

In addition to these benefits, undertaking insider research provides far greater opportunities for using research for positive change; once you have answered your research question, you have more scope for using your results to influence or inform developments in practice within your organisation, something which may not be practicable as an outsider, unless your study has been commissioned by the organisation. Further, undertaking research as an insider also offers considerable economic benefits in terms of time and the potential financial costs associated with undertaking research as an outsider, sometimes in settings geographically distant from home or work. This broad range of 'possibilities and potentialities' offered by insider research is summarised by Sikes and Potts (2008: 177) as:

> inside researchers readily know the language of those being studied, along with its particular jargon and are more likely to empathise with those they study because of in-depth understanding of them, less likely to foster distrust and hostility among those they study, are often more willing to discuss private knowledge with those who are personally part of their world, are often more likely to understand the events under investigation and are less likely to be afflicted by outsiders' arrogance where researchers fail to understand what they observe. Inside researchers find that those they study are often more likely to volunteer information to them than they would to outsiders.

Challenges in insider research

The principal challenges associated with undertaking insider research are those associated with role identity and boundary conflict, confidentiality, relationships, power relations and impartiality. It is a paradox that these same issues – albeit from a different perspective – also present challenges in outsider research. It is essential, therefore, that at the planning stage you consider and address the debates and dilemmas associated with your study, since not to do so will leave your work open to significant – and justifiable – criticism.

Similar to other qualitative approaches in educational research, insider research can be subject to criticisms that it lacks rigour, credibility and reliability. Sometimes such critiques arise from differences in perspective, as in the positivist versus interpretivist debates discussed in Chapter 1. Frequently, however, such criticisms are perfectly valid in the context of the way in which a study has been planned, executed, analysed and/or reported. As a researcher, therefore, it becomes your responsibility – some would say your moral responsibility – to ensure that the process is as systematic, rigorous, credible and reliable as possible. In this way you can generate understandings that can contribute to positive changes in education.

A key aspect of this rigour is the development of a theoretical framework (sometimes referred to as a conceptual framework) for the study. Put simply, a theory is a model, or set of ideas, which is used as a way of understanding or explaining something. Therefore, a theoretical framework uses a particular set or type of explanations in order to interpret or analyse a situation, phenomenon or set of data. The particular set of ideas used in a study (for example, social justice or feminist/Marxist perspectives) will be explored in the literature review, and will influence the approach to the study, the methods used and the analysis. Without this, the study stands alone and cannot be contextualised within, or supported by, similar work. By placing the study within a clear and well constructed framework, you are more likely to avoid criticisms associated with completing a project which is not credible and rigorous – for example, by making weakly supported or unsupported assertions. In other words, there is less scope for sloppy research. The theoretical framework thus becomes a means, together with an ethical and methodologically rigorous approach to the research process, of undertaking research which is 'systematic, credible, verifiable, justifiable, useful, valuable and trustworthy' (Wellington, 2000: 14). We will return to these words later, in the context of impartiality.

It is useful to consider your role of insider researcher as being on a continuum and to use this to guide the decisions you make about the ethical and methodological issues that arise in your study. Both Hammersley and Atkinson (2007: 82), and Wellington (2000: 93) reproduce Junker's model of social roles for fieldwork (1960: 36), outlining the advantages and disadvantages of each end of a continuum in which the researcher is complete participant or complete observer, and this is a useful model to help you determine where you stand as an insider researcher. Within the context of this continuum, the complete participant end of the scale refers to a researcher who is embedded within an organisation undertaking covert research. However, for an insider researcher investigating their own setting, it is likely to be impossible to undertake a complete participant data collection. This is as a consequence of the ethical and contractual issues that exist in terms of professional responsibilities to students, employers and the wider organisation. This point is noted by Hammersley and Atkinson, (1983: 95) who argue that 'the complete participant has to act in accordance with existing role expectations'. In addition, for anyone working within a relatively closed organisation, such as a school, college or university, their role and identity are often familiar to others, also rendering covert research impossible.

Similarly, and paradoxically, the same ethical and contractual responsibilities also render the position of complete observer impractical for the insider researcher. The necessity of carrying on with an organisational role precludes this level of observation and the close working relationships with colleagues and students mean that an 'outside' detached and objective view of a situation or phenomenon is not possible. Indeed, as Hammersley and Atkinson (2007: 86–7) have argued, there is more of a risk of 'over-rapport' which in itself can limit data-gathering opportunities and, owing to the close identification the researcher has developed with the participants, may result in the research participants being presented in an unrealistically favourable light at the reporting stage.

As well as these issues, other influences on the researcher as a member of the organisation in which the research is being conducted include a range of ethical and practical difficulties, such as access, confidentiality, and political and other constraints on participants, and the reporting and disclosure of data. Potts (2000: 369–403) discusses these difficulties at length in his insider research on college academics, although he argues in favour of such research not only by outlining the advantages such as ease of access and the economic benefits, but also by developing a clear theoretical framework, which in his case included concepts such as symbolic interactionism and situational adjustment.

The issues Potts faced, such as the reporting and disclosure of data while maintaining the confidentiality of individuals and organisations, form a particular challenge in insider research in educational settings. The smaller the organisation, the greater the challenges involved in maintaining confidentiality and this is a particular problem in education where constant scrutiny and inspection means that apparently insignificant facts or information can have an alarming impact on individuals or organisations. It is not enough to anonymise here, or even to warn participants that anonymity may be difficult to achieve. It is also necessary to consider for participants, what the possible implications might be of inadvertently releasing information, and considering how that could be avoided. One student, alluded to in Chapter 2, used non-gendered names (capital cities) as pseudonyms for his participants, and avoided giving geographical and other information which might have identified them. This was effective, but the use of these strategies has to be balanced against other imperatives – if gender is significant in the context of your study, for example, then participants will need to have gender-specific names, and if status is important this will have to be defined and these characteristics may well compromise confidentiality. It is your responsibility, as the researcher, to find ethically and methodologically acceptable ways of addressing these issues, which are explored in the activity below.

Building critical research skills: activity

Tom's study explored specific skills acquisition among 20 engineering apprentices doing an NVQ 3 at the engineering company where he worked as training manager. He had guaranteed anonymity to all participants. The company director was keen to see the results, as they had implications for competitiveness in a difficult economic climate. Tom spent a year gathering data, using a range of mixed methods, as the apprentices moved between departments to develop different skills and achieve different competencies. Analysis of data demonstrated that although 18 of the apprentices completed the course and gained their NVQ (two having left for alternative employment) the time frame for achievement of competencies varied significantly between departments and the specific skills gained in one department were weak. Here, the data suggested that additional training might be necessary.

What are the implications of these results:

- for Tom?
- for the company?
- for the apprentices?
- for individual staff and departments?

Impartiality in insider research

Positivists would argue that a degree of objectivity is critical to the reliability and validity of a research project. This requirement to achieve objectivity arises from the history of educational research, which originally drew on research in the natural sciences. Scientific research has always laid emphasis on objectivity, validity and reliability. However, as Wellington (2000: 14) has argued, it is a 'mystery' why so many educational researchers subscribe to these ideas, rather than aspiring to undertake research which is 'systematic, credible, verifiable, justifiable, useful, valuable and trustworthy'. We would argue that it is never possible to be truly objective within a subjective situation, and since all educational research involves people it is inevitable that it will be subjective in nature. What is important is that it meets the criteria proposed by Wellington (above). That said, impartiality, or the ability to step back and look at a situation differently, is a major consideration in undertaking insider research, and is, perhaps, something which is often overlooked by novice (and some not-so-novice) researchers. Impartiality becomes a consideration because, as a 'proper' member of the community you are investigating, the challenges around maintaining a distance 'in order to be able to take a clear and an unbiased non-partisan approach are significant and complicated' (Sikes and Potts, 2008: 7).

The implications arising from the way in which the researcher views their own organisation have also been explored by Taylor and Bogdan (1984: 19–20) who highlight the tendency for researchers to believe that their own view of their organisation is the only one, or the 'right' interpretation. They warn that every researcher should be aware that their own interpretation is only one of many possible views of a situation or phenomenon. This concept of relativity, based in the philosophical belief that all interpretations and the value of those interpretations vary, also illustrates the fact that as an insider with particular insights and understandings of your setting and the people who work there, it can be very difficult to step back and 'make the familiar strange', or to take something which is taken for granted and accepted as normal within your organisation and problematise it.

Reflective activity

Which practices in your own organisation might be mystifying to an outsider? Considering these is the first step in 'making the familiar strange'. Questions that might help you to identify some of these practices might include asking: 'How do we do x?' 'Why do we do it this way?' 'To whose benefit is it?'

Relationships and power relations

While you are undertaking your research, a whole host of issues may arise which can present difficulties with impartiality. For example, your relationships with others within the organisation will be different, and some will be stronger or more challenging than others. Such differences in interpersonal relationships can create bias and it can be very difficult to acknowledge this and step back, and consider the implications of this particular relationship in ethical and methodological terms. Similarly, the different relationships arising from your role as researcher (and hence, as 'outsider', since you have taken on a different role) may impact on future professional relationships. For example, people may trust you less as a researcher than they did as a fellow professional. It is not only relationships with colleagues that can change; the role of researcher may come into conflict with the job you are employed to do, or leave you with competing loyalties as you uncover different pictures to those that are accepted as reality by the organisation and the people within it. This is illustrated in Grace's story, below.

Vignette 1

Grace was a teacher in a school for children with special educational needs. Many of the children had autistic spectrum disorders. The school prided itself on its pastoral care and there was a common belief among the staff, written into self-evaluation reports, that they were providing the best possible service for these young people. Grace's PhD research explored the curriculum in some depth. Her findings implied that, for most of the children, the curriculum was not challenging or stretching and by extension they were not fulfilling their potential. This directly challenged the belief among staff at the school that they were doing a 'good job'. Grace's findings and the research process (both of which were commended at her PhD viva) were challenged and heavily criticised by her colleagues. Relationships deteriorated and Grace eventually moved to a new post.

Of course, conflict arising from a research project will not always have negative outcomes to the extent that Grace's did. However, there is still the possibility that your research, or possibly the expectations that others have of that research, may have the potential for conflict, something which is explored in the following activity.

> ## Reflective activity
>
> As a condition of being flexibly timetabled to facilitate her research, which explored assessment practices in a *lycée technologique* in France, Jolie was told that she had to present the completed study to her head of department so that it could be used to support *lycée* policy. This implied that the *lycée* expected a particular set of outcomes from the study. Reflecting on Jolie's experience, how do you think that this might have influenced the integrity of her study and her relationship with her manager?

Power relations

Power relations are also likely to play a part in these changing and developing relationships. Power relations, and some of the issues around this concept, are also discussed at some length in Chapter 7, 'Action research'. To a great extent, what is written there also applies to insider research, much of which uses ethnographic techniques. This raises questions about people's motives for participating in the study, particularly where students/pupils are concerned. Despite potential participants being given the 'choice' of whether or not to participate, you should always give consideration to the possibility that they are making choices that are not their own, because they feel pressured in some way. This does not have to be as overt as a person in a less powerful position being 'told' to participate, but may be related to an individual's wish to 'do the right thing' or create a positive impression. Power relations will also be influenced by subtle positioning among those who are apparently 'equal', as well as by characteristics such as race, gender, disability, sexuality age and level of experience or time in the organisation. For example, there will be subtle differences between two teachers at the same grade where one is an ambitious young male, and the other is an older female planning to see out her career as a classroom teacher. Andy's story below, illustrates some of the tensions that can arise in insider research as a consequence of power relations within a setting or organisation.

Vignette 2

Andy was part-way through his MA when he was appointed Assistant Head at a specialist pupil referral unit. The unit catered for up to 50 11–16 pupils, all excluded from school, most of whom had complex social, emotional and behavioural problems. A significant proportion of the pupils were also known to the youth justice system. The school had been graded satisfactory during its last inspection, two years previously, but was the subject of significant intervention by the local education authority (LEA) following a perceived decline in attainment and behaviour. For his dissertation, Andy decided to investigate behaviour across the school. He specifically wanted to establish whether the behaviour policy was applied consistently (it wasn't) and what led staff to deviate from the policy. He used the opportunities for peer observation presented by his new role, as well as interviews and documentary evidence such as behaviour reports as data. Andy was able to establish that, with one exception, all teaching staff deviated from the policy when faced with persistent, low-level disruption in the class.

It is useful to consider some of the implications of this study in terms of insider research. These included the blurring of role identity, ethical complications and power relations. In Andy's case, his new role of Assistant Head provided many opportunities for insider research, particularly in terms of observations of staff teaching and access to a broad range of school data. However, it raised particular issues in terms of the blurring of boundaries, since he negotiated the use of scheduled peer observations as 'dual' observations during which he used the standard observation documentation, with some additions to collect data on classroom behaviour and its management. This was pragmatic in terms of minimising disruption and saving on staff time. However, it presented ethical issues in terms of how the data might be used, who would have access to it and what the implications might be for the ongoing LEA concerns about the school and individual teachers. Further complications were presented by the power relations within the study; although the (mainly female) staff team were keen to improve and to address behaviour management, which they recognised was a problem, and although Andy presented his study as an opportunity to identify common problems and develop practice, it is likely that his management position persuaded some staff to participate in the study, particularly since, as a relatively new member of staff, his interpersonal relationships with other staff were not yet fully established.

In addition to these concerns, there were the more 'usual' ethical and methodological challenges, such as how to anonymise a small staff team and how to address the ethical challenges associated with observing behaviour among young people already deemed to be vulnerable or at risk, some of whom were looked after by the local authority and others of whom had parents and carers hostile to the school and unwilling to support research activity.

Reflective activity

In all studies, any potential ethical or methodological issue is important. However, there are always some which are 'big' issues, and others which are 'small' and largely instrumental (anonymisation, for example). Reflect on a study you have done, or have planned, as an insider researcher and consider the big and small issues raised by Andy's work. What are the big issues in your study? What are the smaller, instrumental issues? Make lists of these then move on to the next activity.

Building critical research skills: activity

Using your list, create a chart or mind-map (as in Figures 3.1 and 3.2), which breaks your issues down and relates them to texts which problematise or explain them in ways which would be useful to your project.

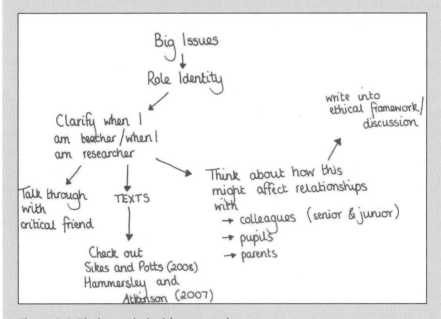

Figure 3.1 Big issues in insider research

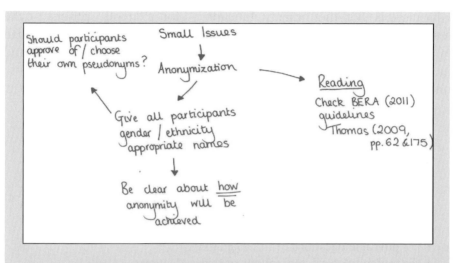

Figure 3.2 Smaller issues in insider research

Using your chart or mind-map as a starting point, you can then discuss the issues you have identified in the methodology section of your research report, supporting your ideas with the literature you have also identified.

Other challenges

Different challenges can be presented when the data tells you stories that cannot be told in turn, perhaps because they would be exploitative, would compromise an individual's confidentiality or have other negative consequences for the individual or the organisation. In a study that Liz did, young people made disclosures about criminal and self-harming activity. While this was pertinent to the focus of the study – identity – some of the stories could not be put into the public domain, as they had the potential for harm to the individual. In response to these concerns, these data were acknowledged as a brief, general summary which reported that many of the young people were engaged in risky behaviour involving alcohol, drugs and sexual activity, or were known to mental health or youth justice systems. Other issues such as individuals' competence in their job role can arise (as in Tom's story) and in these cases, how do you balance the risks of an individual being disciplined or losing their job, and the personal implications of that, with the risks of being trained or educated by someone who is not 'up to the job'? Finally, in some settings, particularly where education is not the primary function – for example, prisons – the researcher may be seen as more threatening or may be at greater risk than in others, such as schools, where education is the primary function and most of those working with the organisation will be committed to understanding the setting and using research as a means of positive change.

Building critical research skills: activity

You have been asked to formally evaluate training needs in your institution/department in advance of the implementation of a major curriculum reform, to which some staff are vehemently opposed. You plan to do this as part of your MA studies. Discuss with a colleague:

- the ethical implications of this evaluation;
- the methodological implications of this evaluation;
- the relationship implications of this evaluation;
- the practical challenges;

and how these might be addressed.

Triangulation

So, how can these challenges be addressed, while ensuring that the study is 'systematic, credible, verifiable, justifiable, useful, valuable and "trustworthy"' (Lincoln and Guba, 1985) (Wellington, 2000: 14)? A key means of achieving this is by ensuring that the study is effectively triangulated. This is more than just using mixed methods. Silverman (2010: 134) draws on earlier work by Fielding and Fielding (1986) to argue that triangulation should:

- always begin from a theoretical perspective;
- always make use of methods and data which provide an account of structure and meaning from within that perspective.

This again emphasises the importance of working within a clear theoretical framework as we discussed in Chapter 2. The most common means of triangulation uses existing theory (in the form of your literature review) and a variety of methods to investigate the same questions. This is a form of *methodological triangulation* known as between-method triangulation.

Alternatively, you could use the same method on different occasions, which is known as 'within method triangulation'. There are, however, other forms of triangulation as well, all of which can contribute to ensuring that your study is verifiable and trustworthy. These include using the same methods over time, using different researchers within the same investigation, collecting and analysing data within more than one (usually competing) theoretical framework or undertaking comparative studies. Many people use triangulation as a means of confirming that all the data is telling the same story, and this is indeed a primary function of it since it generates more confidence that the story is credible and trustworthy. However, focusing entirely on a particular picture can lead you to ignore data which have discrepancies, but which can illuminate particular (important) points or issues (Hammersley and Atkinson, 2007: 184).

At a practical level, Liz used different forms of triangulation in a study exploring the aspirations and learning identities of young people. The study, which was conducted within a theoretical framework drawing on concepts of social justice, involved gathering data over time using multiple methods within a broadly ethnographic approach. The key methods used were observation and interview. Data were gathered and interpreted over time and Liz returned to the young participants in the study at each stage of analysis to discuss the emerging themes with them and establish whether they thought these themes reflected the contributions they had made. Those contributions from the young people formed part of the data reporting.

Reflective activity

At the beginning of this chapter you were asked to place yourself and your study on the TLRP continuum of insider/outsider research, and to ask yourself how your positioning on that continuum affected: your relationships with others (both participants and non-participants) and what the possible implications are for your research and for future working relationships. Now you have read this chapter, return to those questions and consider them again. When you have made notes, compare these with your originals. What differences do you find? What do you now consider to be the key issues facing you, in your particular setting, in undertaking insider research?

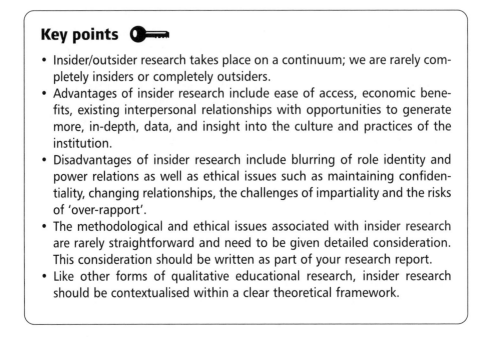

Key points

- Insider/outsider research takes place on a continuum; we are rarely completely insiders or completely outsiders.
- Advantages of insider research include ease of access, economic benefits, existing interpersonal relationships with opportunities to generate more, in-depth, data, and insight into the culture and practices of the institution.
- Disadvantages of insider research include blurring of role identity and power relations as well as ethical issues such as maintaining confidentiality, changing relationships, the challenges of impartiality and the risks of 'over-rapport'.
- The methodological and ethical issues associated with insider research are rarely straightforward and need to be given detailed consideration. This consideration should be written as part of your research report.
- Like other forms of qualitative educational research, insider research should be contextualised within a clear theoretical framework.

Websites

http://www.bera.ac.uk/theory-in-qualitative-educational-research/roles-for-theory/ This BERA online resource explores the use of theory in educational research.

http://www.tlrp.org/capacity/rm/wt/bridges/bridges7.html This page, which draws on the Teaching and Learning Research Project, is useful in outlining some of the epistemological issues associated with insider/outsider research.

References and further reading

British Educational Research Association (BERA) (2011) *Ethical Guidelines for Educational Research*. Available at: www.bera.ac.uk/publications/guidelines/.

Costley, C., Elliot, G. and Gibbs, P. (2010) *Doing Work-based Research: Approaches to Inquiry for Insider-researchers*. London: Sage.

Fielding, N. and Fielding, J. (1986) *Linking Data*. London: Sage.

Geertz, C. (1973) 'Thick description: toward an interpretive theory of culture', in C. Geertz (ed.), *The Interpretation of Cultures*. New York: Basic Books.

Goghlan, D. and Brannick, T. (2010) 'Issues and challenges in researching your own organisation', Part 3, in D. Goghlan and T. Brannick, *Doing Action Research in Your Own Organisation*. London: Sage.

Hammersley, M. and Atkinson, P. (1983) *Ethnography Principles in Practice*. London: Routledge.

Hammersley, M. and Atkinson, P. (2007) *Ethnography: Principles in Practice*. 3rd edn. London: Routledge.

Junker, B. (1960) *Field Work*. Chicago, IL: University of Chicago Press.

Potts, A. (2000) 'Academic occupations and institutional change: reflections on researching academic life', *Academic Work and Life*, 1: 369–403.

Sikes, P. and Potts, A. (eds) (2008) *Researching education from the inside: investigations from within*. Abingdon: Routledge. This edited book provides a broad range of discussions from academics who have conducted insider research in different contexts, and the implications and dilemmas arising from each study.

Silverman, D. (2010) *Doing Qualitative Research*. 3rd edn. London: Sage.

Taylor, S. and Bogdan, R. (1984) *Introduction to Qualitative Research Methods*. New York: Wiley.

Teaching and Learning Research Programme (TLRP) (2011) *Capacity Building Resources: Insider and Outsider Research*. Available at: http://www.tlrp.org/capacity/rm/wt/bridges/bridges7.html (accessed 31 October 2011).

Thomas, G. (2009) *How to Do Your Research Project*. London: Sage.

Trowler, P. (2011) *Researching Your Own Institution: Higher Education*. British Educational Research Association online resource. Available at: http://www.bera.ac.uk/files/2011/06/researching_your_own_institution_higher_education.pdf (accessed 4 November 2011).

Wellington, J. (2000) *Educational Research: Contemporary Issues and Practical Approaches*. London: Continuum.

Wellington, J. and Sikes, P. (2006) 'A doctorate in a tight compartment: why students choose to do a professional doctorate and its impact on their personal & professional lives', *Studies in Higher Education,* 31(6): 723–34.

CHAPTER 4

WRITING A LITERATURE REVIEW

Summary

The literature review is a key component of any research project. It familiarises the researcher with current knowledge in their field of interest, informs the methodology of the study and provides a framework for the analysis. It is a form of scholarship which is 'a prerequisite for increased methodological sophistication and for improving the usefulness of education research' (Boote and Beile, 2005: 3). This chapter explores ways in which a literature search can be conducted and, drawing on the questions most frequently raised by students, goes on to discuss how the literature should be analysed, synthesised and finally structured into a critical review. The chapter also includes guidance on referencing and citation, which, done correctly, is a critical part of developing a really good literature review.

Key words used in this chapter: *literature, critical, criticality, theoretical framework, referencing, citation.*

Introduction

The literature review is a key component of most research projects, and is perhaps the part that many students initially find the most daunting. A part of that concern is focused on the nature of the description of the literature review – usually described as 'critical literature review' – and the requirement to 'engage with the literature'. While these are skills which can be developed with practice over time, the expressions are bewildering to many students who want specific definitions of the terms and concrete advice on how to achieve the appropriate levels of engagement and criticality. It is difficult to give concrete advice, since guidance will differ according to the nature of the literature, the specific university requirements and the experience and writing ability of the individual, and the general advice given by most supervisors never quite manages to pre-empt all the queries and concerns felt by anxious students approaching a literature review for the first time. Many of these queries and concerns recur regularly and will be familiar to any tutor who has supervised students with research projects. This chapter has been structured around these frequently asked questions with detailed responses to each. The questions include the following:

- What is a literature review for? How does it relate to the rest of my study?
- Do I have to do a literature review?
- What do you mean by a critical literature review?
- How many books do I have to include? Is anything more than five years old too old?
- What counts as literature? Can I use newspaper articles or government papers?
- How do I start?
- There isn't any literature on my subject!
- There is too much literature in my subject – how do I know which books/papers are relevant?
- How should I structure my literative review?

However, there is good general advice which should be applied to any review. First, always make notes of the literature you read, and include full bibliographical information to avoid the frustration of having to spend hours searching for a missing citation – one of us once spent three days in a library searching for a citation, finally discovering it in an edited book. Some suggestions are given in this chapter of different ways in which this might be done. Read as widely as possible and, if you have not previously written a literature review, read the experts in your field and take note of how they structure their work – academic papers will normally include a section on the literature. Sometimes, this section of the paper will have literature review as a sub-heading (for example, see Reay et al., 2010 or Taylor et al., 2010). On other occasions, however, the sub-heading will be different. For example, in his paper '"It sort of feels uncomfortable": problematising the assessment of reflective practice' (2011) Jonathan Tummons uses the introduction to position reflective practice and in doing so draws on the extensive literature in this area. He moves on to a report of the research he undertook, and later in the paper, draws on this literature again as he analyses his findings within the context of an approach known as New Literacy Studies. Irrespective of how the literature is presented in a published paper, the work will always be grounded in the literature and can provide a model for you to use for your own work.

Another general point is to avoid the use of secondary citation (for example, 'It is also worth noting that participants' voices are already mediated when they come to interview (Lewin, 1991, cited Olesen, 2000: 231')). The problem with secondary citation is that you are relying on an interpretation of the original made by another person. Your interpretation may differ, or you may inadvertently use the original out of context since you have not actually read it all, and in doing so run the risk of misrepresenting the original author. Another risk is that you will miss reading something of major significance to your study; additionally, use of secondary citation suggests that you have not fully engaged with the literature, so you should always track down the original and use your own interpretation. Other useful advice is to write in clear, cogent English. This is actually much more difficult than it sounds. There is often a temptation to try and adopt the style of language you have been reading but if this does not come naturally to you it will come across as confused. It is more effective to use clear and simple language where possible, and to check carefully for spelling and grammatical errors as this will get your argument across with greater clarity. Finally, ensure that your referencing and citation is consistent and technically correct according to your university guidance. Most education departments in the UK use Harvard referencing. While there are a number of variations on a theme, some broad examples are given below.

Referencing and citation

Most education departments in the UK use Harvard referencing. This approach is also the most commonly used in educational research journals. There are many variations on the theme, and it is essential to be consistent in following your institutional guidance. In Harvard, the surname only of the author is used in the text followed by year and page number, as in the example below, and the full reference is given in the reference list. The reference list should include all the texts you have used.

Avis (2007: 161) in his critique of different pedagogical models has argued that 'narrow, outcome led learning is out of kilter with the needs of a knowledge economy'.

This is referenced at the end of the document as:

Avis, J. (2007) *Education, Policy and Social Justice: Learning and Skills.* London: Continuum.

Complexities arise with multiple authors, edited books, journal articles, online and corporate publications. Your institutional guidance will probably give a model for each of these. Government documents can be particularly difficult as numerous policy papers, reports, legislation and other documents are published each year. In this case, they would be differentiated in the text and reference list by letter of the alphabet, indicating which one was the earlier publication. This is demonstrated in the example below:

Department for Education and Skills (2003a) *14–19 Opportunity and Excellence.* London: The Stationery Office.
Department for Education and Skills (2003b) *21st Century Skills: Realising Our Potential: Individuals, Employers, Nation.* London: The Stationery Office.

What is a literature review for? How does it relate to the rest of my study?

The literature review serves a number of different purposes. It demonstrates your knowledge of your field and locates your study in the context of that field of enquiry at a particular moment in time. It will include both what is known and what is currently being explored or is not fully understood, and, particularly in the context of doctoral research, will identify the gaps in the literature which your study is aiming to address. In doing this it helps to refine – or even generate – research questions and thus the approach or methodology of the study. It also forms a framework for analysis of the data, forms part of the argument you will be making throughout your project, and is a key part of the final discussion and conclusions of the study, as you situate your conclusions in the context of existing knowledge (for MA studies), or make a contribution to that knowledge (for PhD studies and beyond). In this sense, we like to think of it as a hook, on which the analysis and, indeed, the rest of the study hangs. It is important to be mindful throughout of the fact that, while the literature review is absolutely integral to the study, you should continue to engage with the literature throughout, rather than just in one or two chapters (McNiff and Whitehead, 2009: 65). All too often, students write a literature review and then undertake a short study without any further reference to the literature. This weakens research, leaving it open to criticism for lacking rigour.

It is important to read extensively and that reading will be ongoing. New work is published all the time, so your final review must include the most recent work on the subject, and discuss its implications for your own study. However, this does not mean that you have to read everything that has ever been written about a particular subject. It does mean, though, that you will be aware of the key issues and contemporary debates in your area of interest.

Do I have to do a literature review?

Most traditional research reports will include a separate chapter which explores the literature in which the study is situated. However, there is a school of thought (Wolcott, 1990) which argues that the literature should be integrated throughout the study as appropriate, rather than standing alone. Kevin Orr used this approach in his 2010 PhD study of trainee teachers. In his own words: 'I did not write a traditional literature review but allowed my review of literature to leak across the introductory chapter, the chapter on conceptualisations and methodology and the chapter on policy, informing each one.'

It is difficult to do this well unless, like Kevin, you are experienced at writing within the context of a body of literature or theoretical concept. We usually advise students to begin the review first, keep up to date with any developments in the field, and present it both as a separate chapter and draw on it as appropriate throughout the study. The only exception to this would be where the student is using a grounded theory approach to their research. Grounded theory, based on the work of Glaser and Strauss (1967), attempts to generate theory from the data *before* using analytic frameworks (literature). Using this approach, the use of literature would be dictated by the outcomes of the empirical research, rather than beginning by situating the research in the literature. The approach is open to criticism: as Silverman (2010: 236) has argued, it can degenerate into a 'mere smokescreen to legitimize purely empiricist research'. Irrespective of the approach you take, undertaking a wide range of reading is essential not only to familiarise yourself with the subject, but to enable you to discriminate between the good and not-so-good research, and to make informed decisions about what should, or should not, be prioritised in the review. This understanding and discrimination is the first step in developing a *critical* literature review.

What do you mean by a critical literature review?

All research projects are expected to *critically* review the literature associated with the field of study. At MA level this review is normally expected to be a summary of current knowledge which situates the study being undertaken in the context of that knowledge. In relation to doctoral-level study, the review is also expected to identify the gaps in the literature which will be addressed by the study being undertaken. However, the meaning of *critically* is rarely explained, possibly because it is such a subjective term. To discuss the literature critically is broader than identifying strengths and weaknesses in the research you read, although this is a part of it. It also means to discuss that work in the context of your own study, and to be aware of its implications for your study, and in particular, for the institutions and participants involved in your study. This is illustrated in the extract from Jon Melville's (2010) literature review below:

In none of the above policy documents is there more than passing considera-tion of the work of Further Education colleges in delivering higher education (Medhat 2007a, Moreland 2005). The majority of engineering learners in uni-versities study full time and since UK-SPEC in 2003 have been involved in developing their "employability" skills (HEA 2005, Hind and Moss 2005). The majority of engineering learners in further education study their higher educa-tion qualifications part-time (Kumar 2007). Many of these have entered the profession as apprentices, progressing to higher education at approximately the same age as full-time undergraduates after undertaking work-based and work-related study on a block- or day-release basis (fdf 2008b).

How many books/papers do I have to include? Is anything more than five years old too old?

It is always a bad idea to try to quantify how many texts should be included. It is more important to be concerned about finding the most relevant and robust research on the subject you are investigating and then considering how you can report on that literature in the context of the arguments you are making and within the approximate word limits you have to work with. Because the literature review is to locate the study in a particular field, it is essential to use up-to-date literature, something most tutors emphasise. This leads many students to believe that they should only include very recent texts – some will come up with a time frame, such as five or ten years. This is not helpful. A literature review must be current, so it should always include the most recent work on the subject; however, it should also cover seminal work, major studies and, if appropriate, give a historical context to 'where we are now'.

The most recent work is most likely to be found in academic papers, which normally go to publication far more quickly than books – research is usually at least two or three years old before it is reported in a book due to the time frames involved in writing and publication. However, because of its length, a book provides greater breadth than a paper, which normally addresses one small aspect of a research study. Good examples of this include the work done by the *Cambridge Primary Review* (2006–2009) and the *Nuffield Review of 14–19 Education and Training*. The Nuffield Review ran from 2003 to 2009 and drew on a broad range of research projects as well as taking submissions from individual academics working in the field of 14–19 education. As the review concluded, the team produced the book *Education for All* (Pring et al., 2009), which reports on the findings of the review and presents an analysis of contemporary education and training in the context of existing research. It goes on to make recommendations based on this analysis. Anyone exploring issues related to 14–19 education would draw on this text, yet although the book was not published until 2009, the earliest submissions to the review date from 2003/04 and the book draws on these papers – as well as a wealth of other writing and research. In exploring an aspect of 14–19 education it would be necessary to follow up some of the citations in the book (which include, for example, research by Dewey (1902) as well as research undertaken during the life of the review), illustrating some of the difficulties of applying a rigid time frame to a literature review. Similarly, the final report of the *Cambridge Primary Review* draws on a broad range of research undertaken during its lifetime, much of which remains pertinent today.

Further issues in using a rigid time frame are those of seminal work, and historical context. In a literature review which explores aspects of reflective practice, for example, the here and now would be contextualised in terms of the origins of reflective practice, something which would draw on Donald Schon's seminal work *The Reflective Practitioner: How Professionals Think in Action* (1983), while one on assessment for learning would include Black and Wiliam's 1998 study and their subsequent work. Similarly, a review on aspects of vocational education is likely to make reference to the new vocationalism of the 1980s, from which contemporary vocational education and training programmes are descended. Inevitably, this would mean reading the works of authors such as Bates (1984) or Cohen (1984), who were influential and contemporary critics of new vocationalism. Ultimately, what is important is balance. If historical context is important to the wider subject, then it must be addressed, but it is essential to avoid a detailed history at the expense of reporting on current thinking. Based on this, you would read the subject thoroughly, allude to the history briefly, citing the key authors who were researching or critiquing your area at that time. Once you have positioned your subject in this way, you would move on to contemporary research and ideas and it is in this section that you would use the most recent research.

What counts as literature? Can I use newspaper articles or government papers?

Generally, the answers to the latter questions are yes and yes, but with some qualifications. First, sources such as government or media reports are non-academic sources which should be balanced within a literature review by appropriate reference to academic sources. Media articles have an agenda and a particular readership demographic to please. Therefore, the reporting will, in general, lack criticality and be sympathetic to particular viewpoints.

You can see this illustrated by reading the editorial comment in a range of newspapers (a good range would be the *Sun, Daily Mail, The Times* and *Guardian*) on a political issue such as free schools or academy status for primary schools. Despite this, it may be relevant to report on public opinion represented by the media at a particular time. For example, Ecclestone and Hayes (2009: 3) draw on the publication *psychologies* to illustrate a particular mindset which they argue has serious implications for education. Elsewhere, and in a chapter on the historical context of 14–19 education newspaper headlines are cited as evidence of the wider public furore which arose following discrepancies in A-level marking in 2002 and led to the establishment of the Tomlinson Committee (see Peart and Atkins, 2011: 22).

Secondly, like newspaper articles, government papers are also biased, albeit for different reasons. The purpose of any government paper is to 'sell' particular policy for reasons which are primarily political. Therefore, such documents tend to use a lot of rhetoric which sounds very plausible and positive but which, if read carefully, means very little or is merely persuasive to a particular viewpoint – for example, that credentials are a good thing, or that all 5-year-olds should be able to write their names. This is illustrated in the following activity.

Building critical research skills: activity

1. Define the words 'opportunity' and 'excellence' in an educational context. Spend some time doing this and consider the constraints that might be placed on opportunities for children, young people or adults in your sector of the education system, and what excellence might mean for them.
2. Obtain copies of two of the following White Papers. Try to use one recent and one older paper as they were published by governments of different political persuasions. All are available online. Read the papers, taking particular note of the way in which the words 'opportunity' and 'excellence' are used.

Department for Business, Innovation and Skills (2010) *Skills for Sustainable Growth*. Available at: http://www.bis.gov.uk/policies/further-education-skills/skills-for-sustainable-growth.

Department for Education (2010) *The Importance of Teaching: The Schools White Paper 2010*. Available at: https://www.education.gov.uk/publications/standard/publicationDetail/Page1/CM%207980.

Department for Education and Skills (2006) *Further Education: Raising Skills, Improving Life Chances*. Norwich: The Stationery Office. Available at: http://www.official-documents.gov.uk/document/cm67/6768/6768.pdf.

(Continues)

(Continued)

Department for Education and Skills (2005) *Higher Standards, Better Schools for All*. Norwich: HMSO. Available at: https://www.education.gov.uk/ publications/standard/_arc_SOP/Page20/Cm%206677.

3. Now discuss the following questions with a colleague:
   (a) How is the word 'opportunity' used in these papers?
   (b) How is it defined?
   (c) How realistic are those opportunities for Jodie, whose parents have never worked and have no qualifications, and who left school at 16 with 5 GCSEs at grades E–G? Will the implementation of these policies make a difference to the potential educational outcomes of her 4-year-old brother?
   (d) How meaningful is the use of discourse around concepts such as excellence and opportunity?

This illustrates the care that should be taken in using government papers. It may be that policy documents are a key part of the literature that you need to access. If so, read them critically, checking for assumptions (for example, that all opportunities are equal opportunities) and taken-for-granteds. If they cite research, check to see whether that research is independent (non-government funded) and robust. It is also important to remember that documents published by organisations such as the Office for Standards in Education, Children's Services and Skills (Ofsted) reflect government thinking and policy – Ofsted, like many other organisations, is a quango and as such defers to government policy and guidance. Finally, such documents can only be examined critically in the context of research and writing around the same issue, so a review which included government documents might discuss the intentions and actual or possible impact of that policy, supporting the discussion with wider literature examining similar issues as illustrated in the following extract, written as part of an MA study, which critiques government policy on post-16 education in engineering. Note how the critique is supported by reference to other sources:

The government's policy for investment in post-compulsory education appears to be firmly grounded in human capital theory (Coffield 1999, Schultz 1961, 1971, Becker 1964, Sweetland 1996) and has been so since 1976 (Callaghan 1976). This approach is flawed in that it presupposes investment in the technology and infrastructure to support developments in education (Olaniyan and Okimakinde 2008) and neglects the effects of 'diploma creep' (Ferguson 1998), where the value of education qualifications is diminished by the increasing proportion of people achieving them. The government permits itself, through investment in education, to transfer some of the blame for poor economic performance onto educators and the trainees themselves (Coffield 1999). (J. Melville, 2010)

How do I start?

Reading for and preparing to write a literature review is a wonderful experience which provides a great opportunity to read without feeling guilty that you should be doing something else. However, there is no doubt that undertaking the work is time-consuming, so it is important to be highly organised and methodical. This does not come readily to all of us, but there are a few things you can do at the beginning which will make the process much more efficient. Some of these are illustrated in the steps Catherine took, when writing a literature review for the first time.

Vignette 1

Catherine is a primary teacher and numeracy co-ordinator at her school, which is a large primary school in an inner city area with high levels of deprivation. Sixty per cent of children speak English as an additional language. During her MA (Education) Catherine completed an independent research module in which she explored ways of communicating mathematical concepts to non-English speaking children. Her first degree was a BSc in Mathematics and she had not previously completed a literature review; she was daunted by the prospect. Catherine sought out her tutor for a meeting to discuss this and also arranged to meet the subject librarian at the university for additional help on searching the literature. She then approached the review very methodically. Using two recent papers on her subject as a starting point, she began to explore the literature. She kept colour-coded notes on the papers and chapters she read. The hard copy notes, one page for each text, included bibliographical information, a two-sentence summary of each paper/chapter and a list of key themes. The themes were colour coded to facilitate comparisons between studies and to inform Catherine's own data analysis. She also gave each paper a numerical grade from 1 to 5 in which 1 was of extreme relevance to her study and 5 was of minimal or no relevance. This strategy was very helpful and contributed to Catherine's completed study which gained a high mark (over 70 per cent). She has subsequently implemented some of the strategies she identified and continues to evaluate and develop them.

Catherine's methodical approach paid dividends in terms not only of the grade awarded to her project, but also, more importantly, in its application in the classroom. This could not have been achieved without a methodical and organised approach.

To achieve such an approach, first you should be absolutely clear about the research questions you want to answer, as this will dictate the content of the review. It is essential to have clear and focused questions at this point, which bear only one interpretation. If appropriate, break down the questions into themes. Seek advice from your supervisor or subject librarian on the best sources to access and set aside some blocks of time to do the initial search. Always keep notes on what you do. You could use a very traditional, hard copy method such as that adopted by Catherine in the vignette in this chapter, but there are also alternative methods. There are now a range of electronic systems such as Endnote, many of which are freely available as resources through university libraries. If you have access to one of these, try it out. Many people find them invaluable and time-saving. Other methods include drafting a reference list as you go along, and using Post-it notes in books and papers to make comments on particular sections. This has the advantage of avoiding marginalisations which damage books and papers, but it is important to be rigorous about recording every reference as you go along. Other systems include hard-copy card indexes or similar systems developed electronically. Ideally, the system will allow you to prioritise your literature, perhaps by colour coding or, as in Catherine's case, applying a numerical level of relevance to each document, and to categorise your reading into themes. This helps not only with the literature review, but also with the analysis and discussion sections of your research project.

By this point, you will have spent time in the library and made notes on some of the literature using your chosen method. Your problem now will be deciding how to limit the literature appropriately in the context of your study. As Wellington (2000: 34) has suggested, knowing where to stop is far more difficult than knowing where to start!

Reflective activity

Think about the approach that Catherine used to note-taking. How efficient do you think this approach was for Catherine? What benefits did she accrue from it? Would this system work for you? If not, what sort of approach could you use?

There isn't any literature on my subject!

Despite the fact that there will *always* be literature relevant to a research study, since all research builds on existing understandings and knowledge, this concern is raised regularly by students. The issue here is that some students, unfamiliar with search engines or the electronic resources at their institution, look in the wrong places for literature. This can be a particular issue for more mature students who are less confident using electronic resources and happier wandering round a library. Occasionally, the issue is one of specificity in that the student has undertaken too narrow a search in an area which is relatively under-researched. We will address these two issues separately.

In terms of sources, there is no alternative to using the electronic sources which every institution has available. It is important to remember that there is a wide range of potential sources from which you might elicit useful literature, and not merely to restrict yourself to the most readily available books and journals. These include the more obvious, such as the periodical indexes (for example, the British Education Index), but might also include theses and dissertations held in university libraries, reports, conference proceedings or statistical data. In terms of trying to decide where to start, there is considerable help and support available for you to access. For example, your tutor/supervisor will be able to suggest a starting point, and the university library subject librarian will be able to offer help in accessing the university resources and advising on issues such as which are the most relevant indexes to use. Some students use widely available search engines such as Google, but this should be done with caution as they often throw up vast quantities of useless information, and the validity and authenticity of some of the sources are questionable. The most important thing is not to panic, and to approach the literature review – and indeed the whole study – methodically.

In terms of specificity, a student exploring different strategies for assessment for learning among a small group of autistic children in mainstream primary school would be unlikely to find many articles dealing with AfL among primary-aged children with autistic conditions. However, there is a considerable body of literature around AfL, a separate body around the education and assessment of autistic children and a wider body of literature relating to the education of children with different types of special educational need. There is literature on both appertaining to the primary phase. Therefore, there is always something which is relevant and can be synthesised as part of a literature review informing a research study.

This is the case even if there is a paucity of literature in a particular area.

When Liz began her EdD thesis, which explored the aspirations and learning identities of post-16 level 1 GNVQ (General National Vocational Qualification) students in English further education colleges (very specific!) only one paper had previously addressed the education of students on vocational programmes at this level (Bathmaker, 2001). This in itself was telling, as it confirmed Liz's view, discussed throughout the thesis, that these learners had little societal value placed on them. It also meant that the literature review would have to consider broader aspects of vocational education, and lead to an understanding of the positioning of level 1 students at that time. Therefore the review, which formed a 7500 word chapter, encompassed the historical and policy contexts of pre-vocational education, drawing comparisons between this and contemporary level 1 programmes, the development of GNVQ programmes generally, and level 1 specifically, and the relationship between vocational education and social inequality. It went on to explore the positioning of level 1 students within a contemporary social and political context and a separate chapter addressed the conceptual framework for the thesis.

There is too much literature in my subject – how do I know which books/papers are relevant?

The literature can be somewhat overwhelming, particularly in an area which is very well researched, such as literacy in Key Stages 1 and 2, assessment for learning or aspects of science education. It is also a particular problem for students undertaking short research projects on modular programmes which are constrained by both time and word limits. The key here is to prioritise the literature, selecting only that which is directly relevant to your research questions and disregarding the wider literature. Searching through dozens, sometimes hundreds, of publications is certainly time-consuming. A good tip is to read the abstract and let that inform you whether the paper itself is relevant. If there is nothing in the abstract which seems relevant to your research questions, leave it and move on. If there is something relevant, then read the publication in full to assess its relevance. The exception to this would be if a particular publication was consistently cited by others whose work was directly relevant – you may then wish to read the whole publication just to double-check whether or not it was relevant to your study.

How should I structure my literature review?

The literature review must be clearly and cogently written, with the literature synthesised to present a clear argument. It should be organised thematically, and the themes within the literature should be clearly related to the research questions. Always begin with the broader themes, and move to the more specific. Subsequently, those themes will provide a framework for your data analysis and for the conclusions that you draw. Jon Melville's MA study 'Developing higher-level transferable skills in engineering work-based learners' broke the literature review down into six themes: a historical perspective on the engineering profession, the government skills context, employer engagement with higher education, higher education in further education, transferable skills and the nature of learning. These themes recurred later in his analysis and conclusions.

Presenting the literature review thematically will also help you to avoid the pitfall of listing your literature on an author-by-author basis which results in a description or regurgitation of literature rather than a critical review in which the author constructs their own argument and expresses their own ideas. Such a description of the literature tends to be uncritical (everything is included, irrespective of merit) and invariably reads rather like a shopping list, or, as Haywood and Wragg (1982: 2) eloquently put it, a 'furniture sale catalogue' in which 'everything merits a one-paragraph entry no matter how skilfully it has been conducted: Bloggs (1975) found this, Smith (1976) found that, Jones (1977) found the other, Bloggs, Smith and Jones (1978) found happiness in heaven'. A catalogue approach such as that described by Haywood and Wragg is also often associated with the multiple use of direct quotes, something else which should be avoided in a literature review. The use of multiple quotes means that you are merely repeating what someone else said, rather than generating your own argument. In general, direct quotes should only be used where the words are particularly eloquent (witness Haywood and Wragg's quote above, which appears in many later writings), or where you want to use words and phrases which have specific meanings in the context of your study, but which were coined by others, as in the example below:

> One aspect of social justice is the concept of the 'common good' which is found in both Aristotelian philosophy and Christian teaching ...

Direct quotes might also be useful to contrast and compare opposing arguments, and may be useful in helping you to justify your own arguments. You should, however, avoid the use of long quotes and multiple quotes from the same author as well as over-using quotes. It is generally much better to synthesise what you have read, making sure, of course, that any ideas you have derived from the writing of others are correctly cited.

You should also summarise your reading. If you are including a particular study in your literature review, much of the detail in the original paper can be excluded. For example, it is probably unnecessary to describe the methodology in detail (unless you are writing about methodology). It is certainly unnecessary to summarise the whole paper, which the author will have done (more clearly and cogently than you could!) in the abstract. Summarising key points and relating these to the themes in your own work is an essential part of producing a critical review of the literature. It can be done using very few words. Liz's 60,000 word EdD thesis was summarised thus in just 137 words:

> As Elizabeth Atkins shows in her detailed study of teachers and students on a level 1 general vocational course, images of students at risk, vulnerable, and in need of 'emotional attachment and nurturing' lead [teachers] to regard students' emotional needs as integral to a progressive educational ethos. Despite their reservations about the quality and usefulness of the qualification students were taking, their concern for confidence and esteem led them to prioritise positive attitudes and dispositions to engagement rather than pushing students to learn content or to do difficult tasks. Although students enjoyed the course and its activities, and believed they worked hard, Atkins argues that their positive views were predicated on lack of demand placed on them and on feeling valued. She concludes that their experience cannot be called education in any meaningful sense.
>
> Ecclestone and Hayes (2009: 74)

Of course, this summary does not allude to all the themes in the thesis which also included culture, gendered and classed dispositions, fantasy futures, learning and leisure identities, but it does draw on the themes of nurturing and therapeutic education which was the subject of Ecclestone's and Hayes' book.

A final note of caution on things to avoid in the literature review is that of misrepresentation, or using a person's work to support an argument they did not make or do not agree with. It is, unfortunately, easy to do this in error so there are two cardinal rules to help you avoid this pitfall:

- Do not use any work whose meaning seems unclear to you – you may misinterpret it.
- Particularly if using an index, always avoid reading a single phrase or paragraph in isolation. Read the whole section – preferably the whole chapter – to ensure you have understood the context in which the argument was made.

In summary, when structuring your literature review you should ensure that you:

- choose the most relevant literature from what you have read;
- prioritise the literature, beginning with the general and moving to the specific;
- present it as a clear and organised narrative discussion which gives a picture of 'how it is now' and outlines the emerging issues and questions in the field;
- ensure that the 'how it is now' is up to date and includes the most recent thinking and research on the topic;
- focus on the themes in the literature, rather than on individual authors. The themes should be guided by the research questions.

Theoretical/conceptual frameworks

Put simply, a conceptual or theoretical framework is simply a particular theory or set of understandings about how the world works. When applied to research, empirical work and data analysis are conducted around and related to the framework of understandings and ideas as reflected in the literature. As a result, the study will draw heavily on literature written from a similar perspective, and/or on literature *about* that particular perspective. Commonly used frameworks in educational research include Marxist perspectives (useful for analysing power relations in the education system), social justice (useful for exploring inequalities), and feminist approaches (useful for investigating the implications of gender). This can form part of a literature review or appear as a separate section or chapter. For example, in Atkins (2009) the conceptual framework for the study (social justice) is discussed in a discrete chapter, informed both by contemporary academic literature in the field of social justice and by ancient philosophic and religious texts. The discussion in the chapter explores the concept of social justice with particular reference to inequalities in post-compulsory education in England and in the context of a belief in the equal value of each individual. Kevin Orr's work (alluded to above) drew on Marxist perspectives as he sought to understand the institutional cultural influences on trainee teachers.

Building critical research skills: activity

Ideally, you will undertake this activity with one or more colleagues. You will access and read in detail a peer reviewed paper from a reputable journal which is relevant to your own area of interest. If you have not yet identified a specific area of interest for your research, you could use any of the papers referenced in this chapter. Once you have chosen a paper, read it carefully and make notes on the following points:

- Decide why this paper was judged to be worthy of publication.
- Consider how the paper is written (its format, language and any other issues you deem to be important).
- Why this is (or is not) a robust piece of research in terms of its literature, methodological approach, analysis and conclusions.
- What questions or issues might this document raise for your own piece of independent research?

Once you have made notes, discuss your findings with your colleagues. Did you make similar points? What were the differences? What further understandings did you gain from the discussion?

Key points

- Read around the subject.
- Sort literature into themes.
- Begin with general, working through to the specifics. Integrate literature into discussion, rather than using multiple long quotes.
- Ensure that the review is balanced (for example, between historical and contemporary work, between academic and non-academic sources).
- Ensure that the review presents the fullest possible picture of the area you are exploring.
- As you write the narrative, remember that you are telling a story, not writing a shopping list!
- Ensure that referencing and citation are technically correct according to your institutional guidance.

References and further reading

Atkins, L. (2009) *Invisible Students, Impossible Dreams: Experiencing Vocational Education 14–19*. Stoke-on-Trent: Trentham Books.

Bates, I. (1984) 'From vocational guidance to life skills: historical perspectives on careers education', in I. Bates, J. Clark, J. Cohen, D. Finn, R. Moore and P. Willis, *Schooling for the Dole? The New Vocationalism*. Basingstoke: Macmillan.

Bathmaker, A.-M. (2001) 'It's a perfect education': lifelong learning and the experience of foundation-level GNVQ students', *Journal of Vocational Education and Training*, 53(1): 81–100.

Black, P. and Wiliam, D. (1998) 'Assessment and classroom learning', *Assessment in Education*, 5(1): 7–74.

Boote, D.N. and Beile, P. (2005) 'Scholars before researchers: on the centrality of the dissertation literature review in research preparation', *Educational Researcher*, 34(6): 3–15.

Bourdieu, P. (1990) *The Logic of Practice*. Cambridge: Polity Press.

Cambridge Primary Review (2009). Available at: http://www.primaryreview.org.uk/index.php accessed 19 September 2011.

Cohen, P. (1984) 'Against the new vocationalism', in I. Bates, J. Clark, J. Cohen, D. Finn, R. Moore and P. Willis, *Schooling for the Dole? The New Vocationalism*. Basingstoke: Macmillan.

Dewey, J. (1902) *The Child and the Curriculum*. Available at: http://www.archive.org/details/childandcurricul00deweuoft (accessed 10 August 2011).

Ecclestone, K. and Hayes, D. (2009) *The Dangerous Rise of Therapeutic Education*. London: Routledge.

Fisher, D. and Harrison, T. (n.d.) *Citing References*. Oxford: Blackwell. This very useful little book gives examples of how to cite references from a wide range of publications.

Glaser, B.G. and Strauss, A.L. (1967) *The Discovery of Grounded Theory: Strategies for Qualitative Research*. Chicago, IL: Aldine.

Haywood, P. and Wragg, E.C. (1982) *Evaluating the Literature*. Rediguide 2. University of Nottingham School of Education.

McNiff, J. and Whitehead, J. (2009) *Doing and Writing Action Research*. London: Sage.

Melville, J. (2010) 'Developing higher-level transferable skills in engineering work-based learners'. Unpublished MA assignment, Nottingham Trent University.

Nuffield Review of 14–19 Education and Training. Available at: http://www.nuffieldfoundation.org/14–19review (accessed 10 August 2011).

Orr, K. (2010) '*College cultures and pre-service trainee teachers: a study in the creation and transmission of ideas about teaching*'. Unpublished PhD thesis, University of Huddersfield.

Peart, S. and Atkins, L. (2011) *Teaching 14–19 Learners in the Lifelong Learning Sector*. Exeter: Learning Matters.

Pring, R., Hayward, G., Hodgson, A., Johnson, J., Keep, E., Oancea, A., Rees, G., Spours, K. and Wilde, S. (2009) *Education for All: The Future of Education and Training for 14–19 Year Olds*. London: Routledge.

Reay, D., Crozier, G. and Clayton, J. (2010) '"Fitting in" or "standing out": working class students in UK higher education', *British Educational Research Journal*, 36(1): 107–24.

Schon, D. (1983) *The Reflective Practitioner: How Professionals Think in Action*. New York: Basic Books.

Silverman, D. (2010) *Doing Qualitative Research*. 3rd edn. London: Sage. Chapter 18 discusses some of the issues around writing a literature review and includes some useful examples and activities.

Taylor, M., Baskett, M. and Wren, C. (2010) 'Managing the transition to university for disabled students', *Education and Training*, 52(2): 165–75.

Tummons, J. (2011) '"It sort of feels uncomfortable" problematising the assessment of reflective practice', *Studies in Higher Education*, 36(4): 471–83.

Wellington, J. (2000) *Educational Research: Contemporary Issues and Practical Approaches*. London: Continuum. Chapter 3 of this book provides ten sources for literature searches, which provides a good starting point. There is also a very useful section titled 'Judging other people's research' which gives comprehensive advice on critical reading.

Wolcott, H. (1990) *Writing up Qualitative Research*. Newbury Park, CA: Sage.

Wyse, D. (2008) *The Good Writing Guide for Education Students*. 2nd edn. London: Sage. This very practical and accessible guide provides lots of good tips for searching the literature, as well as on the writing and structuring of your work.

CHAPTER 5

INTERVIEWING IN EDUCATIONAL RESEARCH

Summary

In this chapter the reader is introduced to the use of interview as a method for collecting research data. The chapter discusses the stages of the interview process, including the choice of interviewees, the drawing up of questions, the conduct of the interview and subsequent considerations of ethics and interpretation. It draws attention both to the advantages and to the difficulties of this method of research, and uses a series of examples to illustrate and explore the various practical epistemological issues which the use of interviews may raise. Towards the end of the chapter the reader is presented with an extract from a postgraduate assignment for critical comment, in which the use of interviews is described and discussed.

Key words used in this chapter are: *interview, respondent, informant, transcription, interpretation, confidentiality, epistemology.*

Interviewing in educational research

Interviews are a frequently used method for collecting qualitative data in educational research. There are several good reasons for this, not the least of which is that they allow us to engage with our research participants individually face to face in a way that questionnaires or focus groups, for example, do not. They are also a very flexible research tool which can be used to gather a range of different types of information, including factual data, views and opinions, personal narratives and histories, which makes them useful as a means of answering a wide range of research questions. The opportunity for dialogue which they provide allows the interviewer to probe and clarify and to check that they have understood correctly what is being said. Encouraging participants to talk will help provide us with insight into their thought processes and the value judgements they bring to bear. But this also, of course, requires us to honour our guarantees of confidentiality and to handle the data which the interview provides in a way which is consistent with an ethical research framework.

However, there are disadvantages, too. Transcribing and analysing an interview can be an arduous and lengthy task, though often a necessary one if we are to get the most we can from our data. And the analysis of interview responses is also a complex and often difficult process, despite the growing availability of software designed to help in the interrogation of qualitative data. Drawing conclusions or constructing theories based on what someone has said can very often come down to a matter of interpretation, and this means that we have to be scrupulous and methodical in presenting a sound argument for our choice of interviewing as a method and for any claims to knowledge which we make based upon the results. We will also have to address the questions of *trustworthiness* and *reliability*. That is, to what extent we can know that what the interviewee is telling us is 'true'; and how certain we can be that a different interviewer asking the same questions of the same interviewee would receive the same answers as we did.

Power relationships and putting interviewees at ease

Once we have decided that interviews are the best method for collecting the data we need, we then have to consider carefully our choice of interviewee. If our research is taking place in schools, should we interview the head teacher, or the entire teaching staff, or selected teachers, or all of those plus teaching assistants and parents? This will depend very much on the nature of our research question, and it is important to remember that we will need to present a detailed justification for our choice of interviewees when we come to write up our research. In this way we can demonstrate that we have made an appropriate and informed decision.

You will have noticed that we did not include pupils in the list of possible interviewees in the previous paragraph. This is because, working within an ethical framework, we are required to gain our interviewees' 'informed consent' before the interview can take place, and it is not considered possible for anyone under 18 to give *informed* consent, as they may be unable to fully understand the implications of participating in the research. This raises a range of complex ethical issues and questions, which are debated at more length in Chapter 2. The involvement of young participants also raises the question of the power relationship between interviewer and interviewee. But, of course, this is not a problem confined to age differential. Let's imagine, for example, that you have chosen to conduct research within your own institution (see Chapter 3, 'Insider research'). As we have seen, you may find yourself being more deferential when interviewing your line manager than you are, say, when interviewing a colleague. But a more serious problem is that your manager may be less inclined to tell you the whole story than she would be if you were one of her peers. And if you were to interview one of your adult students, your role as teacher might be an inhibiting factor in getting the interviewee to talk freely. The significance of power relationships within an interview setting should never be underestimated and needs careful consideration by the researcher. This may be a simple matter of choosing an appropriate setting. The relative status of yourself and your head teacher will be very much in evidence if they are sitting behind their big desk and you are perched in front of them on a hard chair. And similarly if you're the one who gets to sit at a big desk, the process may feel to your participant less like an interview and more like an interrogation. A comfortable and informal setting is usually considered the most useful, with chairs set at right angles to one another rather than face to face, signalling that this is a conversation rather than a confrontation. And, as most academic researchers will tell you, it is always useful to begin with a question which will put your interviewee at ease and allow them to remain safely for the time being in their comfort zone (Cohen et al., 2011).

Respondents or informants

Once we have decided whom to interview and why, we need to think about what style of interviewing will be most useful in helping us to answer our research question. Powney and Watts (1987) draw a distinction between two main types of approach: the *respondent* interview and the *informant* interview. The respondent interview is one in which the interviewer keeps a tight control over the process. The pre-prepared list of questions is fairly strictly adhered to and the interviewee's role is to *respond* to these. In such a process it is the interviewer alone who sets the agenda. The only questions to be explored are questions the interviewer has thought to ask. This very structured and relatively rigid approach means that the researcher is unlikely to glean any information which might lie outside the limits of knowledge and understanding they had when devising the questions. The informant interview, on the other hand, allows the interviewee room to contribute to the agenda. Their input is not confined only to responses to set questions, and therefore there is the potential for uncovering issues and questions which are relevant to the research question but about which the researcher had not known to ask. It will typically open a question with, 'Tell me about ...' or 'Can we talk a bit about ...', which will open up a topic without specifying a particular aspect or line of enquiry. This type of interview provides the scope for the participant to *inform* the research in ways the researcher may not have anticipated. It also allows the researcher to 'gain some insight in to the perceptions of a particular person or persons within a situation' (Powney and Watts, 1987: 18) taking the interview beyond the gathering of facts and allowing the participant an authentic voice.

Each of these approaches is useful, and it is the researcher's task to decide which will best serve their purpose. One important point to bear in mind is that the respondent interview can make the analysis and comparison of data more straightforward, as questions and response will follow the same pattern and fall into the same potential categories over a series of interviews; whereas the use of the informant approach may result in every interview following a different track.

Drawing up the interview schedule and phrasing your questions

The next useful step is to draw up an interview schedule. This is the list of questions or topics you intend to cover in your interviews. Part of its purpose is to help you reflect on wording and sequence, and to avoid asking leading questions, or closed questions requiring a one word answer which could just as easily be asked via a questionnaire.

Reflective activity

Look at the list of questions below. It includes one usefully phrased open question. The rest are either leading, loaded, over-complex or closed, and should be carefully avoided. See whether you can identify which is which.

- To what extent do you believe that seating pupils in rows is counter-productive to their learning?
- What seating arrangements do you think are most conducive to pupil learning?
- Do you think the way pupils are seated has an impact on their learning?
- What are your most favoured and least favoured seating arrangements for pupils, and is your own preference in line with school policy or does the school or the head teacher not take a line on this?
- What is your view on the regimented and some would say punitive approach of having pupils seated in rows?

Your list can also act as an aid to memory and will help you to estimate practical issues such as timing. In the case of lengthy respondent interviews, a clear schedule of questions will help to minimise bias by ensuring that all interviewees are asked the same questions about the same things – although this won't be the case if the researcher doesn't stick to it, as we shall soon see.

Practical and tactical considerations: recording, transcribing and piloting

The researcher will need to make a decision about how the interview is to be recorded. There are three main options: note-taking, audio recording and video recording. Consider for a moment the opportunities and disadvantages presented by each of these, and then compare your ideas to the list we've set out in Table 5.1.

Listening to or watching a recording of ourselves conducting an interview can be very useful in developing the researcher's skills. It allows us to hear whether we are asking our questions clearly; whether we are giving our interviewee time to answer and – just as important – time to think; whether we are doing too much of the talking or interrupting the interviewee just as their answers get interesting; whether we are distracting the interviewee with our verbal mannerisms or body language; and so on. For this reason it is a very good idea to treat the first interview we conduct in the course of our research as a pilot or practice interview. We can still use the data it produces, but in addition it will help us to spot our mistakes and to review and improve our technique for the interviews which follow.

Table 5.1 Recording the interview

Methods of recording the interview	Advantages	Disadvantages
Note-taking	Interviewer can identify key points and jot down relevant quotes as the interview goes along Rules out a transcript which can be time-consuming	No complete record of the interview Reduced opportunity to review data Difficult to check accuracy of quotes with interviewee Impedes eye contact between researcher and interviewee and so may interrupt their communication
Audio recording	Captures the entire interview and allows for careful review of data Makes a complete transcription possible Allows accurate partial transcription (e.g. of quotable extracts) Allows researcher to check accuracy of transcript with interviewee Allows the researcher to evaluate his or her own interview skills	The technology may fail leaving no record of the interview The use of recording equipment may make the interviewee self-conscious and inhibit their responses Does not capture body language which could provide a more nuanced reading of the interviewee's discourse
Video recording	This has all the advantages of an audio recording, and in addition can record body language, analysis of which could be used to present a more nuanced reading of the interviewee's discourse	The technology may fail leaving no record of the interview The presence of a camera may make the interviewee self-conscious and inhibit their responses Can be difficult to organise and set up without technician support Does not preserve the anonymity of the interviewee

Vignette

Bashir is an MPhil student who is researching head teachers' attitudes towards vocational qualifications, and in particular the status they attribute to them in relation to general academic qualifications such as A levels. After careful reading of the research literature and a discussion with his tutor, he decides that a useful place to start in his data collection is by interviewing a number of head teachers. He chooses five local secondary schools which seem fairly representative, or typical, of the majority of non-selective comprehensive schools in the region. Four out of the five head teachers approached agree to be interviewed. Bashir explains the purpose of his research to them clearly in order to ensure that he has their *informed consent* (BERA, 2011). He knows that this is an important ethical consideration when planning a research strategy.

His next step is to design an interview schedule. This is a list of the questions he will ask, and it serves several important purposes. On a practical level it will make sure he remembers what he wants to ask and in what order. It will also ensure that all interviewees are asked the same questions. This will make the eventual comparison of responses much more straightforward. It will also increase the reliability of the data. If interviewees are asked different sets of questions or asked questions in a different order or asked questions which are worded in different ways, this could have an impact on their responses. Imagine, for example, the researcher posing a question about the status of qualifications to two head teachers, but wording that question to the first like this:

- 'How would you see the relative status of vocational and academic qualifications?'

And to the second like this:

- 'Do you think vocational qualifications have a lower status than academic ones?'

He might claim he's asking the same question, but in the second example he is *leading* or *prompting* the interviewee towards a particular response or point of view. We refer to this as a *leading question,* and part of the purpose of drawing up an interview schedule is that it gives the researcher an opportunity to think carefully about how questions should be worded in such a way as to minimise the risk of them eliciting a biased response. It also allows the researcher to reflect on the range and topic of questioning. Often this will be informed not only by the research question which the researcher has come up with, but also by the literature the researcher has explored while reading around the topic.

Bashir, having done a lot of reading and having thought carefully about the sort of data he needs from his interviewees, has come up with the following framework of open-ended questions:

Bashir's interview schedule

1. Can you tell me little bit about your sixth form provision here at X School?
2. Where did the idea of offering vocational provision post-16 in this school originate?
3. What research was carried out to gauge the likely take-up rate?
4. What are the characteristics of those students at whom the vocational provision is aimed in this school?
5. How do the staff feel about the introduction of this provision?
6. How would you define the differences between those students who will take up this provision and those who will take up A levels?
7. What new skills will the vocational provision demand from staff at the school?
8. How would you see the relative status of vocational and academic qualifications?'

There are some important things to note about this list of questions. First, they are numbered sequentially. This may seem a small point, but it does suggest that Bashir has thought carefully about the order in which he wants to ask them. You'll see that question 1 is a broad, open question which casts the head teacher in the role of informant rather than respondent. It allows her to focus on her own agenda, and in this way it may bring areas of data to light which Bashir could not have anticipated and therefore would not have discovered through straightforward respondent questioning. Setting this question at the beginning may well give him some unexpected insight at the outset which he can then explore further as the interview progresses. Also, look again at questions 4 and 6. You will see that these are both asking more or less the same thing, but in different ways. The responses can be checked against one another for consistency, which will give the researcher some indication of whether the responses can be treated as reliable and therefore whether this key piece of data is trustworthy. This cross-checking within the same data collection instrument is a form of internal *triangulation*. It can also be used, of course, in questionnaires. So we can see that the question order here may be quite deliberately designed by Bashir to suit his own research purposes.

What else do we notice about the list? Look at questions 1, 2, 3 and 7. They are all relatively straightforward queries requiring a factual answer. They are unlikely to make the interviewee feel as though she has been put on the spot. They are not asking for value judgements or opinions. And those questions themselves, in their phrasing, are value-free, carrying no implication that there could be a 'right' or 'wrong' answer. All this is designed to put the interviewee at ease. The crucial questions for Bashir's research are 4, 5, 6 and 8. Perhaps he is hoping that his interviewees will feel sufficiently at ease answering the factual questions that they will be open and honest in their answers to these rather more complex ones.

Armed with his carefully thought-out list of questions, Bashir sets out to conduct his first interview. He has decided, with the head teacher's permission, to record it on a small dictaphone. The resulting interview has then been transcribed and is set out below. Read it through carefully with particular attention to the questions asked and to Bashir's interview technique. We shall be focusing on the interrogation and analysis of data in Chapter 11, but for the purposes of this chapter we are looking at the structure and conduct of the interview rather than the content of the interviewee's discourse. To start with, you might find it useful to compare the interview as it happened in practice with the schedule of questions which were originally planned. This is the issue we shall be exploring first.

Interview 1

> *BP*   Can you tell me a little bit about your sixth form provision here at X School?
>
> *Head*   Yes, we provide two progression routes here from GCSE. First, there is the A-level strand, which constitutes most of our post-16 provision. And then there is the vocational pathway which is a smaller and more recent strand, which is to say that it recruits at present a smaller number of students than the traditional academic sixth form. But numbers are growing, year on year, so that it may eventually match, in numbers terms, the A-level cohort.
>
> *BP*   Why do you think recruitment is expanding so rapidly on the vocational course?
>
> *Head*   Well, several reasons, really. I mean, these are the youngsters who in the past would have left school with a GCSE or two and gone into employment or to the further education college – that sort of thing. And, of course, there aren't the jobs now, and the FE college is some distance away and public transport around here is expensive and infrequent. So really staying on at school has become the preferred option.
>
> (Continues)

(Continued)

BP   But what I mean is, why is it the vocational sixth form that's expanding, rather than the A-level sixth form?

Head   Oh well, you're talking now as if there were two different, separate sixth forms, and that's not the case. It's one sixth form – we're very clear about that. There's one sixth form common room, and one set of rules and one collective assembly. So I don't want you to get the idea that this is some sort of sheep and goats set up. It's not. Not at all. But the vocational numbers are expanding because these are the youngsters, as I said, who wouldn't traditionally have stayed on. They're not suited for A-level study and they're not qualified for it – in the sense that they don't have a firm foundation of good GCSE grades. And given the choice, they wouldn't opt for A levels in any case.

BP   So they're given the choice?

Head   No. What I'm saying is that if they *were* given the choice they probably wouldn't want to do A levels. It's not an academic future that they're after. They sights are fixed on employment in the much shorter term.

BP   But these vocational qualifications can be used for entry to higher education, can't they?

Head   Well yes, of course. That is to say, you know, that er, that er many universities consider them now and they are part of the points system for entry, of course. But I think it would be fair to say that most of our sixth formers who are aiming to progress to higher education will do so through the A-level route.

BP   So how many of the vocational students apply for university entrance – let's say, last year.

Head   Well, none of them last year. Because, you see, that's not what they're aiming for.

BP   And this year?

Head   None. But I don't think you're hearing what I'm saying here. Progression to higher education isn't part of the purpose of our vocational stream post-16.

BP   So how would you describe its purpose? In a nutshell.

Head   The purpose is in line with government policy, which is to prepare young people for the world of work and for their role in contributing to the country's economy.

BP   OK. So I'd like to ask you one more question, if I may. And that's about how you select which route – A level or vocational – each student will take when they enter the sixth form.

Head   Well, that's very straightforward. They self-select. That's to say, if they don't have good sound GCSE results – five A to C grades including maths and English, we don't accept them into the A level stream.

BP   So they don't have choice.

Head   No. And nor should they.

BP   And what if a student with good GCSEs wants to take the vocational option?

Head   I think you said a couple of questions ago that that was the last one. So we'll finish there, if you don't mind.

Discussion

So, focusing on the structure and conduct of the interview, let's have a look at how the progression of the interview as it took place in practice compares with the pre-prepared schedule which was designed to provide a framework for the purposes of consistency over the series of interviews which are planned. And, of course, you'll have seen straight away that after the initial question ('Can you tell me little bit about your sixth form provision here at X School?') the interviewer deviates from the schedule and doesn't return to it again until near the end of the interview when he seems suddenly to remember some of what he intended to ask: ('OK. So I'd like to ask you one more question, if I may. And that's about how you select which route – A level or vocational – each student will take when they enter the sixth form') which is an approximate combination of questions 4 and 6 from the list he'd planned.

- Why do you think this happened?
- How important do you think it is to keep to the questions and sequencing set out in the schedule?

There are a number of reasons why Bashir may not have followed his planned sequence of questions. Here is his own reflective account of what happened which he gives during a meeting with his tutor.

> *Bashir* I suppose I could come up with all sorts of explanations. For a start, I could say that it seemed better to paraphrase the questions rather than use the exact wording in the schedule because then I could keep the tone more conversational, or that I was hoping to clarify my meaning. Or I could say that I used the flexibility the interview process provides so that I could probe for clarification or further information – and I do really do this, as you can see from the transcript. And I could also say that I wanted to allow the interviewee to run with her own agenda in case there were issues I hadn't thought to formulate questions about. In other words, that I turned it at the last minute into an informant interview. But the *real* reason, as I suppose you've guessed, is that I was so struck by the head's first point about the rapid expansion of the vocational provision, and then so drawn in by what appeared to be a hidden agenda of selection at 16, that I found myself hunting for honest answers like a fox after a rabbit. Is that sufficient justification, do you think? Would it be an acceptable reason for deviating so far from the planned schedule of questions? Just saying I felt I was on the trail of something significant?

What Bashir is presenting here is a dilemma which many researchers encounter between achieving the goal of consistency where each interview follows the same pattern so that like can be compared with like, or taking advantage of the interview's potential for exploration and probing. How would you answer his question about whether the approach he took was justifiable in research terms? You might find it useful to reflect on this and perhaps discuss it with colleagues or fellow-students.

Interpretation and confidentiality: questions of truthfulness, tone and hesitation

It is useful for the interviewer in qualitative research to think of their role as that of an explorer in uncharted territory investigating and reflecting on what is there, rather than that of a surveyor whose task is to exactly measure the lie of the land. This does not mean, however, that the researcher should forget for one moment what their role and purpose is. There is a fine line between incisive questioning and aggressive enquiry, and you may have noticed that there are points in the interview transcript where Bashir seems in danger of crossing it. As he pushes the head teacher for an answer he comes close to assuming the manner of an investigative journalist or perhaps even the detective who we meet in Chapter 11. For example, here is a piece of dialogue taken from the middle of the interview transcript.

BP   But these vocational qualifications can be used for entry to higher education, can't they?

Head   Well yes, of course. That is to say, you know, that er, that er many universities consider them now and they are part of the points system for entry, of course. But I think it would be fair to say that most of our sixth formers who are aiming to progress to higher education will do so through the A-level route.

BP   So how many of the vocational students apply for university entrance – let's say, last year.

Head   Well, none of them last year. Because, you see, that's not what they're aiming for.

BP   And this year?

Bashir has abandoned his pre-prepared questions and academic interviewer persona entirely at this point, and appears to be suddenly modelling himself on Jeremy Paxman. If we accept his argument that this confrontational style of questioning is justifiable in order to elicit 'an honest answer', how far are we prepared to see this investigative approach go? Would it be appropriate, for example, to comment on the interviewee's eye movements, citing research which suggests we look up and to the left when drawing on our imagination rather than our memory ('making things up', in other words)? Very few academic researchers would think so. But it is essential that we can feel confident about where to draw the line, and to help us do this we have, thankfully, the set of ethical guidelines (BERA, 2011) which are explored in detail in Chapter 2. It is important, from an ethical point of view, that interviewees are not subjected to a 'grilling' but are treated with courtesy and respect. And this is important from a purely practical point of view, too. Bashir's transcript shows that the head teacher quickly feels she has had enough of this line of questioning and abruptly brings the interview to a close. If the original questions and sequence, designed to avoid confrontation or the suggestion of there being 'correct' answers, had been a little more closely adhered to, the researcher might well have obtained more useful data from this interview.

In the short extract we've just quoted we see that Bashir has transcribed some hesitations in the head's speech:

> 'Well yes, of course. That is to say, you know, that er, that er many universities consider them now ...'

Whether or not to transcribe such 'ums' and 'ahs' is a decision researchers have to make. Those who claim it is a desirable practice argue that such hesitations give us a more nuanced understanding of the interviewee's discourse. It helps us to identify the questions which touch a nerve or cause resistance or expose uncertainty, and so on. Without them we lose the flavour of the live interview and have instead a bland unemphasised dialogue. If we ignore such hesitations and vocalisations, argue some, we only exacerbate the problem identified by Whitehurst (1979), which is that collecting talk, whether by interview or any other means, is 'like catching rain in a bucket for future display. What you end up with is water, which is only a little like rain' (cited in Powney and Watts, 1987: 16).

Other researchers, however, might argue that there are dangers in attempting to psychoanalyse the interviewee's responses in this way, because doing so opens up a broader opportunity not only for interpretation but also for misinterpretation; and the greater the scope for misinterpretation, the more risk there is of researcher bias creeping in. Moreover, they might argue, if every hesitation is to be transcribed on the grounds of creating a more nuanced record of the interview, then what about the emphasis placed on certain words or phrases, or the tone of voice, or a smile or the failure to smile? These are surely just as important as hesitations, so how shall we keep a record of them? Certainly, there is a well argued case in the research literature for doing all of this. A major practical consideration, however, is that an audio recording alone will not pick up the smiles, frowns and other body language of the interviewee. This would require either a video recording or detailed note-taking (Wellington, 2000). And an important methodological question is raised, too, which is again about *interpretation*. What may sound emphatic or hesitant to one transcriber might not to another.

There is one further problem which Bashir must now face. When, following ethical guidelines, he shows the interview transcript to the interviewee for approval and agreement, the head teacher in question gives permission for it to be used in the research only on condition that some of his words are deleted. The words in question are those which are underlined below:

'Well yes, of course. That is to say, you know, that er, that er many universities consider them now and they are part of the points system for entry, of course.'

Bashir, as an ethical researcher, has no option but to abide by this, even though it means relinquishing evidence which he sees as crucial to his emerging theory that a relatively low status is attributed to vocational courses in schools.

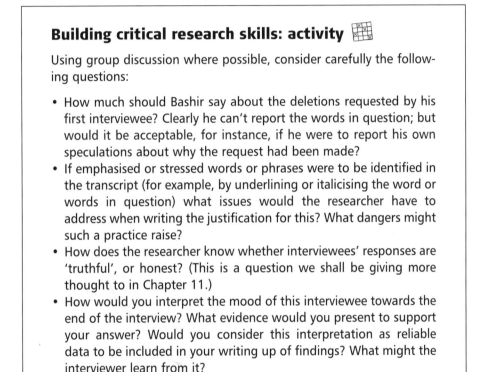

Building critical research skills: activity

Using group discussion where possible, consider carefully the following questions:

- How much should Bashir say about the deletions requested by his first interviewee? Clearly he can't report the words in question; but would it be acceptable, for instance, if he were to report his own speculations about why the request had been made?
- If emphasised or stressed words or phrases were to be identified in the transcript (for example, by underlining or italicising the word or words in question) what issues would the researcher have to address when writing the justification for this? What dangers might such a practice raise?
- How does the researcher know whether interviewees' responses are 'truthful', or honest? (This is a question we shall be giving more thought to in Chapter 11.)
- How would you interpret the mood of this interviewee towards the end of the interview? What evidence would you present to support your answer? Would you consider this interpretation as reliable data to be included in your writing up of findings? What might the interviewer learn from it?

Evaluating the pilot interview

Bashir has learnt a great deal from this initial interview, both in terms of his own interviewing skills and in terms of the potential pitfalls awaiting the unwary interviewer. Here we see the value of conducting and evaluating a pilot interview. It can be an important developmental experience for the researcher. When he goes on to conduct his interview with a second head teacher Bashir will hopefully remain focused and will manage the encounter in an appropriately academic and professional manner. You'll find the transcript of this second interview below. Look at it carefully. In your view, does he make a better job of it this time?

Interview 2

BP	Can you tell me a little bit about your sixth form provision here at X School?
Head	In terms of numbers, do you mean? Or what?
BP	In terms of the provision. What does the school offer in terms of qualifications post-16?
Head	I see. Well, we have a wide range of AS and A level subjects, including modern and classical languages, a full range of sciences, humanities and arts, and soft subjects such as drama, art, music. And alongside those we have vocational qualifications in the areas of sport management, travel and tourism and erm another one, something to do with social care. And those, the vocational subjects, are offered at both level 2 and 3, so there's something for pupils who didn't do well at GCSE but don't want to re-sit them. You know, they've lost interest in all that, but they'll engage with subjects they've not done before, subjects they consider to be more to do with the adult world I suppose you could say.
BP	And how well do these subjects recruit? All of them. In terms of numbers.
Head	We had a problem a couple of years ago of falling rolls in the sixth form. At that time it was just a normal sixth form, of course, catering for the more able pupils and offering only A levels. But numbers were falling and we faced a position where we were having to think about dropping some A levels from the curriculum and even perhaps making cuts in staffing. But then our curriculum deputy came up with the idea of building up numbers by setting up a suitable provision for pupils whom we wouldn't normally have encouraged to stay on at school. And the vocational curriculum was ideal for this purpose. So this is what we did, and of course it saved our proper sixth form from cuts and curriculum shrinkage. So we have nice buoyant numbers now overall post-16. The majority are pupils we would never have envisaged retaining in the sixth form, but they and their vocational programme have allowed our high quality A level provision to continue.

> *BP*   So do pupils have a choice over which route they take in the sixth form?
>
> *Head*   There's a wide range of AS and A levels, as I said, yes.
>
> *BP*   No. I mean are pupils able to choose whether to go the A level or the vocational route?
>
> *Head*   I don't quite understand the question.
>
> *BP*   Well, could a pupil on entering the sixth form here say, 'I'd like to do AS levels'. Or 'I'd like to do a vocational course'?
>
> *Head*   No, that's not how it works. It wouldn't work that way. Pupils have to have the necessary qualifications to enter the AS and A2 programme. They have to have grade 1 or 2 at GCSE in the subjects they wish to study. Which is only common sense really. So the more academically able pupils enter the sixth form – by which I mean the AS/A level programme. And the rest we put on the vocational programme – I was going to say 'of their choice', but we have to exercise a bit of caution there because some of them we know are going to be trouble.
>
> *BP*   So what proportion of pupils at this school use their vocational qualifications to progress to higher education?
>
> *Head*   Oh, I think there was someone this year who got a place on a sports science course somewhere or other. But normally, if a pupil is aiming for university we steer them towards the sixth form proper.

We shall have an opportunity in Chapter 11 to discover what Bashir makes of this second interview.

Writing up the findings – an example for critical analysis

We're going to look now at a section of his drafted work in which Bashir writes about his choice of interview as a research method. Read it through carefully and, as you do so, keep a critical and analytical eye on his argument. Ask yourself, for example:

- Does he convincingly justify his choice of method?
- Does he identify and address any potential weaknesses in his approach?

- Does he present evidence to support the points he is making?
- Does he ground his argument in appropriate literature from current research methods and practices?

You might like to note down some of your comments and compare them with the tutor's remarks which follow the extract.

Extract from Bashir's assignment

Method and methodology
Having chosen the four schools as a representative cross-section of local provision, I had to devise a way of gathering my data in order to provide an answer to my research question: 'Are vocational qualifications held in the same esteem as GCE A levels in Xshire's secondary schools?' I decided to interview the head teachers on the grounds that they play a major role in shaping the culture and values of the school. A fairly structured interview schedule was used (see Appendix 1). It was not always rigidly adhered to, but was used as a framework to identify points of comparison in the data collected from different heads. The advantages of the structured interview (Cohen et al., 2011) had to be weighed against the need to respond flexibly to each set of responses and the freedom to explore points further where necessary. As Schostak (2005) points out, interviewing is about more than simply information gathering. I would categorise my approach, therefore, as being of the 'informant interview' type described by Powney and Watts (1987) in which 'the goal is to gain some insights into the perceptions of a particular person (or persons) within a situation' (p. 18) as opposed to the 'respondent interview' (Powney and Watts, 1987) where all control and initiative rest with the interviewer. I reasoned that the more formal 'respondent' interview would tend to present me as the 'expert' and would be less likely to encourage the interviewees to talk openly about their values and beliefs.

The interviews were recorded, with the interviewees' permission, on a small dictaphone. The tapes were then transcribed and the recordings archived in a safe place to maintain confidentiality. Transcription was time-consuming, but it allowed me to show the transcripts to the interviewees later in order to gain their approval to quote from them. At this stage, one of the interviewees asked that several lines of his interview be deleted. This caused me some difficulty because the words he wished to have expunged would have been significant and useful data, and the fact that he asked for them to be deleted gave me some insight into his values. And I could not use any of this as evidence in my findings because of ethical constraints (BERA, 2011).

The research is intended to throw light on the current situation in schools' post-16 provision. It is too limited in scale to produce any generalisable findings, but it may open up further lines of enquiry in this area. I am aware that the nature of the evidence is to some extent unreliable because there is a possibility that the interviewees' statements about their values were inaccurate, either intentionally so or because they themselves are not consciously aware of the value judgements that they make. And, added to this, there is the danger with interviews that the researcher, in interpreting what is said, may bring their own biases and preconceptions to bear. Using 'informant' style interviews has been one way of minimising the risk of me imposing my own ideas on the interviewees through my selection and wording of questions. And in using personal narratives and statements of value as my main source of data I am taking the position that subjective truths – the accounts of themselves and their schools given by the head teachers – can be counted as knowledge. My research places value upon individual responses and perceptions as data which provide a representation of the status of vocational courses in the sample schools.

Bashir then goes on to explain and justify his choice and phrasing of questions, the order in which he planned to ask them, and the detailed reasons for and possible consequences of his deviation from the original plan. Now, keeping in mind your own evaluation of this extract, have a look at the written feedback on this section which Bashir receives from his tutor. Does she pick up any points in addition to those which you noted down?

Your section on method and methodology is well written. You have achieved an appropriate academic style and you use the research-related vocabulary accurately and with confidence. Important questions about the nature of knowledge are raised and discussed, and you draw on a relevant range of literature to support this discussion. In all these ways your work meets the standard you're aiming at. There are some

(Continues)

(Continued)

points, however, which you could have developed further and which I'd like you to think carefully about:

1. You write that the four schools are 'representative of local provision', but 'representative' in what way? Size? Catchment? GCSE Results? Academies? Selective? And does each of the four represent a different category of local school, or are they all four similar and 'typical'? I hope you can see why this statement of yours needs careful elaboration. The choice of your 'sample' is where bias in the findings can start to creep in. So it's a crucial stage, and you do need to explain very carefully how and why it was the heads of *those particular schools* who were chosen as your interviewees.

2. You present a well-reasoned argument for the type of interview approach you used. But you don't really address the question of why you chose interviews in the first place rather than some other method such as open-ended questionnaire, focus group or heads' written narratives. It's important that you establish the reasons for your choice. This doesn't mean that you have to list every other method, explaining its advantages and disadvantages; but it does mean that you have to demonstrate you have considered alternatives and come up with the best tool for the job. You can achieve this by drawing on research literature and citing what others have said about the use of interviews in a similar context to yours.

3. You explain how the interviews were recorded and then transcribed, but there's little to explain your decision to do this. What are the advantages of making a recording? (E.g. you can maintain eye-contact with the interviewee, which is often not possible if you're taking notes.) And what are the disadvantages? (E.g. a recording device whirring away on the table can be inhibiting for the interviewee). You describe later how you gave the interviewees transcripts to check before you used them. This, of course, is another advantage of recording – it helps prevent misquoting. So you should explain this, as well as giving the ethical reasons.

4. Your final two sentences of this section would carry more weight if you had cited relevant sources in support of your argument for construing personal accounts as 'knowledge'. This is an aspect of qualitative research that often comes under criticism, and so it's particularly important that we present supporting evidence for value statements of this kind.

5. You are quite right to point out the dangers of researcher bias in the interpretation of interview data, and you explain that 'informant' interviews help guard against this. But there are other essential procedures, too, in the interrogation of interview data which will also help to minimise bias, and some of these could have been mentioned here.

How did your evaluation compare with the tutor's? Did you pick up similar points? It's useful to see here that, although some aspects of his work are praised, there is still room for further reflection and improvement. The tutor's questions are designed to help this researcher to think more deeply and engage more critically with the idea of interviews as a reliable and valid means of generating meaningful and trustworthy data. You'll see that she also draws his attention to the crucial issue of interpreting interview data, and this is something we shall explore in detail in Chapter 11 where we encounter Bashir and his interviews again.

Key points 🔑

The key points covered in this chapter are:

- The advantages and disadvantages of interviews as a method of data collection.
- The choice of interviewees.
- Power relationships.
- Choosing your setting.
- The distinction between respondent and informant interviews.
- Drawing up an interview schedule.
- Minimising bias and avoiding leading questions.
- Recording and transcribing.
- The pilot: evaluating and developing your skills as an interviewer.
- Interpretation and confidentiality: questions of truthfulness, tone and hesitation.
- Writing up the findings: an exemplar for critical evaluation.

References and further reading 📖

British Education Research Association (BERA) (2011) *Guidelines for Educational Research*. Available at: www.bera.ac.uk.

Cohen, L., Manion, L. and Morrison, K. (2011) *Research Methods in Education*. 7th edn. London: Routledge.

Hammersley, M. (2008) *Questioning Qualitative Inquiry*. London: Sage.

Powney, J. and Watts, M. (1987) *Interviewing in Educational Research*. London: Routledge and Kegan Paul.

Schostak, J. (2005) *Interviewing and Representation in Qualitative Research*. Milton Keynes: Open University Press.

Sikes, P., Nixon, J. and Carr, W. (eds) (2003) *The Moral Foundations of Educational Research*. Maidenhead: Open University Press.

Wellington, J. (2000) *Educational Research: Contemporary Issues and Practical Approaches*. London: Continuum.

CHAPTER 6

CASE STUDY

Summary

In this chapter the reader is introduced to a range of ways in which case study research can be applied in an educational context. The chapter discusses the stages of case study research from design and preparation, through the collection and analysis of data, to the drawing of conclusions or the framing of further questions. It draws attention both to the strengths and to the dangers of this method of research, and uses a series of examples to illustrate and explore the epistemological questions which the use of case studies may raise.

Key words in this chapter: *case study, research question, grounded theory, unit of analysis, iterative, triangulation, construct validity.*

Making a case for case studies

Case studies have been defined as empirical enquiries that 'investigate a contemporary phenomenon within its real-life context especially when the boundaries between phenomenon and context are not clearly evident' (Yin, 2003: 13). They are used extensively in educational research. One of the reasons often given for this is that they provide a means for the researcher to capture or interrogate the 'real world' – be that a situation, an organisation or a set of relationships – in all its complexity, in a way that quantitative approaches cannot do. Of course, the fact that we can still use such expressions as 'capture' and 'interrogate' in relation to case studies should warn us at once that this approach to research does not automatically or necessarily mean that the researcher is in no danger of falling into difficulties over such issues as ownership and power relationships. Moreover, as Hammersley (2008) points out, case studies, like the other qualitative approaches we have been considering, can be vulnerable to the accusation that they attempt to generalise from the particular and that they make claims or assumptions about cause and effect which go beyond the evidence presented. For example, we might notice that a class of learners shows improved behaviour when they get a new teacher. Can we assume that the improvement is as a result of the new teacher's approach? No, of course we can't, any more than we can safely conclude from this one case that all classes will show an improvement in behaviour if we change their teacher. As long as we keep these warnings in mind, case studies will prove a useful and fascinating method of enquiry.

In educational research the case study provides a means of conducting a small-scale investigation in order to explore a research question or theory. Its flexibility means that it can be used to explore a variety of contexts and situations, from the experiences of individuals to the workings of large institutions such as universities, and from single cases of people, classes or organisations to multiple cases – comparing policy implementation in a number of schools, for example, or searching for common factors in the attitudes and values of particular groups (units of analysis). Most researchers will find that the case study approach is useful for exploring questions which are more complex than simply 'What?' or 'How many?' It provides a way of investigating connections, patterns and context, and of reflecting on the bigger picture as well as on the detail.

Planning and process

Yin (2009: 1) describes the case study process as 'linear but iterative', and consisting of six key stages:

- planning;
- designing;
- preparing;
- collecting;
- analysing;
- sharing (or disseminating).

It is an 'iterative' process in that it involves links between non-consecutive stages for the purposes of reflection and clarification; so that, for example, we might decide to return to our research design and make some changes in the light of our initial experience of collecting or analysing the data.

The planning stage is, of course, crucial. It is the point at which we have to frame our research question and make a decision about the *unit of analysis*. The wording of our question is very important, even at this early stage. It will serve to give us a clear focus on what it is we are investigating, and it will help us to identify what is and what is not central to our enquiry, whether we're doing a literature search or combing through the data we've collected. If you look at the two examples below you will see how a carefully articulated question is much more helpful in this respect than a title which indicates a general topic or intent.

Framing your research question: 1

For her research project Alex tells her tutor she wants to 'look at classroom behaviour'. The title she's thinking of using is, 'Classroom behaviour: a case study'. Her tutor asks her to consider the following points in order to decide exactly what it is she wants to find out, and then use that question as her title.

- Whose behaviour?
- What aspect of their behaviour?
- What is it you want to find out about this aspect of their behaviour?
- Where are you looking (Primary? Secondary? Nursery?)
- When? Are you looking at behaviour over time?
- Why do you want to explore this? What's the purpose of your enquiry?

Having thought carefully about these points, Alex comes up with a revised title:

'How does pupil behaviour impact on teaching styles in Year 10? A case study of one large secondary school'.

Framing your research question: 2

Pascal is interested in discovering why adults in his region choose to enrol on Foundation degrees, and whether these degrees in reality deliver all that is expected of them. He's hoping to use his research to gain an MPhil. On his tutor's advice he decides to take a case study approach and, to clarify his focus for himself, he frames his working question like this: 'What are the motivating factors in choosing to study for a Foundation degree, and to what extent are students' hopes and expectations being met? A West Midlands case study.'

Each of these researchers now has what we sometimes call 'a working title' for their enquiry which sets out the parameters of their research. It will keep them focused and on task, and will act as a guide for what to include and what not. It also helps to ensure *construct validity*. In other words, in thinking carefully about the way their question is expressed and aiming for clarity and precision in their terminology and phrasing, the researcher will be able to avoid ambiguity over how their terms of reference are to be *construed* and what constitutes 'evidence'. A precisely worded title will also provide a useful signpost to anyone else reading their work, because it explains where the lines of enquiry are going and why. And, in the process of refining their question, they have also arrived at a decision about their *unit of analysis*. For Alex it is one secondary school, while for Pascal it is foundation degree provision in the West Midlands – or at least a cross-section of that provision yet to be specified. In other types of research method the unit of analysis might be smaller: one or more individual pupils or individual teachers, for example; or one set of examination results; or a policy document. Or the unit of analysis could be much larger, as would be the case if a survey were carried out into primary provision nationally.

In Alex's and Pascal's case the unit of analysis they have chosen will allow them to implement a number of different methods of data collection. Alex, for example, investigating how pupil behaviour impacts on teaching styles in Year 10, could do any or all of the following:

- carry out classroom observations;
- set up participant observations;
- interview teachers;
- set up pupil focus groups;
- devise questionnaires for teachers and/or pupils;

- request written personal narratives;
- look at documentary evidence (for example, on disciplinaries and exclusion).

Using more than one method of data collection will allow her to compare and cross-check her findings. She will be looking to see whether there is a *convergence of evidence* (Yin, 2009); that is, whether most or all of the different sources of evidence she is using seem to point to the same conclusions. If there is no convergence – if the data from her classroom observations appears to be at odds with what pupils are saying in their focus group, for example, she will need to consider the trustworthiness of her evidence and the reliability of her methods. If, however, the data collected through both these methods seems to be saying the same thing – that is, the one corroborates the other – she will have more confidence in the reliability of her findings. If we build opportunities into the research plan to compare the evidence produced by two or more methods, we are using what is known as *methodological triangulation*. Triangulation can also refer to the comparison of information provided by more than one data source, but using the same method, as when we compare information from two different teachers in response to the same factual question, for example. This process is known as *data triangulation*.

Potential pitfalls

Clearly, as we've seen, there are many advantages to using a case study approach. There are pitfalls too, however; and we need to make sure we're aware of them.

- *The danger of generalising from the particular.* We must be wary of making generalised claims based on one specific case. If we look again at Alex's and Pascal's titles for their case study research we can see that they have very sensibly and quite rightly made the context and parameters of their enquiry explicit. Pascal's research is going to tell us something about people taking a particular qualification in one specific region of the country. Anyone reading Alex's research knows right from the start that they are going to learn something about what's happening inside one secondary school. There is no suggestion that Alex is hoping to make claims about the relevance of her findings for any other school or organisation. But in that case, you might ask, what is the point of anyone outside that school bothering to read her research? The answer is that there could be very good reasons. Her findings may illuminate similar situations in other schools and provide other researchers with a starting point from which to embark on their own investigations. Her methods and her methodology may serve as useful examples to others wishing to do research into the same issue. There may be other case study researchers looking into the same or a similar question in other schools who find it useful to compare Alex's findings with their own. What's essential is that the limitations of the research, in terms of scope and transferability, are acknowledged and no grandiose claims made on the basis of one case. Generalised statements along the lines of, 'Problems with pupil behaviour in Year 10 of second-ary schools can be solved by ...' are to be avoided at all costs!

- *Accusations of lack of rigour.* Here is what Yin (2009: 14) has to say:

> Perhaps the greatest concern has been over the lack of rigour of case study research. Too many times, the case study investigator has been sloppy, has not followed systematic procedures, or has allowed equivocal evidence or biased views to influence the direction of the findings and conclusions.

We have already discussed some of the ways in which we can build rigour into our investigation – by having a clearly defined research question; by ensuring construct validity and opportunities for triangulation; by avoiding unrealistic claims of generalised relevance or transferability. In the next section of this chapter we shall look at a case where the researcher has indeed been *'sloppy'*, and we shall examine how such lack of rigour may be avoided, including the important question of how to design our research process in such a way as to minimise opportunities for bias.

- *Ethics and access.* We cannot use a school or indeed any institution or community as the basis of a case study unless we can be sure of access to the people and events and documentation and whatever other sources of data we seek to include in our investigation. The question of access is inseparable from the issue of research ethics because it will necessarily involve the researcher in requesting and gaining *informed consent* and, as a rule, giving an undertaking to protect the *privacy and confidential-ity* of participants (see Chapter 2). This is a matter of the utmost importance and should be a major consideration at the planning stage of the case study.

Vignette 1

Let's look now at an example of case study research in practice. We suggest you read the following vignette carefully while keeping in mind the potential pitfalls we have just discussed. To what extent does Stan manage to avoid these dangers? Is there anything you think he should have done differently? What advice would you give him, as a critical friend?

Stan, a retired teacher enrolled on a part-time Master's programme in education, wants to find out whether there is some link between elderly people's experience of ageing and the value they place on their own continuing learning. He decides that, to keep his research project manageable, he will restrict his sample to the elderly residents of the small village where he himself lives. They will constitute his case study. The village itself has grown up around the fishing industry – now in terminal decline – and is developing its tourist trade. Its population is predominantly white, with an ageing demographic, and it is well equipped in terms of facilities for the elderly. Stan decides to gather his data about attitudes and values by using, in the first instance, a questionnaire. He leaves copies for distribution in three key locations in the village where he knows elderly residents will find them: the library, the church and the health centre. The questionnaires include a final line which asks for volunteers to be interviewed. Several respondents tick this box, and so Stan is able to follow up some of the questionnaires with more in-depth questions face to face. All this work is undertaken without consultation with his tutor; and he is disappointed to hear his tutor, at their next meeting, express a number of serious concerns about his approach.

Building critical research skills: activity

Using group discussion where possible, consider the following questions:

- Why might we call Stan's enquiry a case study?
- How consistent is the wording of his research question with a case study approach?
- What problems can you identify in Stan's design and data collection?
- What are the existing and potential pitfalls here in terms of (a) generalising and (b) reasoning about cause and effect?

Reflective activity

What advice would you give Stan about planning his research into age and learning? Key points to think about here are:

- the wording of his research question or principal aim;
- the design of the case study;
- how the data could be collected and analysed.

Discussion

We shall look now at what Stan's tutor has to say. This is an opportunity for you to compare the issues he raises with those which you yourself identified as a result of engaging in the two analytical activities above. The following is a dialogue which takes place between Stan and his tutor during a formal tutorial session.

Tutor So you've dived right in with your data collection, Stan. It looks as though you've been very busy. Can you just tell me a little bit about how your reading of research methods informed your decisions about data collection?

Stan I haven't done any reading yet because I'm using grounded theory.

Tutor Ah. But you still need to read around research methods and methodology, though. I think you might have misunderstood something about grounded theory. It's only the literature related to your field of enquiry that you can leave until you've started your data collection.

Stan Well, I decided not to read anything.

Tutor Hmm. Let's just go through what you've done and see whether we can sort things out a bit. Can we look at your research question first? I'm not sure what the first bit of it is actually asking. What do you mean by 'experience of ageing'? Do you mean how they feel about growing old?

Stan No. It means how they've experienced it.

Tutor Well, I'm quite old, Stan, but if you asked me that question I really wouldn't know what you were getting at. Wouldn't it be more straightforward, from a data collection point of view, to ask them – for example – about what criteria they'd use to categorise someone as 'old'.

Stan But that's it. That's exactly what I'm asking them: what do they experience age to *be*.

Tutor So how about rephrasing it as: 'What criteria do you use to categorise someone as "old"?'

Stan Well, I've asked them my question now.

Tutor But if they didn't understand that question, or if some of them understood it to mean one thing and some of them thought it meant something else, what are the consequences going to be for

	your data? How meaningful is it going to be if there's a lack of consistency in how the question's understood?
Stan	But I can't start all over again, can I?
Tutor	You know, Stan, it might be a good idea if you did. Let's just go through one or two other points. Your unit of analysis for the case study, for example. You've said this is a predominantly white, elderly, seaside community. That's OK; but have you considered what level of predictive validity your findings are likely to have for other communities, for urban populations, for example, or for our multicultural society as a whole? How relevant would your findings or theory be to other researchers working in the same field?
Stan	Does that matter?
Tutor	Not necessarily. But it'll be important, when you write up your research, that you demonstrate that you've thought through the implications of this choice you've made. You'll need to construct a convincing argument for it and also show that you recognise its disadvantages.
Stan	What sort of an argument?
Tutor	Well, you tell me. What were your reasons for choosing that particular community?
Stan	It was accessible. And there were plenty of old people.
Tutor	OK. But you'll need to think very carefully about how you're going to present that as a convincing argument. Let's just go on to look at what you're doing with these questionnaires. You say you're going to leave them at the church and at the library. Can you see what might be the problem with that?
Stan	No. I've got permission from the vicar and …
Tutor	No. Sorry to interrupt, but I meant a problem from a methodological point of view, rather than a practical one. Who will you be getting completed questionnaires from?
Stan	From elderly people who use the library and the church?
Tutor	Right. And so that means …?
Stan	What?
Tutor	Well, if the questionnaires are only available to those who attend church and the doctor's and use the library, your data will be specific to those limited groups, not to the elderly population as a whole within that community. So you're not going to be able

(Continues)

(Continued)

> to develop a theory about 'the elderly'; only about 'the elderly who attend church or visit the doctor or use the library'. And they'll have other particular characteristics, too, won't they? I mean if they're picking up questionnaires at those places they'll be unlikely to be housebound or non-readers or non-Christians for a start. So the way you're distributing your questionnaires is immediately excluding all those groups from your sample.

Stan   Does that matter?

Tutor   Well, you keep asking me that, Stan. Let me turn the question around and ask you: Do *you* think it matters?

Stan   I don't know.

Tutor   The thing is, you have to present a convincing argument, supported by references to the research methods literature, for every decision you make at each stage in designing and carrying out the data collection. So in your case at the very least you'll have to demonstrate that you're aware you're building a bias into your enquiry right from the start, so that the case study only focuses on the mobile, literate, Christian elderly and that any theory developed from it can't be applied beyond that group. And on the same basis, think about your request for interviewees – what do you think might be a potential problem there?

Stan   Oh, I see, yes. If the interviewees are self-selected – volunteers – they're not random and not necessarily representative of the group as a whole, because they're likely to be the ones who are most interested in this research or research in general?

Tutor   Yes! That's right! Good! Or they could be lonely and wanting someone to talk to. But, whatever the case, they're not necessarily going to be typical and so their interview responses won't necessarily be representative of the views of the majority. OK, so what I'd like you to do now is to take that reading list I gave you on method and methodology relating to case studies and do some careful reading, focusing particularly on framing the question and selecting the unit of analysis, and on key concepts such as reliability, validity, generalisation, triangulation, the trustworthiness of data, and the question of cause and effect. And then I'd like you to write me 500 words or so explaining and justifying your own methods of data collection.

Let's summarise the tutor's advice here:

- The question you are exploring in your case study – and indeed any question you ask your participants to answer – needs to be clear and meaningful both to yourself and to those who will be responding to it. If there's ambiguity or lack of clarity in the way the question is phrased, you risk participants interpreting it in ways you didn't intend. This makes your data unreliable.
- When choosing the unit of enquiry for your case study you need to consider how useful or relevant your findings will be to others, and discuss this issue in your written account of your methodology.
- Beware of building bias into your research design. Stan leaves questionnaires where only certain groups from his intended sample of participants will find them. If he had a reason to do this and was able to write a convincing justification his tutor would perhaps not have been so worried. But Stan has obviously not even recognised the implications of what he has done. He has not thought through this aspect of his case study sufficiently. Considering the implications and ramifications of each stage of our method is essential before we begin our collection of data.
- Make sure your method and strategies are informed by a careful reading of appropriate literature about research methods.
- Discuss your ideas with your tutor and listen to your tutor's advice before diving in and getting started. In the dialogue we've just read we can sense the tutor's frustration that Stan has neglected to do this and has thereby created unnecessary difficulties for himself.

As well as these specific points, the tutor also addresses Stan's mistaken understanding of the relationship between grounded theory and the use the researcher makes of literature and other published sources.

Grounded theory and case study

The concept and practice of grounded theory is widely used in qualitative research and was developed by Glaser and Strauss in 1967. Their publication, *The Discovery of Grounded Theory*, is available in a more recent edition (Glaser and Strauss, 1999). Unlike traditional or positivist methods of research where the starting point is a theoretical perspective or hypothesis, grounded theory starts with the collection of data and goes on to develop a theory or theoretical framework based on an analysis of that data. In other words, the resulting *theory* is constructed from, or *grounded* in, the data which the researcher has gathered, rather than applying a previously identified theory to drive the direction of data collection. Since Glaser and Strauss's original publication, diverging versions of grounded theory have been developed, not least by the two original authors themselves, who have each taken the work in different directions. However, the common factor that identifies grounded theory is the idea of 'data first', and its aim, which is to investigate and explain participants' values, motives, actions or interactions. Some researchers would argue that it takes as its unit of analysis not the individual participant but their situation, predicament or collective interaction. From this point of view it fits very well with a case study approach.

Because grounded theory does not take a theoretical perspective as a starting point, the reading of literature relevant to the field of enquiry usually happens later in the research process as the data is being interrogated and sorted into codes, concepts and categories. This analysis of the data will then inform the direction the researcher's reading will take; and the literature and data will be compared in an ongoing process from which an evidence-based theory will take shape. Stan, as his tutor points out, has mistakenly taken this 'data first, literature second' approach to mean that he needs to read nothing at all before collecting his data. In fact it is essential, with grounded theory as with any other approach, that *the researcher reads carefully around the method and methodology they propose to use before embarking on their data collection.* In Stan's case we see what happens when this reading is neglected.

But now, we hope, he has acted on his tutor's advice, done some reading and produced a written rationale for his method so far. Below you will find the piece of work his tutor asked him for. Read it through and, using a critical and analytical approach, make some notes about what you see as its strengths and weaknesses in terms of:

- the justification for using a case study approach;
- the evaluation of the data collection strategies;
- the use of appropriate literature to support both these arguments.

Stan's written rationale

Age and learning

I am basing this enquiry on a case study of the elderly residents of a fishing village in the South West of England. It has grown from an ancient settlement mentioned in the Domesday Book into a thriving modern community situated away from major roads and motorways. It has a church, three public houses, a library, a primary school and a medical centre as well as a range of shops. The population is around 10,000. It also has a circle of standing stones nearby which attracts tourists during the summer months and causes a build-up of traffic in the village.

A case study approach was chosen because I am interested in finding out more about the community I live in. The case study allows me to research people's attitudes and values in a specific setting. It is an appropriate approach for the sort of question I am asking, which is a complex one about 'how' and 'why' and focuses on values and attitudes, rather than on facts about 'what' or 'when' or 'how many'. My unit of analysis is the elderly population of a small community, which again is appropriate to a case study approach. One of the criticisms of case study research is that it lacks rigour and allows the researcher to make claims based on impressions rather than on evidence. In order to avoid this I am employing research instruments which provide documentary evidence of the data collected, such as completed questionnaires and interview notes.

I will first of all put out a questionnaire aimed at all residents over 60 years of age. To distribute the questionnaire I have decided not to post it through people's letter boxes because I don't know where all the elderly people live. Instead I will leave questionnaires to be collected at the church and library and also, because those will only reach a certain section of the elderly residents, I'll leave some at the medical centre for people who are not mobile or cannot read or do not go to church. I will also put a notice in the village magazine telling people what I'm doing and explaining where the questionnaires can be found. Questionnaires are a useful way of gathering data from a large number of respondents (Wellington, 2000). They will have a mix of questions. Some will be closed questions which will allow me to gather statistical data such as what percentage of my respondents are currently attending courses which could be defined as education or training, and some will

(Continues)

(Continued)

be open questions which will allow me to find out respondents' views and opinions. Responses to open questions are much more time-consuming to analyse and categorise (Wellington, 2000). At the bottom of each questionnaire I have left my phone number and asked for volunteers to be interviewed as part of the case study. In the interests of research ethics I have also promised confidentiality and anonymity (BERA, 2011).

The interviews will be conducted in the village library, which is neutral territory. I have obtained the librarian's permission to do this. The interviews will allow me to probe more deeply into participants' questionnaire responses. I shall take notes during the interviews rather than make audio recordings because I think a recording might intimidate the interviewees and make them less willing to answer freely. Note-taking will allow me to record the key points of what they are saying for future categorisation and analysis (Wellington, 2000). The questionnaires will be focusing on participants' feelings about education and about what it means to grow old. One of the disadvantages of interviews is that they can produce a lot of qualitative data which is time-consuming to analyse and categorise.

Another source of data that I plan to use is attendance statistics for local day and evening classes in academic and leisure subjects and a breakdown of how these relate to age. I shall also be researching how many local residents over 60 are registered with the Open University. I also plan to interview the nurses attached to the medical centre who do home visits for the elderly, and the local representative of Age Concern.

My case study uses grounded theory (Strauss and Corbin, 1997). This means that I will be collecting and analysing my data and beginning to theorise based on this before I do a review of relevant literature. My theory will be grounded in the data in the first instance. The direction my exploration of the literature will take will be to some extent decided by the theory emerging from the data I have collected. I will then begin analysing the literature in the light of my data, and my data in the light of the literature.

Stan emails this piece of work to his tutor who reads it through and adds his comments. You will find this annotated version below. As you read it, compare the tutor's comments (Figure 6.1) with the notes you have made.

Tutor's feedback

Age and learning

I am basing this enquiry on a case study of the elderly residents of a fishing village in the South West of England. It has grown from an ancient settlement mentioned in the Domesday Book into a thriving modern community situated away from major roads and motorways. It has a church, three public houses, a library, a primary school and a medical centre as well as a range of shops. The population is around 10,000. It also has a circle of standing stones nearby which attracts tourists during the summer months and caused a build-up of traffic in the village.

A case study approach was chosen because I am interested in finding out more about the community I live in. The case study allows me to research people's attitudes and values in a specific setting. It is an appropriate approach for the sort of question I am asking, which is a complex one about 'how' and 'why' and focuses on values and attitudes, rather than on facts about 'what' or 'when' or 'how many'. My unit of analysis is the elderly population of a small community, which again is appropriate to a case study approach. One of the criticisms of case study research is that it lacks rigour and allows the researcher to make claims based on impressions rather than on evidence. In order to avoid this I am employing research instruments which provide documentary evidence of the data collected, such as completed questionnaires and interview notes.

I will first of all put out a questionnaire aimed at all residents over 60 years of age. To distribute the questionnaire I have decided not to post it through people's letter boxes because I don't know where all the elderly people live. Instead I will leave questionnaires to be collected at the church and library and also, because those will only reach a certain section of the elderly residents, I'll leave some at the medical centre for people who are not mobile or cannot read or do not go to church. I will also put a notice in the village magazine telling people what I'm doing and explaining where the questionnaires can be found. Questionnaires are a useful way of gathering data from a large number of respondents (Wellington, 2000). They will have a mix of questions. Some will be closed questions which will allow me to gather statistical data such as what percentage of my respondents are currently attending courses which could be defined as education or training, and some will be open questions which will allow me to find out respondents' views and opinions. Responses to open questions are much more time-consuming to analyse and categorise (Wellington, 2000). At the bottom of each questionnaire I have left my phone number and asked for volunteers to be interviewed as part of the case study. In the interests of research ethics I have also promised confidentiality and anonymity (BERA, 2011).

The interviews will be conducted in the village library, which is neutral territory. I have obtained the librarian's permission to do this. The interviews will allow me to probe more deeply into participants' questionnaire responses. I shall take notes during the interviews rather than make audio recordings because I think a recording might intimidate the interviewees and make them less willing to answer freely. Note-taking will allow me to record the key points of what they are saying for future categorisation and analysis (Wellington, 2000). The questionnaires will be focusing on participants' feelings about

Comment [S1]: You need a title which clearly articulates your research question. Nowhere in this written piece do you explain clearly what your research question is. Neither is any explanation of what it is you will be asking your case study participants about, either in the questionnaire or the interviews. Without a clear statement of your research question the reader can make only limited sense of your arguments here.

Comment [S2]: Why do we need to know this? You aren't writing a guidebook. It's OK to give some description of the village in order to provide a context and bring the case study to life. But its traffic problems surely aren't relevant.

Comment [S3]: Here was another opportunity to explain your research question. Instead you've made a very general comment which doesn't really add anything to your argument.

Comment [S4]: This is a good point, but you need to make a reference to relevant literature here to show that you can substantiate what you are saying. Yin (2009) would be an appropriate source to cite, as he makes this point on p.14.

Comment [S5]: Is this sufficient to ensure rigour? What other things might you have to consider?

Comment [S6]: You don't need to explain what you didn't do. It's sufficient to explain what you did do, so long as you also explain clearly why you did it that way.

Comment [S7]: I think you need to rephrase this. The way you've worded it makes it sound as though only non-mobile, illiterate non-church-goers attend the medical centre! Your choice of locations needs a much more detailed discussion than this, with reference to the avoidance of bias, for example.

Comment [S8]: I don't want to press this point too much, but you need to think about who is NOT going to read the Village News. This may include people with sight impairment or difficulties with literacy or with English. It therefore has a bearing again on the eventual profile of your participant group and the dangers of building in bias.

Comment [S9]: You should provide a copy of your questionnaire (or draft) as an appendix and refer the reader to it. This will allow you to discuss the structure and content in much more detail.

Comment [S10]: Think back to our last conversation. What are the implications of your interviewees all being volunteers?

Comment [S11]: But the questionnaires will be anonymous. So how will you do this?

Comment [S12]: A good point. But what are the disadvantages of not having a full audio record?

(Continues)

(Continued)

education and about what it means to grow old. One of the disadvantages of interviews is that they can produce a lot of qualitative data which is time-consuming to analyse and categorise.

Comment [S13]: You need to consider here the extent to which such data can be considered to be 'knowledge'. How do we trust people's own accounts of their values and feelings? What are the potential problems here, about trustworthiness of data, for example?

Another source of data that I plan to use are attendance statistics for local day and evening classes in academic and leisure subjects and a breakdown of how these relate to age. I shall also be researching how many local residents over 60 are registered with the Open University. I also plan to interview the nurses attached to the medical centre who do home visits for the elderly, and the local representative of Age Concern.

Comment [S14]: Do you know whether statistics relating to adult learners' age are actually available? If so, how would you access them?

Comment [S15]: How will you find this information? What about other open learning and flexible learning providers?

My case study uses grounded theory (Strauss and Corbin, 1997). This means that I will be collecting and analysing my data and beginning to theorise based on this before I do a review of relevant literature. My theory will be grounded in the data in the first instance. The direction my exploration of the literature will take will be to some extent decided by the theory emerging from the data I have collected. I will then begin analysing the literature in the light of my data, and my data in the light of the literature.

Comment [S16]: Why? What questions will you ask? You need to explain why the nurses' views are relevant.

Comment [S17]: Why? You need to explain what you'll be asking and why this is relevant to your research question.

Comment [S18]: Good. I'm reassured that you understand this process better now.

General comments

Stan, you've done as I asked and – although there are still things you need to address here – I can already see that you are thinking things through more carefully and using the research literature to inform your thinking.

To summarise the comments I've made in the margins of your work, here are the eight most important aspects of your work that you now need to address:

1. The working title and the research question. These are an essential part of the planning stage of the case study, and it will help you to keep focused if the title incorporates the question. And you must explain what that question is. Nowhere in this piece of work do you clarify exactly what issue your case study is designed to explore.
2. Make sure that everything you include is relevant to your research question. For example, you must avoid lapsing into a travelogue about your village.
3. Support your methodological argument with references to the literature at every opportunity. And don't rely on only one or two sources as you've done here.
4. When you describe your methods, make sure you thoroughly explore questions of rigour: reliability and validity and the risk of bias.
5. Provide a copy of your questionnaire and your interview questions as appendices to your work. This will allow you to discuss them in more detail, explaining your reasons for the choice and sequence of questions, for example.
6. You need to discuss the 'trustworthiness' of the questionnaire and interview responses. How do you know the participants in this case study aren't simply telling you what they think you want to hear? What is your justification for treating these data as a source of 'knowledge'?
7. Always explain your reasons for each stage in your case study design. For example, why do you include the nurses and charity worker as interviewees? This isn't clear or obvious from what you have written about your original plan.

Remember to include a list of your references!

Figure 6.1 Tutor's feedback

Reflective activity ▦

Did you identify the same strengths and weaknesses? Is there any issue raised by the tutor which you missed on your first reading of Stan's work? If so, make a note for yourself of useful points that *you* have learnt from the tutor's feedback.

Review of key terms

Before we finish this chapter, you might find it useful to look again at some of the key terms we've used, particularly if they are new to you. You may like to read some sections through again and check your understanding of:

- grounded theory;
- unit of analysis;
- triangulation;
- construct validity.

Key points 🔑

- The appropriate use of case studies.
- Advantages and limitations of a case study approach.
- Designing a case study: unit of analysis and framing the question.
- The use of grounded theory.
- Conducting a case study: methods and methodology.
- Writing up a case study.

References and further reading 📖

British Educational Research Association (BERA) (2011) *Ethical Guidelines for Educational Research*. Available at: www.bera.ac.uk/publications/guidelines.

Glaser, B.J. and Strauss, A.L. (1999) *The Discovery of Grounded Theory*. Chicago, IL: Aldine Transactions.

Hammersley, M. (2008) *Questioning Qualitative Inquiry*. London: Sage.

Sikes, P., Nixon, J. and Carr, W. (eds) (2003) *The Moral Foundations of Educational Research*. Maidenhead: Open University Press.

Strauss, A.L. and Corbin, J. (1997) *Grounded Theory in Practice*. London: Sage.

Wellington, J. (2000) *Educational Research: Contemporary Issues and Practical Approaches*. London: Continuum.

Yin, R. (2009) *Case Study Research: Design and Methods*. 4th edn. London: Sage.

CHAPTER 7

ACTION RESEARCH

Summary

This chapter discusses the principles and practices of action research and considers, with the use of real examples, how these might be applied as part of practitioner research in an educational context. The chapter briefly covers the history and practice of action research: this is used to contextualise the theoretical, philosophical and values basis for action research as well as approaches such as participatory action research (PAR), transformational action research and living educational theory. It also differentiates between action research and action enquiry. The chapter goes on to provide practical guidance on undertaking an action research project, from early consideration of the identification of an issue or problem through to the point of re-evaluation, and including a discussion of the potential ethical and methodological issues associated with undertaking action research. The chapter concludes with suggested additional reading, and also identifies useful websites which can provide resources and guidance for action research.

Key words in this chapter: *action research, change, values, ethics, morality, reflexivity.*

History and practice of action research

Action research originated in the mid twentieth century. While most people tend to associate action research with cycles of investigation or observation, it is much more than this. The term 'action research' alludes less to a process and more to a philosophy. That philosophy, discussed in more detail later in this chapter, emphasises social change as an outcome of research and may be seen in the original definition of action research which emphasises the need for social practice. The term originates in the works of Kurt Lewin, a highly influential American scholar who produced some of the seminal thinking on groups and experiential learning as well as action research. He defined action research as:

> The research needed for social practice can best be characterized as research for social management or social engineering. It is a type of action-research, a comparative research on the conditions and effects of various forms of social action, and research leading to social action. Research that produces nothing but books will not suffice. (Lewin, 1946, reproduced in Lewin, 1948: 202–3)

Lewin was not referring to education in this argument, and action research subsequently experienced a loss of popularity in the US. However, the approach came to be applied to education in the UK from the 1970s as the potential for practitioner research using action research became clear. Lawrence Stenhouse (1975) was a major influence on educational action research. In his book *An Introduction to Curriculum Research and Development* he called for a research-based model of teaching and argued that 'curriculum research and development ought to belong to the teacher' (Stenhouse, 1975: 142) and also asserted that 'it is not enough that teachers' work should be studied: they need to study it themselves' (ibid.: 143).Considerable development in the use of action research in education also took place in the 1980s, and includes work by Carr and Kemmis (1986) and Kemmis and McTaggart (1988).

Carr and Kemmis (1986: 162) defined action research as 'simply a form of self-reflective enquiry undertaken by participants in social situations' which is undertaken in order to achieve three possible outcomes:

- improving practice;
- improving understanding of practice;
- improving the situation in which the practice takes place.

Carr and Kemmis's approach has many parallels with notions of reflective practice (for example, see Schon, 1983) although, in action research, the commitment to social action and change implies *personal* development and growth as well as *professional* development and growth. Therefore, action research might more properly be described as self-*reflexive*, rather than self-*reflective*. Reflexivity is rather more than the self-examination which is implied in reflection. Reflexivity demands that the researcher reflects on and evaluates not only their own impact on the research, but also how such things as personal values, past experiences, attitudes and assumptions might impact on the research. This process of reflexivity should be ongoing, and discussion of the issues it raises is one of the ways in which the integrity and reliability of the research can be demonstrated. Reflexivity can be supported by using the perspectives of others. By this, we mean to use a critical friend. This person might be a colleague – someone who is familiar with the situation you are working to change. The role of the critical friend is to *question* rather than to *criticise*, to provide a different pair of spectacles through which to explore situations and contexts, and to interrogate values, beliefs and assumptions. They will do this on an ongoing basis, contributing to each iteration of your research.

Because the planned improvement and development of practice is something that teachers are always involved in, to some extent you may already be involved in action research, albeit in an informal manner. Changes in education are ongoing, and as a teacher, you are continually responding to and implementing change in a planned and reflective manner, making adjustments and changes as you evaluate. This iterative process is the basis of much action research, although to be defined as *action research* the process would be informed by a theoretical framework or body of literature. Where the process is one of the practitioner engaging in ongoing critical reflection based on a critical questioning of their own assumptions and practice, but not informed by a body of literature, this would be more appropriately termed *action enquiry*. For the purpose of this chapter, it is assumed that any research undertaken is action informed by theory: thus, all the references made are to action research. You can use the activity below to reflect on the extent of your ongoing involvement in Action Research or Action Enquiry.

Reflective activity

Think about the last time you had to institute a major change in your practice as a consequence of changes in institutional or government policy. Examples might be the introduction of a new behaviour policy or curriculum changes. Consider the following:

• What was the intention behind the change?
• What planning did you do before implementing the change?
• How did you evaluate the change?
• What evidence did you use?
• Did you make any further changes?
• What were the intended and unintended outcomes of the change?
• How did the changes influence your thinking on this issue?

Values in action research

Throughout this book, we have emphasised the importance of undertaking research which is both moral and has outcomes that make a positive change. This thinking has close parallels with the philosophy and values underpinning action research.

Action research emphasises moral and ethical issues, considering these in both the practical learning and research contexts as well as in the context of values and beliefs. Examples of values might be respect, honesty or integrity. These are abstract in nature, but most people who hold particular values will enact them in their daily lives. We try to live by those values – honesty and respect for others – which are important to us in the situations we find ourselves in and with the people we meet, and this is expressed in some of our work (for example, see Atkins, 2009: ch. 3). Therefore, as well as holding abstract values (talking the talk) they have become part of our lived lives (walking the walk). The values we hold are embodied not only in what we do, but in how we practise as educational professionals and in what is of importance to us in that practice. These values, and the practice they inform, become part of the research as they are examined and questioned. The values are often the starting point for the research, in that the researcher has a problem or dilemma which conflicts with their educational values. This is discussed later in this chapter while the application of values to research, with particular reference to social justice, has been discussed in detail by Morwenna Griffiths (for example, see Griffiths, 1998; 2003).

Reflective activity

McNiff (2002) is among those who have argued that action research (AR) begins with the values of the researcher. Since AR is a development of reflective practice this assumes that action researchers are self-reflective – and self-*reflexive* – practitioners. Such self-reflectivity enables you to be aware of what drives your life and work. Reflexivity enables you to respond to methodological challenges and issues in a thoughtful and moral way. It may be useful at this point to consider the values which you hold, both personally and in respect of education as these will influence your research interests. For example, our personal and educational values include: valuing every individual; respect for others; social justice and honesty. These commitments influence our research interests, for example by leading Liz to be more interested in excluded student groups such as level 1 vocational learners than, for example, in concerns about the value of the A-level curriculum. You may have similar or different concerns. Reflecting on your values in this way will enable you to have greater clarity about what you are doing, and, more importantly, why you are doing it.

Using the following four questions to focus your reflection, try to identify two or three key values which guide your life and your practice. Write these down and then return to them at each stage of your action research project and ask yourself, and record, how these values are influencing your research at this moment in time.

- What values/principles do you hold?
- How do you enact these in your daily life? How do you 'walk the walk'?
- How does this relate to your role as a teacher or other education professional?

Theories in action research

There are a number of influential approaches and theories in action research. Broadly speaking, action research is considered by its advocates to be a political, democratic and emancipatory approach to research. By this we mean that it engages with political issues such as inequalities in education through democratic processes. Eventually, emancipatory social change occurs as a result of the action taken and the new knowledge gained. The notion of emancipation originates in Carr's and Kemmis's work of the 1980s, which also emphasises the collaborative nature of action research. There are tensions between those who emphasise the individual nature of action research, and those who emphasise more collaborative or participative perspectives.

Participatory action research (PAR) has its roots in the critical pedagogy developed by Paolo Freire in South America as a response to traditional forms of pedagogy in which, rather like Gradgrind in Dickens's *Hard Times*, teachers imparted information to passive students who were 'empty vessels' waiting to be filled. Participatory action research developed from these ideas as a democratic means of initiating and implementing change and development in communities and groups. While used extensively by organisations such as international development agencies, PAR is also used in educational contexts, such as involving pupils in change for school improvement. Essentially, in PAR, the action research process – identifying a problem, imagining a solution and so on – is undertaken by all the relevant parties in the research. This actively democratic approach – in which all parties are equal, including those who are intended to be 'helped' by the research – means that the group critically reflects on current action and the contexts in which it happens, in order to make positive social change.

While it may not be truly participatory, much action research is collaborative in nature. In part, this is because education is collaborative – it never involves only one person. Indeed, it can be argued that true action research must always be collaborative as groups of people work together to change and improve their professional lives and practice. There is also an argument that individual reflection on data and outcomes is insufficient, in terms of both the validity of the research and in using the widest possible range of ideas about the data. This might involve, for example, all participants analysing aspects of data together, doing the analysis separately then sharing their ideas, or one or two people undertaking the analysis, then returning to other participants with their ideas so the others can feed back and comment on the interpretation, in other words, validate it. Although much action research is collaborative, some writers, such as Whitehead, emphasise the individual nature of the process, and individual outcomes such as personal change, as in living educational theory.

Educational theory originates in the work of Jack Whitehead and has been developed by Whitehead and McNiff in later work (for example, see McNiff and Whitehead, 2009). It is predicated on ongoing personal and social growth leading to development of, and changes in, practice and ideas within the learning environment. According to McNiff and Whitehead (citing Foucault, 2001), the theory is influenced by critical transformational theories of social change as well as (citing Rayner, 2008, and Whitehead, 2008c) drawing on critical transformational theories of epistemological change in which personal and social change are rooted. In discussion with us, Billy Barry reflected on the nature of living educational theory (LET), which he used in his PhD thesis. In the course of our discussion he proposed the following definition of LET:

> [It is] a critical and transformational approach to action research. It confronts the researcher to challenge the status quo of their educational practice and to answer the question, 'How can I improve what I am doing?' Researchers who use this approach must be willing to recognise and assume responsibility for being a 'living contradiction' in their professional practice – thinking one way and acting in another. The mission of the LET action researcher is to overcome workplace norms and self-behaviour which contradict the researcher's values and beliefs. The vision of the LET researcher is to make an original contribution to knowledge through generating an educational theory proven to improve the learning of people within a social learning space. The standard of judgement for theory validity is evidence of workplace reform, transformational growth of the researcher, and improved learning by the people the researcher claimed to have influenced. The LET approach has been successfully used by action researchers across the globe at the post-graduate level.
> (Barry, 2012)

Reflective activity 🔲

- Which of these theories do you feel most comfortable with? Why?
- How easy or difficult would it be to undertake collaborative or participative action research in your setting? What are the reasons for this?

Action research: what makes it different?

Many students believe they are undertaking an action research project when what they are doing would more properly be described as case study. This is because many students conduct practice-based, insider research and, indeed, a key feature of AR is that it is about practitioners trying to understand and improve their practice on a day to day basis. However, there are aspects of AR which make it very different to case study. First, in AR the practitioner is a key actor in the research, while case study research can be undertaken by someone who is not actively involved *in* the group or situation under investigation, but is conducting research *on* that group or situation. Secondly, the case study looks at a particular case in depth at a moment in time in order to *illuminate* that case, while a key aspect of action research is that you revise and develop your study in cycles, gathering data as you go, in order to make a *positive change.*

Vignette 1

George and Alice were both completing MA dissertations. They were working in similar settings (primary education; George was Assistant Head in his school and Alice was a classroom teacher) and, as both were gifted amateur musicians who had co-ordinated arts and music in their schools, shared concerns about similar issues.

Alice was concerned about the teaching of music in school. In order to develop her understanding of the practices in school and the strategies used by individual teachers, she interviewed eight teachers, three from Key Stage 1 and 2 and two from Foundation stage. She also observed the teaching of music in each of those classes, spoke to the children about their experiences and sent a questionnaire out to parents. She drew on school policy, Ofsted reports and government guidance as additional data. She concluded that there was considerable variation in the quality and practice of music teaching and that this directly correlated to the teachers' previous experience of music: those with some formal musical knowledge (for example, those who had learned to play instruments as children) were much more confident and innovative than those without. She recommended that the school developed an in-service CPD programme to support those teachers with less confidence and also proposed minor timetable changes which would facilitate each class to have some teaching by a more confident music teacher. Both recommendations were taken on board by the school head.

George recognised that cultural practices in the catchment area meant that, for boys, music – particularly the learning of an instrument – was seen as a 'soft' and feminine subject, inconsistent with their own emerging masculine identities. He wanted to change his practice in the teaching of instrumental music in such a way that boys would be more readily engaged and have the freedom and opportunity to enjoy instrumental music. He identified three different strategies he could use which included the use of instrumental music in football and gymnastic lessons; the introduction of a broader range of instruments in school, supported by the peripatetic music service and exploring the lives of contemporary instrumentalists as part of a literacy project. He also arranged for a local amateur cellist to visit and meet the children. He introduced these strategies over a three-month period and then evaluated the data he had collected. His data included a detailed evaluation of every lesson in which music was used, external observation of some of those sessions by colleagues, interviews with some of the children, a questionnaire to parents and school data on uptake of instrumental lessons through the peripatetic music service. George evaluated his interventions and built on them in subsequent curriculum developments.

Reflective activity 🔲

Read the vignette above and consider the following:

- In what ways were the studies fundamentally different?
- Which of the projects might be described as action research? Why?

What concerns and philosophies do you think underpinned each study?

Since changes made in action research are specific to you and the participants in the study, another feature of this approach is that it is about improving knowledge in a particular situation, and therefore is not generalisable. While generalisability is also a debate in case study, most *rigorous* case study is considered relatable if not generalisable. Action research is also *political*. It is grounded in the philosophy of social action which is 'acting with social intent, doing things in order to influence someone somewhere' (McNiff and Whitehead, 2009: 11) and which is also about working towards *social justice*. Therefore, the active nature of the philosophical and conceptual basis for action research, which is about *change*, differentiates it from other forms of research, including case study. Acting with social intent, and effecting social change, mean that action research is transformative, in that it makes a difference to the lives of both the researcher and the researched.

Because it is about change, AR is an ongoing process. You will identify a theme or problem you want to explore and address, gather data in a structured and systematic manner to establish what is happening now (reconnaissance) evaluate those data, plan and implement changes in the light of your conclusions, observe and evaluate again and make further changes. These will then inform a further data-gathering phase as you continue to try to make ongoing improvements. This process, which will also involve changes to your thinking about the problem, is referred to as the action research spiral. This action then *is* the research tool, and the research is *on* the action. In other words, both aspects are of equal importance in an action research study. There are a number of models of this spiral (for example, see Wellington, 2000: 22). While we particularly like this early one from Kemmis and McTaggart, as it is very clear and illustrates the ongoing nature of AR (see Figure 7.1), do be aware that all research is messy, and AR is no exception, so at times the spiral may become a little confused or messy round the edges, as you explore different aspects of the same problem.

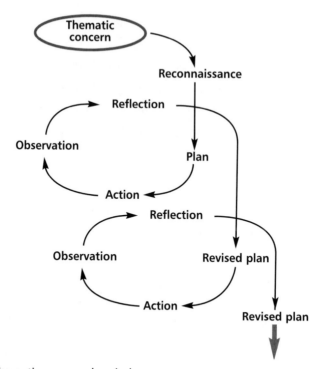

Figure 7.1   The action research spiral
(Kemmis, S. & McTaggart, R. (1988). *The action research planner* (3rd ed). Victoria, Australia: Deakin University Press.)

Many students ask 'How many cycles is enough?' However, this reduces AR to the procedural. McTaggart (1996: 248) has warned against thinking that following a spiral necessarily constitutes action research. He argues that, rather than a method or procedure, AR is 'a series of commitments' which involves observing and problematising through professional practice 'a series of principles for conducting social enquiry'.

For action research practitioners, who are committed to continually developing educational practice in a socially active context, observations and reflections on particular situations are ongoing and never-ending. However, it is also necessary to be pragmatic and if, for example, you are undertaking a study as part of an MA programme, you will have a submission deadline. Therefore, for the purpose of your assignment you might be obliged to limit the study to two or three cycles, depending how long the data gathering takes and the extent of your developments. However, as a practitioner committed to social action, you will carry on your research, albeit with less extensive 'writing up' than was required for your assignment. A more extended formal study might be carried out over one or two academic years if this is a subject you have a particular interest in and/or are, for example, undertaking your AR for a PhD or EdD study. Here, the difficulty is knowing when to stop for the purpose of writing up. Once you have made that decision you can 'write up' the study to that point in time, although again, you will continue your investigations and development of practice.

Undertaking an action research project: planning

Action research as practitioner research is grounded in the question 'How do I improve my practice?' (you will have noted that the first of Carr and Kemmis's outcomes of action research is improvement in practice). In order to improve practice, you may first need to investigate a particular situation or phenomenon in order to understand exactly what is happening and why. Therefore, the first thing you need is a clear focus or concern for your project. This focus or concern should be clear and simple. You should bear in mind that improving practice is an incremental process and you are not going to change the world overnight. Therefore, the focus for your action research study should be:

small

In general, small means manageable! You should also bear in mind any statutory constraints on what you do. As Whitehead (2011) has suggested, teachers in the UK have, in recent years, been subjected to oppressive statutory regulations that have not supported their creativity in improving practice. Such constraints may mean that you are unable to implement all your ideas in full but also challenge you to be still more creative in your ideas and practice. It is also important to be clear about the philosophy and values underpinning your study, as well as about data gathering and analytical methods and ethical concerns, and how they might be addressed. This means ensuring that your research is rigorously planned and organised. Jack Whitehead (see McNiff and Whitehead, 2002: 72) has produced a framework for planning action research which takes the form of the following questions:

- What is my concern?
- Why am I concerned?
- What do I think I can do about it?
- What will I do about it?
- How will I gather evidence to show that I am influencing the situation?
- How will I ensure that any judgements I make are fair and accurate?
- What will I do then?

These planning questions build on Whitehead's earlier work (1985: 98), which emphasises the individual nature of much action research. In this, he proposes five questions which illustrate how the process *feels*. This approach is outlined in McNiff et al. (2003) and was used by Billy Barry to frame his PhD study:

> *I experience a concern when some of my educational values are denied in my practice*
> My concern was my values and beliefs about educational quality were often denied by the implied expectation of my role as school principal to maintain the status quo.

> *I imagine a solution to the concern*
> I sought to recognize school situations where my values and beliefs about educational quality were being denied by the status quo and influence others to do the same. Using data from semi-structured interviews, my reflective journal, and discussions with participants, I created a meta-model of transformational quality that represented the collective values and beliefs of people in the school and local community. The model served as a guide for planning, nurturing, and assessing quality in my school leadership decisions and actions.

I act in the direction of the imagined solution
I initiated school reform in critical areas where the status quo meaning of quality was notably contradictory of students', staffs' and my own values and beliefs.

I evaluate the outcome of the solution
I looked for contradiction between my 'quality' intentions and the consequences of my actions. In order to gather more detailed and personal feedback, I met with a group of three critical friends, a school principal, psychologist, and secretary. The critical friends observed me on a routine basis in my role as principal and their feedback came from their first-hand experience of my leadership. I also met with a participatory action planning committee of teachers, students, and parents twice a month for a year and a half to gather feedback.

I modify my practice, plans and ideas in the light of the evaluation
Based on the feedback I gathered from the participatory action research committee and critical friends, I modified my leadership approach and understanding to limit the contradictions between my intentions toward promoting transformational quality and the consequences of my decisions and actions.
(Barry, 2012)

Undertaking an action research project: data collection

Part of the planning process in doing action research is deciding what methods to use. In terms of method, it is important that those chosen should be fit for purpose, that is, they will generate data which will help to resolve your concern or answer your question. While other factors (see below) will also influence this, there is a broad range of qualitative methods to choose from. Many students restrict themselves to interviews and questionnaires, thus limiting the range (and in the case of questionnaires) the quality of data they generate. Other sources of data might include:

- focus groups;
- observations (of or by you);
- images such as photographs or film of your setting;
- images, products or writing generated by participants to reflect their feelings about a situation or experience;
- research diary;
- school/college/institutional data such as standardised assessment records,

Individual Education Plans, socio-economic information – in fact, anything the organisation keeps in text or electronic form;
- inspection reports, policies and procedures.

Using a range of methods, sometimes called between method triangulation (Wellington, 2000: 24) will help to confirm the reliability of your data.

As well as fitness for purpose, two other significant factors will influence the choice of research methods. First, the nature of the research questions and issues such as time and accessibility, and secondly, the imperative to evolve a research process which reflects the underpinning values and philosophy of the study. Thus, if your values include respect for others and you are framing your study around concepts of social justice, you will want to be sure that your methods demonstrate respect for the participant group and their needs and preferences consistent with your social justice framework.

Vignette 2

This vignette further develops Billy's experiences of action research (see planning, p. 135). Billy holds educational values concerned with providing the best possible comprehensive education for every child and a belief that each child should and can be enabled to achieve and reach their potential. On his appointment as Principal of Pirsig High School in the USA he found a situation where certain groups of students – mainly the less academically able – were treated less favourably, where those who were good at sport where held in the highest esteem, and where, even among the staff, racist, homophobic and other discriminatory behaviours were commonplace. Billy addressed these issues by working to change systems and behaviours using a process of action research. This had the added benefit of enabling him to respond reflexively to any critical incidents as they arose. Changes involved at school level included removing 'setting' and introducing a compre-hensive curriculum, and at a personal level included using only forms of language and behaviour which focused on the needs of the 'other'. Using this process, he was able to resolve many of the very significant problems the school experienced. His research snowballed – as one issue was resolved further development was needed or another issue arose – and, given that the action research he was undertaking concerned the behaviours, systems and structures across a whole school, his study became very large.

Building critical research skills: activity

Billy used a range of existing school data – attendance records and assessment outcomes for example – to determine the effectiveness of the move to a comprehensive curriculum. Identifying clear criteria for monitoring and evaluating improvements in relationships was more difficult.

Discuss the issues which may have arisen here with a colleague and consider:

• What sort of criteria could he have used to evaluate the success of his intervention?
• What kind of data might have contributed to this?
• What ethical and methodological issues might arise from a project which attempts to improve relationships? How might these be overcome?

Undertaking an action research project: data analysis

Undertaking an action research project will generate large quantities of qualitative data. Analysis of this can be very time-consuming, however, the significant advantage that an action researcher has is that the analysis is part of an ongoing cycle which can be built into daily practice. We have produced a 'how to' chapter on data analysis elsewhere in this book (see Chapter 11) but there are a couple of points to be made in the context of data analysis for action research. One is pragmatic – your analysis has to be organised and systematic, and built into your daily practice simply to avoid it being overwhelming, or leading to a situation where your study goes on and on, because you cannot progress until the data analysis is complete. The second is an ethical and methodological issue. That is, the data analysis, like all other phases in action research, must be completed as rigorously as possible. The change which is inherent in action research can significantly impact on people's lives. It is essential, therefore, that your data analysis is rigorous – and your interpretations reasonable and grounded in the data – before you introduce change and develop your practice. It would be highly unethical to make a change which was not evidence based, where that has implications for the educational well-being – or otherwise – of others. However, once you are confident in your data and its analysis, that provides a point at which you can make changes based on your new knowledge, and in doing so, develop practice and generate positive change.

Criticisms of action research and how to avoid them

Action research, similar to many other qualitative approaches to research, has been subject to some criticism. This is largely focused around its rigour and the (lack of) training of those undertaking it. There is also considerable debate and rhetoric, not to say confusion, around what is, or is not, action research. This has been addressed elsewhere in this chapter but there is a clear imperative to outline *how* your study is action research if you are to avoid this particular criticism.

Criticisms around lack of training tend to focus on the fact that few practitioners have undertaken formal research training. This implies that there are likely to be methodological or analytical weaknesses or errors in the study, with possible negative consequences for the participants. Addressing such concerns is an ethical, as well as a methodological, issue and requires that you are knowledgeable about the approach, clear about the focus of your study and that you approach it in a systematic and reflexive manner. There is a significant body of 'how to' literature on action research which you should read carefully in addition to attending any seminars or lectures on the subject and seeking guidance from your tutor or supervisor which would support you to do this. Lack of time can be problematic, but only if you do not prioritise your changes in practice and study of them. Good planning and organisation and a systematic approach to every aspect of the study can help to overcome this.

Action research has also been subject to criticisms for the lack of objectivity arising from the practitioner's role of researcher (insider research is discussed in detail in Chapter 3). However, it may be argued that all qualitative research is subjective, particularly in education, irrespective of whether it is done using an action research approach or not. This is because our research interests and the approaches we use are influenced by our values and beliefs which in turn are influenced by our life experiences, cultural and religious beliefs and practices. To avoid the risk of such criticism, it is necessary not only to acknowledge values and beliefs which inform the study but to question your own assumptions and behaviour at each point in the process, in order to achieve a degree of 'reflexivity, or 'introspection and self-examination' (Wellington, 2000: 200). This would involve a consideration of your own values and understanding how they may influence the design of the study, the collection and interpretation of data and relationships with other participants in the research. This approach cannot be disentangled from undertaking research which is moral and ethical, and involves attempting to understand and clarify the relationship between your own values, assumptions and experiences and your research practice, a process of 'interior reflexivity' which Sikes and Goodson (2003: 48) argue is a better 'anchor for moral practice' than any external guidelines.

Building critical research skills: activity

Emma was undertaking an action research project evaluating the phased introduction of a new behaviour policy among Year 7 and Year 8 pupils at a mixed comprehensive school. She had undertaken a research-based dissertation during her degree but this was her first research project at postgraduate level. Data-gathering techniques involved writing observations of children's behaviour where this was deemed to be inappropriate, keeping records of sanctions and detailed observations of Emma herself implementing the new policy. Children were asked for their perspectives on it during class discussions.

The school deputy head, then studying for a PhD, agreed to be a critical friend, as did Emma's supervisor. Emma asked them to look at raw data alongside her interpretations of that data at intervals during the study.

- What were the ethical implications of this?
- What were the methodological implications?
- In what way might the study be open to criticism?
- How might those criticisms be avoided and rigour demonstrated?

Ethical issues in action research

As with all educational research, undertaking AR involves walking through an ethical minefield, because the research must involve people, and, as Sikes and Goodson (2003: 48) have argued, it is not enough to use a framework which emphasises the instrumental, an approach they suggest is both reductive and procedural. By this, they mean that anonymising participants and gaining consent is not sufficient, that there are much more serious questions here which need to be addressed. These might include questions such as: Do participants really consent meaningfully? How many people have such an understanding of research that they can be aware of the possible social and relationship implications of participating in a study? Of being at the receiving end of unforeseen and unintended consequences?

In addition to these issues, which you will come across in any form of qualitative educational research, action research can present us with another layer to those ethical concerns. In the event that you are undertaking cyclical research, in which each cycle involves a change of some description, what if, for some participants at least, this change has unforeseen and negative consequences? Or in a comparative study (in which one group receives an intervention and a parallel group does not) where one group has a very positive outcome but the second group has a very poor outcome? Can those consequences be justified by the argument that you are now better informed or have found a better way of doing something?

Another significant ethical issue in action research is the potential for your values and beliefs, which are fundamental to your study, to conflict with those of others. An obvious example of this might be opposing values in terms of religious versus secular education. However, there are multiple examples of opposing and conflicting perspectives in education, such as the relative value of a vocational education or the low value placed on education by certain cultural sub-groups as opposed to their freedom to choose their own life journey.

Noel's research provides an example of a situation where his values and beliefs came into conflict with those of some of the students participating in his study.

Vignette 3

Noel has a driving commitment to the value of education for all and a strong belief in social justice. He was undertaking action research to develop new strategies for teaching level 1 and 2 vocational programmes in leisure and tourism. During the course of his study, although all had initially agreed to participate, some students were reluctant to try out new learning activities. Three articulated that this was a waste of time, since the qualification would not get them a job anyway – the only value in it was the EMA payment all were then receiving for attending college, which they regarded as 'putting them on' until such a time as they obtained employment. All three subsequently left college before the end of their course to undertake low-pay, low-skill work unrelated to the leisure and tourism industries.

- What dilemmas do you think this raised for Noel?
- How might he have resolved those dilemmas?
- How might this experience have re-framed Noel's values around education?
- In your own area, what potential is there for your values to come into conflict with those of others?

The key to dealing with such issues is to respond to them in a moral and ethical manner. Radnor (2002) proposes three principles of researcher practice which she summarises as: 'The researcher is the research instrument who engages in a transactional process, recognising that the process is ethics-in-action' (Radnor, 2002: 30). This means that the researcher recognises their role and responsibilities in the research process, the implications of their own values and beliefs for that process, and continually questions and considers the impact of these influences on the research process and those involved in it, including him/herself. Additional guidance on undertaking ethical research may be found in Chapter 2.

Writing up your action research project

Action research is, essentially, a story about you and the positive changes you have made. Therefore, it should be written in a narrative style, and the research communicated from a personal, rather than 'objective' standpoint – use the first person and take ownership of your work. It is your study and the story is about your practice, your concerns, your values, your changes, your observations, your reflections, your evaluation, your learning. Because so much of it is about you, it would be inappropriate to write in the third person, even though (particularly for students of a certain age!) this sometimes feels a 'comfortable' way to write.

It is also important not be overly descriptive in an action research report (something which also applies to other qualitative approaches). The written report will begin with an explanation of the situation or problem and while you should outline (describe) *what* you did, you must also explain *why* you did it, as in the extract below:

> I asked Ollie, my critical friend, to undertake detailed observations of me in the classroom as part of the school's peer observation programme. As the students knew Paul well and were likely to interact with him I decided that he should use a participant approach within the spectrum of observation proposed by Wellington (2000: 93). This approach was also informed by both the research questions and the underpinning value of demonstrating respect for the students participating in the study.

Your work will need to be well written (see Chapter 4, 'Writing a literature review', for guidance on this) and clearly communicated. It should be technically correct in respect of citation and referencing, and should be proofread and checked for spelling and grammar before submission, and, since action research uses action as a means of research, your written report must show how your planned change was implemented, monitored and analysed. It is still likely to follow a 'traditional' format, since the approach still requires you to be rigorous about exploring current theory (literature), provide a rationale for your methodology and be able to clearly show how and why you have interpreted data in a particular way. Institutions vary in their requirements, but a traditional format for a research report might include:

- abstract;
- introduction;
- literature review;
- method and methodology;
- presentation of data;
- data analysis/discussion;
- conclusions;
- recommendations (implications for policy, practice and research).

At the risk of stating the obvious, the report should clearly demonstrate an improvement in practice which has been analysed and considered in a reflexive and honest manner, as well as a clear understanding of your own values and the context in which you practise. At Master's level you will demonstrate that your change in practice was undertaken in the context of a framework of critical reflection and analysis which also demonstrates that you are familiar with the current state of knowledge in your field. If you are undertaking your study at doctoral level, your work will be extended to a claim for new knowledge and a discussion of its significance in your field.

Ultimately, the work must be written in a *critical* manner and in this sense critical simply means questioning. To do this you will reflect on each aspect of the study, as it is happening, and interrogate not just what is happening, but what assumptions you are making, or taken-for-granted's you are accepting. These questions – and their answers – will form part of your written report and will provide opportunities for you to relate your research to theory, policy and practice in your area. Because action research is about social change, for the study to have validity you will have to be able to show that your work is authentic and honest. This will also help to address any criticisms of taking an action research approach.

Conclusion

The beauty of the action research approach is in its flexibility – it can be used across all educational settings and contexts, from nursery to university to school to college to prison or charitable institution, and can be used in large or small projects. However, the nature of much action research is to be very local, developing thinking and practice in a classroom by the actions of the teacher, and therefore much educational action research is small scale. Done well, it provides limitless opportunities to improve and develop our practice and our understanding of that practice, and thus to make social change by improving the experience and opportunities of our pupils and students. As Lawrence Stenhouse (1981, cited Rudduck, 1988) said: 'It is teachers who in the end will change the world of the school by understanding it.' (p. 35)

Key points 🔑

- Action research emphasises moral and ethical beliefs.
- Action research begins with the values of the researcher.
- Action research should be contextualised within clear theoretical frameworks.
- Action research is about developing practice for social and educational change.
- This means that action research is inherently political.
- Action research is applicable across all educational settings and contexts.

Websites 🖱

Both these websites include useful resources and information on conducting action research. As the authors of these sites have done considerable work together on action research, you will find a number of links between them:
McNiff, Jean available at http://www.jeanmcniff.com/
Whitehead, Jack available at: http://www.actionresearch.net/writings/jack/arplanner.htm

References and further reading 📖

Atkins, L. (2009) *Invisible Students, Impossible Dreams: Experiencing Vocational Education 14–19*. Stoke-on-Trent: Trentham Books. See Chapter 3 for a discussion of personal values in the context of a theoretical framework, in this case, social justice.

Barry, W. (2012) 'Fostering emotional well-being in school: the use of living theory action research', unpublished PhD thesis, Nottingham Trent University. www.livingleadershiptoday.com

Carr, W. and Kemmis, S. (1986) *Becoming Critical: Education, Knowledge and Action Research*. Geelong, Victoria: Deakin University Press.

Griffiths M. (1998) *Educational Research for Social Justice: Getting Off the Fence*. Buckingham: Open University Press.

Griffiths, M. (2003) *Action Research for Social Justice in Education: Fairly Different*. Buckingham: Open University Press.

Kemmis, S. and McTaggart, R. (1988) *The Action Research Planner.* 3rd edn. Geelong, Victoria: Deakin University Press.

Kemmis, S. and McTaggart, R. (2005) 'Participatory action research: communicative action and the public sphere', in N. Denzin and Y. Lincoln, (eds), *Sage Handbook of Qualitative Research.* 3rd edn. Thousand Oaks, CA: Sage. See this chapter for a theoretical discussion about PAR.

Lewin, K. (1946) 'Action research and minority problems', *Journal of Social Issues*, 2: 34–46.

Lewin, K. (1948) *Resolving Social Conflicts.* New York: Harper and Row.

McNiff, J. (2002) *Action Research for Professional Development: Concise Advice for New Action Researchers.* 3rd edn. Available at: http://www.jeanmcniff.com/ar-booklet.asp (accessed 20 November 2011). This provides exactly what it says 'on the tin' and is an excellent starting point for first time action researchers.

McNiff, J. and Whitehead, J. (2002) *Action Research: Principles and Practice.* 2nd edn. London: Routledge.

McNiff, J. and Whitehead, J. (2009) *Doing and Writing Action Research.* London: Sage.

McNiff, J., Lomax, P. and Whitehead, J. (2003) *You and Your Action Research Project.* 2nd edition. London: Routledge.

McTaggart, R. (1996) 'Issues for participatory action researchers', in O. Zuber-Skerritt (ed.), *New Directions in Action Research.* London: Falmer Press.

Radnor, H. (2002) *Researching your Professional Practice: Doing Interpretive Research.* Buckingham: Open University Press.

Reason, P. and Bradbury, H. (eds) (2008) *The Sage Handbook of Action Research: Participatory Inquiry and Practice.* London: Sage. This text provides a practical guide to PAR.

Rudduck, J. (1988) 'Changing the world of the classroom by understanding it: a review of some aspects of the work of Lawrence Stenhouse', *Journal of Curriculum and Supervision*, 4(1): 30–42.

Schön, D. (1983) *The Reflective Practitioner: How Professionals Think in Action.* New York: Basic Books.

Sikes, P. and Goodson, I. (2003) 'Living research: thoughts on educational research as moral practice', in P. Sikes, J. Nixon, and W. Carr (eds), *The Moral Foundations of Educational Research: Knowledge, Inquiry and Values.* Maidenhead: Open University Press.

Stenhouse, L. (1975) *An Introduction to Curriculum Research and Development.* London: Heinemann. Particularly Chapter 10 – 'The Teacher as Researcher'.

Wellington, J. (2000) *Educational Research: Contemporary Issues and Practical Approaches.* London: Continuum.

Whitehead, J. (1985) 'An analysis of an individual's educational development – the basis for personally orientated action research', in M. Shipman (ed.), *Educational Research: Principles, Policies and Practice.* London: Falmer.

Whitehead, J. (2011). Available at: http://www.actionresearch.net/writings/jack/arplanner.htm (accessed 20 November 2011).

CHAPTER 8

ETHNOGRAPHIC RESEARCH

Summary

This chapter discusses ways in which an ethnographic approach can be used to illuminate phenomena within educational settings such as organisational culture, and institutional and personal interactions. It also highlights some contemporary forms of ethnographic research, such as netnography and institutional ethnography, and provides real-life illustrations of situations in which these may be used. As ethnographic methods are often used to illuminate issues in organisations, the chapter also develops further some of the content of Chapter 3 in highlighting some of the implications of 'insider ethnography'. It goes on to discuss some of the particular methodological implications of doing ethnographic studies in terms of data collection, analysis and presentation. The chapter draws on real-life examples to provide suggestions for overcoming some of the difficulties associated with ethnographic research.

Key words in this chapter: *ethnography/ethnographic approach, anthropology, observation, ethics, fieldnotes, netnography.*

Introduction

The word ethnography originates from the Greek root *ethnos* which relates to race and culture. It has been defined as 'the scientific description of peoples and cultures' (OUP, 2003: 375); however, this is a somewhat simplistic definition of a term whose meaning has also been described as 'complex and ambiguous' (Pole and Morrison, 2003: 2). There are a number of reasons for this complexity and ambiguity. Although ethnography is widely regarded as a qualitative approach, ethnographers frequently use quantitative as well as qualitative approaches: large ethnographies will often include extensive quantitative data analysis, for example. Further, as Pole and Morrison also note (2003: 2) the term is used as both a verb and a noun (as in 'I am doing an ethnographic study of my school' and 'now I have completed my research I have got an ethnography of my school'). Also, as Hammersley and Atkinson (2007: 14) have argued, the term has 'overlaps' with a range of approaches in the broad field of qualitative enquiry. This overlap is illustrated in seven principles for ethnographic research (Walford, 2007, citing his earlier work with Troman et al., 2006), as well as in Stenhouse's (1985) proposal for the use of historical and ethnographic case study, and includes the use of multiple methods, direct involvement of the researcher and an in-depth study generating rich forms of data. You will note that these criteria have parallels with other approaches discussed in this book, including action research and case study. Despite this, it is possible to undertake either action research or case study which is not ethnographic in the strict sense of the word.

Historically, ethnography was associated with the early anthropologists, as well as having roots in sociology (Walford, 2007) and both these origins may be seen in the principles above. In this book, we take ethnography to mean a structured, observational study of activities in a particular setting which fulfils the principles proposed by Troman et al. However, as Wellington (2000: 44) has argued, although much educational research takes an *ethnographic approach*, few studies 'really merit the label *ethnography*' (our emphasis). Those who use an ethnographic approach (as we have both done in different studies) draw on practices used in ethnography, in particular immersion in the setting and the use of interview and observation as data gathering methods. This group of researchers includes those exploring social and cultural issues, such as understanding the lived experiences of particular learner or professional groups, or those seeking to understand policy impact, such as used with trainee teachers. Understanding is a key word here, since 'the immediate goal of ethnography should be the production of knowledge, rather than, for example, the pursuit of political goals' (Hammersley and Atkinson, 2007: 209). As with other forms of educational research, it is conducted within a rigorous theoretical framework, notwithstanding its goal of generating knowledge. This goal, as well as the approach taken, differentiates ethnographic research from some other forms of educational research, such as action research, which are overtly political and seek to make change. That said, however, if ethnographic research is about the pursuit of knowledge, and that knowledge informs positive change in educational understanding and practice, that may of itself be a political action.

Building critical research skills: activity

Think about the research you have undertaken or are planning to undertake. Go to http://www.bera.ac.uk/educational-ethnography/ and check out Troman et al.'s (2006) seven principles for ethnographic research. Consider Wellington's argument in conjunction with these. Is your work an *ethnography* or does it take an *ethnographic approach*? Discuss this with two colleagues. Are they in agreement with you? If your study takes an ethnographic approach, where does it deviate from true ethnography? These are questions that you may want to answer as you write the methodology section of your research report.

Negotiating access

Negotiating access to organisations or groups is almost always much more difficult than anticipated. Irrespective of whether you are doing your study as insider (see Chapter 3) or outsider, educational ethnographic research demands that you negotiate access to the institutions or organisations you hope to involve via their 'gatekeepers'. In educational research, because of the ethical and regulatory implications, it is unlikely that you would be undertaking a completely covert study. Therefore, negotiating access is likely to be your first major hurdle. However, as Pole and Morrison have argued, negotiating access is not merely about getting past the gatekeepers, although this is important, but is also about 'locating a role and managing entry and exit strategies from the educational setting' (2003: 26). Locating a role – which means answering questions such as, Are you a professional? A researcher? Do different groups such as students and staff see you in different roles in the same setting? – can be difficult, with 'different but similar' issues in outsider and insider research. Sometimes, seemingly small things can make a difference. In an 'outsider' study that Jane did which used an ethnographic approach, she was variously introduced to groups of participating students as 'an ex-FE teacher doing some research' – which located her primarily as a teacher with knowledge of FE students – and as 'a researcher from the university', which located her as an academic, with, perhaps, little insight into the lives of the students. These introductions influenced future relationships with the groups. The second group remained more distant, formal and slightly distrustful throughout the year-long study, while the first group welcomed her into their lives. The methodological implication of this was that the first group ultimately provided much more data.

Similarly, if you are undertaking insider research, there may be issues around role identity that you need to resolve. For example, where and when are you a professional and where and when are you a researcher? How might those lines become blurred and what are the implications – for yourself, others and the study – if they do? Who knows how much about the study and to what extent does that influence their view of you? What are the methodological implications of the role you have adopted? In relation to managing entry and exit strategies, it is important to remember that ethnographic research is about relationships, and that these cannot be established overnight; nor is it possible suddenly to withdraw from an established relationship simply because the data gathering is complete, as this raises ethical issues related to harm and exploitation.

In more practical terms, simply 'getting in' to an institution can be particularly difficult in all fields of education, and it is important to consider the institution's perspective. First, organisational policy may dictate that the head teacher or principal alone cannot grant access – a senior management team or board of governors may also be required to consider the application. This is likely to take a considerable amount of time. Secondly, in a world where education is highly regulated, some institutions will have legitimate concerns about the implications for their reputations or future inspection results, if any potentially negative data were to become public. This concern alone can be sufficient for an organisation to deny access. In addition, the organisation may have priorities which they feel could be impeded by having a researcher there, or they may have concerns about the ethical issues of someone doing ethnographic research, or concerns around the possible impact on the students in the organisation, particularly where the students might be deemed vulnerable in some way. For some institutions with educational provision, such as prisons or secure units for young people, there are additional security issues which may prove particularly difficult to overcome.

We could go on, but the point is that many organisations will feel that the possible negatives of granting access to a researcher outweigh any potential benefits. Alternatively, they may place constraints on how or when research activity is allowed to take place. For example, in an ethno-methodological study that Fred was involved in, two organisations refused to allow interviews to impinge on teaching time. Therefore, negotiations had to take place with young people around them giving up lunchtimes or after-school time to participate in the interviews. Research can be further complicated by the fact that the head teacher or principal who first grants access is only the initial gatekeeper. Depending on what you hope to do, there will be others, such as the Head of Department, the classroom teacher, the teaching assistant or the students themselves who might dictate the extent and level of access. Each of these gatekeepers may place constraints on your study and you may have to make some methodological compromises in order to be able to proceed. Alternatively, you may decide that you cannot make the compromises required and maintain the integrity of the study, and at that point you may wish to withdraw and try to negotiate access elsewhere. Equally, some institutions or organisations may have a genuine interest in your study and may wish to support it as it might help to inform them about particular groups or phenomena.

Inevitably, whatever the response from the institution(s) you approach, negotiating access is time-consuming. Even if access is granted, you will then have to spend time negotiating time scales, and agreeing the activities which will take place, and the time frame for this should not be underestimated. This is most difficult if you are going into an organisation 'cold', that is, you have approached an organisation you do not know and to whom you are unknown. For this reason, most student researchers will draw on personal resources and existing relationships in order to negotiate access. As education is a small world, you are likely to know a range of people in other institutions who might facilitate you to negotiate access. Thus, *who* you know may well dictate *where* you undertake your study.

Reflective activity

A team from a local university are undertaking a year-long study into school communities using an ethnographic approach. The study will involve two researchers each spending several weeks in your classroom, ostensibly as classroom assistants, but during this time they will be keeping detailed fieldnotes and observing classroom activity. A full ethical framework has been developed and approved by the university's ethics committee. Parents have given their consent and pupils are aware that the study will be taking place.

- How do you *feel* about having a researcher in your classroom?
- What personal concerns does this raise for you?
- As the researcher, how could you address some of those concerns on the part of the teacher?

Ethical issues in ethnographic research

Ethnography, and any educational research using an ethnographic approach, raises significant ethical issues. Much of this can be about informed consent. Issues around informed consent are a recurring theme in this book and are discussed at length in Chapter 2. However, they have a particular resonance in ethnography, where the researcher's position as participant may be compromised by giving full information. Other ethical issues which are particularly pertinent in ethnography include privacy, exploitation and harm and this is because the nature of ethnography is to observe social phenomena. Therefore, the researcher is making in-depth observations on the lived lives of individuals. Very often those individuals include people with little voice – the young, the disaffected or disadvantaged. This raises the possibility that observing those individuals' lives – even with their consent – may be a form of exploitation by the more educated, articulate and powerful researcher. In terms of privacy, we regard different places as public and private and ethnographic research has a tendency to blur those boundaries. For example, an off-the-cuff comment made by a student to a friend about his home circumstances might be recorded as data if overheard by a researcher. Harm may well arise as a consequence of the relationship issues in ethnographic research. Young people in particular can form strong relationships with teachers and others in authority – all readers will have memories of particular teachers – and it may be devastating to a young person if they become aware that the relationship they place a high value on was simply, from the researcher's perspective, for the purposes of research. As well as causing emotional harm to the individual, such a situation also raises issues of exploitation. Perhaps more commonly, in some situations, it may not be possible to completely anonymise an individual (for example, a head teacher or college principal) which, if a study becomes public, may have a reputational impact on that individual.

These issues raise a number of questions, which are illustrated in the following activity. Consideration of these questions should form a key focus of any ethnographic study.

Building critical research skills: activity

Ray is interested in how the value placed on education differs across ethnic groups and social classes and this forms the focus of his planned study. He is a geography teacher in a large and diverse 11–16 school. He intends to conduct participant research, using the young people taking geography in all years as participants. He also wants to gather data from parents, specifically what they anticipate or hope their child will do post-16, and the support they see they can give their child while they are still at school. He identifies parents' evening as an opportunity to explore these questions with some parents.

With a small group of colleagues discuss and make notes on the following questions. It may be helpful to ask yourself similar questions in respect of your own ethnographic study.

- Is it acceptable to do this questioning covertly?
- If participants are not fully informed does this amount to a deception?
- Can participants ever be fully informed?
- If participants are fully informed of the purpose of the study will this impact on the data gathering?
- How might it impact?
- Would that invalidate the study or the data in any way?
- Is there an alternative?
- What are the implications for the privacy of individuals?
- How might the study inadvertently cause harm to individuals?
- How might the study be criticised on the grounds of exploitation?

Institutional ethnography

First developed by the social theorist, Dorothy E. Smith, institutional ethnography originated as a Marxist feminist sociology designed as a method 'for women' rather than 'about women'. It has developed as a form of ethnographic enquiry which is used across disciplines to explore textually mediated social relations and the way in which they shape everyday lives; in other words, how the everyday world of the institution works and how it is represented through the discourses it creates. All discourse is powerful: it communicates and embeds ideology from powerful groups (for example, policy-makers) in a cascading process, reflected in the policy, procedures and institutional practices followed by those within an institution. These practices impact most on those who are most marginalised in an educational context and profoundly shape the experiences of generations of students and teachers. Representation and institutional practices reflect the lives of the elite group who creates them. Therefore, the reality that is presented to the world is one in which an elite is represented but the lives and experiences of others are not.

Effectively, this denies the experiences of those who differ from the elite, for example in terms of race, gender or class. The emphasis that institutional ethnography places on relationships between sites and situations in the contexts of policy, professional practice and working life make it useful in exploring such relations across sites within an institution in order to explain how they shape the working lives of those within it, for example in (re)producing and legitimating elite groups and marginalising others. Within this context, notions of power and power relations are of critical importance and form an important theoretical aspect of institutional ethnographies.

Multi-sited ethnography

Multi-sited ethnography is an attempt to address the issue that few ethnographic studies establish clear boundaries to the social world under investigation. It also recognises that an attempt to explore a particular group or culture cannot be done in full simply by exploring the social world in a particular geographical space. Rather, multi-sited ethnography implies that the group or actors who constitute the particular social world under investigation, are in fact, multiply situated objects of study; their world is not confined to a single space but extends beyond it, into spaces that are both real and virtual. An example of this might be the way young people construct their lives both within their educational setting and beyond it, using real-life social activities as well as virtual mechanisms such as the school intranet and social networking sites.

Netnography

The term 'netnography' was coined by Robert Kozinets, a Professor of Marketing in the US. The term is a compound word drawn from inter*net* and ethnography and refers to 'a form of ethnographic research adapted to include the internet's influence on contemporary social worlds' (Kozinets, 2010: 1).

Although netnography was originally developed to use ethnographic approaches to study marketing techniques, Kozinets (2010: 2) argues that the approach now has much wider application, given that as many as a billion people worldwide are engaged with different forms of social media and online communities, meaning that it is not possible to adequately understand cultural issues without looking at both online and real-life social worlds. Elsewhere (Kozinets, 2006: 279), he has argued that the advantages of netnography include the use of un-elicited data which he suggests is more 'naturalistic and unobtrusive' than more traditional ethnographic methods. Because of this, the approach is 'faster, simpler, timelier, and much less expensive than traditional ethnography'. However, he also cautions that 'it is still largely text-based, anonymous, poses ethical issues, is often overwhelming, can invite superficial and de-contextualized interpretation, and requires considerable researcher acuity'. Kozinets's approach has significant implications for ethnographic research in education. Teachers themselves are often involved in a broad range of online communities, such as http://www.teach.us/ and http://www. teacherstalk.co.uk/, while a majority of the people they are teach are young, and have grown up in a digital, as well as real-life, world. Thus, their real and digital social worlds are intertwined and embedded one with the other. If we accept Kozinets's argument – which is persuasive – that a failure to include online and real-life social worlds in ethnographic studies will lead to only a partial picture of the group being investigated – then that suggests that any educational ethnographic study must include this facet of the participants' social world. However, given the ethical and other issues that Kozinets warns of, such an approach should not be undertaken lightly, but with serious consideration of methodological and ethical issues, and following a framework such as that provided in Kozinets's *Netnography: Doing Ethnographic Research Online* (2010).

Fieldnotes

Fieldnotes are a key form of data collection in ethnography and, as such, have to be recorded and interpreted with the same meticulous care as any other form of data. Fieldnotes are more than a research diary: they provide the opportunity to record, as you go along, observations and impressions which are relevant to your study. This can be anything which is happening at a particular moment in time, should be as detailed as possible and, as

Hammersley and Atkinson point out, 'it is important to record even things that one does not immediately understand, because these may turn out to be important later' (2007: 143). Fieldnotes should also be descriptive rather than judgemental and may change over time, as you come to understand and interpret meanings in the data and your ideas about what is most significant develop and change. There are two main difficulties with field notes. First, 'they cannot provide a comprehensive record of the research setting' (Hammersley and Atkinson, 2007: 147). This is because the written word cannot encapsulate everything you know about a particular social world. Nor can fieldnotes record every impression, word or action you have observed. Therefore, it is important to recognise their limitations, to keep them in as detailed and meticulous a form as possible, and to support them with other data.

The second difficulty with making fieldnotes is simply finding the time to write them while also being an active participant in the setting or group you are investigating – for example, as a teacher exploring cultural attitudes to learning within your own school. Similar difficulties can arise even during scheduled data gathering events. It may not be possible to make notes related to, say, a person's demeanour or dress during an interview, even though these may be pertinent to your enquiry. In both these cases, if it is not possible to make detailed notes at the time, then they should be made contemporaneously – as soon as possible after the event. This ensures that you have an accurate record before memory becomes clouded by other events and the passage of time. If notes are not contemporaneous, then the data will be as cloudy as the memory and meaningless for the purposes of research. A useful strategy in educational settings (where writing and note-taking are a normal part of day-to-day activity) might be to make very brief one- or two-word notes as and when possible which can be expanded later on, as Matt did in his study of cultural attitudes to the teaching of literacy, during which he used an ethnographic approach.

Vignette 1

Matt's study used an ethnographic approach in his study which formed part of his PhD. During the study he worked as a teaching assistant (TA) at a primary school. The staff were aware of his study and consent had been obtained from parents and children at the start of the academic year. The study was planned to take place over the full academic year. However, by October half-term Matt's fieldnotes recorded:

I haven't noticed any reserve amongst parents for a while now, and no-one has asked me about the study since the end of September (see note 28/9/2009). The relationship with the children has returned to what it was last year, before they were informed of the study – they seem to have forgotten about it. Must consider ethical and methodological implications of this.

By December he was gathering considerable data. Although the children were apparently unaware of his dual role as TA and researcher, he wanted to be as participant as possible during his data collection and minimise any possible disruption that might be caused by his taking notes while he was working. The strategy he developed for making notes was to carry an academic diary and make brief notes in that as and when necessary and feasible, then write them up in detail each evening. On 10 December he was asked to provide cover for a Year 3 class. On that day his diary notes (mainly written while writing up children's reading records and during morning break) read:

AM – Y3 (Mrs B flu)
9–10 tidying
10–12 reading.
Chloe, RR *red well as ushual*
Hassan (s), I read to Miss every day cos *I'm a slow reader and Joe makes fun of me'* RR *Hassan does not lick this book*
George (s), RR *Read his own book to his little sister*
Demetrio, *'I hate reading out loud'* RR no comment
Denim (s), RR *Read pages 2–6*
Rubina (s), RR no comment
Emily-May (s), RR *Read very weel today*
Kara RR – no comment made
Miss H int cancelled – SS meeting re: child X.
1.30 Miss H upset – blames self not picked up on prob
Int 2mo 4pm

The same evening, Matt expanded his jottings into more detailed fieldnotes and a section from that day's entry reads:

Spent much of the morning tidying up and reading with the Y3 children as Mrs. B [regular TA] off sick and class very challenging. (34 children, 18 SEN; 22 FSM and several known to social services). Some children seem not to like reading out loud – one (Hassan) said to me that he had to read to Miss every day because 'I'm a slow reader and Joe makes fun of me'. Not sure who Joe is (sibling? check) but not a child in the class. Demetrio said 'I hate reading out loud'. Made notes in each child's reading record – of the eight I heard read, 5 had parental comments in the record and 4 of these were mis-spelt (e.g. red well as ushual – Chloe). All from lowest ability group, 5 with statements (Hassan, Kara, Emily-May, Denim, Rubina) 3 without (Chloe, George, Demetrio.). Had planned to interview Miss Harding (class teacher) today, but she was called to an emergency meeting with social services. Saw her after lunch – very upset and pre-occupied with child being made subject of care proceedings, said she felt she should have picked up on problem sooner – but remembered interview and agreed to reschedule for after school tomorrow.

Matt has expanded his notes adding in detail what he has remembered and other, demographic information, gained from school records at the end of the day, but pertinent to his study. This included information on the number of children eligible for free school meals, for example, and how many had statements of special educational need. From an ethical perspective he used children's first names so that he would not confuse himself during later data analysis. However, he subsequently changed all children's names and used gender- and ethnicity-appropriate pseudonyms. He made a point of not identifying or using data from the child who was the subject of emergency care proceedings.

Observation

Participant observation is the key research strategy employed in ethnographic research (Wellington, 2000: 45). This means that the researcher becomes, effectively, an 'insider' (see Chapter 3, 'Insider research'), participating in the cultural and social world of the group being studied as she/he attempts to draw meaning from their actions. This observation, again according to Wellington (2000: 93), takes place on a spectrum of participation ranging from complete participant, through participant as observer, observer as participant to complete observer. A complete participant would be someone who is, or appears to be, a full member of the group being studied. However, this can raise ethical issues around the researcher/researched relationship and the transparency and honesty of the research process, particularly where the researcher is pretending to be a member of the group being studied (for example, see Laud Humphreys' *Tearoom Trade*, 1970).

Most ethnographies undertaken in educational settings will fall somewhere around the participant as observer/observer as participant section of the scale. It is also possible for the degree of participation to vary between observations in a single study. The variations in the extent of participation, demonstrated in the vignette below, may be argued to reflect the impossibility of replicating specific sets of circumstances in ethnographic research and highlight the necessity to be conscious of the way in which different relationships and perceptions of the process might influence the outcomes.

Vignette 2

In Beth's study, which used an ethnographic approach and took place in a sixth-form college, she was constrained in what would be possible in terms of observation by the fact that the students already knew her and would expect some degree of interaction. The level of participation varied, however, as it was dictated largely by the teacher on each occasion. She undertook observations of students in three different A-level classes (politics, history and English) at intervals during the year she spent gathering data. During the politics sessions the tutor was only prepared to allow her to sit and take notes, in history classes there was some interaction with both students and tutor, and during the English classes, the teacher and students, aware that she taught this subject with other groups, asked for her contribution to the lessons.

Building critical research skills: activity

Consider Beth's study above. With a colleague:

- Discuss what methodological issues you think this raises in an ethnographic context. (Try to avoid falling back on reliability!)
- Discuss *why* those issues are raised.
- Discuss what lessons you can draw from this for your own research.

When undertaking ethnographic research, observations in different settings (for example, the classroom, the playground and online communities) can provide the opportunity to explore the different cultures, identities and social worlds existing within the same institution and among the same group.

There is a wide range of techniques which may be used for recording participant observation and these, like the observations themselves, may be placed on a spectrum ranging from very structured approaches to the recording of data such as the formal observations and protocols discussed by Yin (2003: 92), and including strategies such as observation schedules, to those using a stream of consciousness or 'open-ended narrative' method (Angrosino and Mays de Perez, 2000: 674). This was the approach used by Jenny, and was chosen partly because she did not want to 'miss' any potentially useful data, but also in recognition of the fact that participant observation is inevitably mediated by a framework of cultural meanings and symbols arising from the observer's own life history (Vidich and Lyman, 2000: 39). Thus, the observer will see (and interpret what they have seen) in the context of their own social and cultural meanings and understandings, rather than in the context of those of the group being studied, something that has significant methodological implications for ethnographic research.

Issues related to mediation of observation may be addressed principally by recognising and questioning the influences of your own values and beliefs in a reflexive manner. Other strategies might include inviting participants to read and comment on observation notes or to contribute their own opinions about what was happening in the observed situation. This 'elicitation of feedback' is a technique which has traditionally been considered to add to the objectivity and reliability of observation data (Angrosino and Mays de Perez, 2000: 676).

Interviewing

While observation may be the key mode of gathering data in ethnographic research, interviews provide opportunities to gather rich and illuminative data from groups and individuals. Chapter 5 provides guidance on undertaking interviews, and Chapter 11 includes guidance on the analysis of interviews, so this chapter will concentrate on some of the implications of using interviews in ethnographic research.

First, interviews have similarities with participant observation in that 'both must take account of the context and the effects of the researcher' (Hammersley and Atkinson 2007: 109). In ethnographic research, much of the researcher influence relates to the relationship between the researcher and the people being studied. This relationship is of considerable significance within any ethnographic study and means that interviews (and, indeed, observations) will not take place as 'one-off' events. Instead, they will be 'embedded within a long-term and developing relationship' (Walford, 2007) and will reflect that relationship in the way they are negotiated and conducted.

Thus, relationships with participants will influence decisions to be made about whether interviews should be individual or group, and the nature of the questions to be asked and mode of recording, as much as methodological considerations such as the most appropriate type of interview to be used. Many students restrict this consideration to structured/semi-structured questions, but the reality is that it is much broader than that and all questions will have some degree of structure (or intent in eliciting particular data) behind them. It may be more helpful to consider issues such as the relative appropriateness of group and individual interviews, or of using unsolicited oral data.

The relative advantages and disadvantages of group v. individual interviews have been widely debated (for example, Denscombe 1998: 114–15; Fontana and Frey, 2000: 652; and Wellington, 2000: 80–1), and the issues around group interviews are very different to those which should be considered in the context of individual interviews or unsolicited oral data. For example, group interviews have the potential for interference with individual expression or domination of the group by one individual and it is clearly important whatever interviewing technique is chosen to be aware of the implications, pitfalls and problems associated with its use (see Fontana and Frey, 2000: 652 for an overview of these). Perceived or actual power dynamics may also impact on individual interviews. Madriz (2000: 838) has suggested that 'In the context of individual interviews, there is the potential to reproduce the power relationships between the researcher and the participants'. This argument is well supported by her earlier reference to the words of a young Dominican woman who participated in a focus group with Madriz in 1995: 'I'd rather talk this way, with a group of women ... when I am alone with an interviewer I feel intimidated, scared' (ibid: 835). Hammersley and Atkinson (2007: 99) also raise this issue – that for some groups or individuals, an interview process may seem threatening or be perceived as inappropriate (in educational ethnography this may be the case with groups such as young children or people with learning disabilities).

What this means in practical terms, is that relationships as well as methodological considerations will also demand that different types of situation require different types of interview (Fontana and Frey, 2000: 667). This means recognising that each individual has different values and experiences, and that interview questions should be sufficiently flexible to facilitate participants to contribute in a way they feel is appropriate. If participants are threatened by an interview process it may be that, as Hammersley and Atkinson (2007) suggest, you receive unsolicited oral accounts from the participants in your study. Such accounts can provide useful and insightful data which may be highly relevant to your study. However, they raise methodological issues around recording and analysing data, and possibly consent. Ultimately, any decision you make on if, and how, to use interviews must be made in the context of your study with regard to the 'fitness for purpose' of the method and the nature of the data you hope to elicit and may fall into a broad spectrum between unsolicited conversations and formal, pre-arranged individual interviews.

Irrespective of the point on the spectrum in which this falls, the relationship with the interviewee(s) is paramount. In ethnographic research, the interviewee will be someone with whom you have an ongoing and developing relationship. While this avoids the necessity for establishing a rapport with a complete stranger, it does present other challenges. For example, these might include the power relationships between yourself and those being interviewed. These can work many ways; you may interview pupils or students who feel obliged to be helpful as you are the teacher, or you may want to interview your head teacher or line manager where negotiation of access and sensitivity of questions may have implications for your relationship. Similar issues may arise in the interview of colleagues who may feel that it is incumbent on them to 'help' by agreeing to be interviewed in order to gain approval for more senior staff. Other negotiations in the interview relationship may be around issues such as personal disclosure. If your research is about aspects of professionalism, for example, would it elicit more data if you disclosed an unprofessional act on your own part? And what would the implications of this be?

Building critical research skills: activity

In relation to Beth's study (above):

- Would a group or individual approach to interviews with pupils be better in the context of this study?
- How do you justify this theoretically?
- How do you justify this in terms of relationships?
- With a colleague, discuss your ideas and make notes on them.

Data analysis

Data analysis and reporting are discussed at some length in Chapter 11, and you may also wish to take guidance from there. This chapter discusses some of the issues in analysing ethnographic research.

Data analysis is about trying to make sense of a particular social world and the relationships and practices within it. This means that there is a relationship between the data gathering and the data analysis, so in ethnographic research the data analysis does not form a separate stage within a study, but is part of an ongoing research process which is informed by the gathering and interpretation of data at different stages.

Ethnographic research generates huge quantities of data even within relatively small-scale projects, and managing that data can be a challenge, particularly for new researchers. Depending on the nature of the data – interviews, observations, documentary evidence and so on – there are many different approaches which can be used, and these are detailed in Chapter 11. However, irrespective of the strategies selected for analysis – which should be informed by the nature of the questions – data analysis is a process of *thinking* and should always begin with immersion in the data, which may be seen as the first stage in an ongoing process. Immersion means to read and reread documents such as interview transcripts and fieldnotes – in fact, anything you have which you consider to be data – until you feel you know it almost by heart. There is no substitute for knowing the data really well, and it is often the intimacy of this knowledge, rather than specific instrumental approaches, which leads to the recognition of particular themes within data sets. Once you have immersed yourself in the data, you should take the opportunity to step back from it and reflect on it, as this provides further opportunities for insights which may not come if you are 'too close' to your data. The third stage in the process is simply to break it down into manageable units or categories for analysis: this might be by type of data, by sub-group of participant or other category which you consider to be appropriate to your study and your data. As you do this, you will move 'backwards and forwards' (Pole and Morrison, 2003: 82) through the data, literally asking the data questions to see what it says to you. Key among these will be:

- What is happening?
- How is it happening?
- Who is involved and what is their involvement?
- What are the themes emerging from these data?
- What if one or other of the characteristics of the group or setting (for example, geography, ethnicity, social class, gender, and so on) had been

different? How might that have influenced the situation? What does that say about what *is* happening?
- How do any emerging themes relate to each other and to my research questions?
- Do they provide any answers to my questions or merely raise more, different questions?

Next, you will need to synthesise your data: compare the emerging themes between categories and reconsider and re-examine them until you feel you have the best possible picture of what is happening. Finally, you will ask yourself what that picture means and how it might be interpreted. This involves relating your data – or picture – to other theory and literature, so that your findings, when written up, are located in and contextualised by existing knowledge.

Of course, this makes the whole process sound simple and straightforward, when the reality is that it is both messy and time-consuming, particularly since the ongoing nature of the process means that earlier ideas have to be continually adjusted, adapted and developed. In addition, in ethnographic research, all these processes are often happening simultaneously with different data-sets as the research process moves on. However, it is this ongoing engagement with the data that will enable you to develop theories and understandings about the meaning of different actions and relationships within the social worlds inhabited by your participant group and facilitate you to develop a thick, qualitative description of what you have observed in the field.

Representing and writing up your data

Once you have completed your analysis, following a process such as that outlined above, you will need to write up and represent your data. In ethnographic research, this is traditionally done using a narrative approach, although you could support that by using tabular or graphical summaries. For example, presenting data on socio-economic background among students on further education programmes could be done in tabular form as in Table 8.1, but this would support a longer narrative:

Table 8.1 Data representation

Student	Mother	Father	Course
Chloe	Unemployed	Not known – absent	Level 1 Hairdressing
Bella	Carer	Disabled	Level 1 Childcare
Imran	Factory worker	Fundraiser (unpaid)	Level 2 Vehicle maintenance

One mother worked in a clothing factory but the nature of her job role was unclear to her son (Imran). Bella's mother was an unpaid carer. In addition to strongly gendered occupational backgrounds, three of the parents of students in this group were reported as disabled and a further three were working as paid or unpaid carers.

Subsequently, you would need to interpret the meaning of that data, contextualising it within current knowledge as in:

Social class characteristics were demonstrated in the context of parental occupation and level of education as well as in the gender-stereotyped and class-specific programmes the young people were pursuing (Colley et al., 2003: 479). The highest level parental credential reliably reported was a level 3 NVQ and fewer than half of all parents had credentials at level 2. In view of their educational backgrounds, as well as the disadvantage conferred by limited material resources, it may be argued that these parents, and others who are similarly positioned, lack the cultural capital to generate academic profits for their children, contributing to labour and social class (re)production.

As you write your narrative it is important to remember that you are telling a story about the people you are researching. That story needs to be represented in a way which is both ethical and consistent with the data: it is important never to make claims that cannot be supported by data. It also needs to be coherent and engaging, but written in an academic style. Many students fall down the 'gap' between coherence and style. In attempting to achieve an academic style, they use unfamiliar language, often in the wrong context. Only use language you are comfortable with, focusing rather on writing received English and avoiding the use of idiom or colloquial English, and remember that you are communicating with an audience. Another point to note is that you should not make assumptions of knowledge, particularly about a specific group or setting, on behalf of the reader. You will write more clearly if you work from the standpoint that the reader has no knowledge of the group or setting under discussion. You could use the following strategies for developing and checking your written work.

- Avoid the use of idiom or colloquial English.
- Always use the spell- and grammar checker on your personal computer

(PC) but do not completely rely on them.

- Remember that your PC can be set to English or American English – make sure that it is on the right setting.
- Always proofread your work several times.
- Read your work out loud to yourself. If it sounds 'wrong' it probably is.
- Ask someone else – who speaks and writes English well – to proofread your work.
- Make use of texts on writing correctly. Some are listed in further reading.
- If you speak with a strong regional accent you will tend to write colloquially or 'in accent'. It can be helpful to read work by twentieth-century authors such as Dorothy L. Sayers or Colin Dexter as a model for good use of English.

Building critical research skills: activity

Anni is an educated, middle-aged, middle-class female teacher. She is ethnically white English and has values reflecting her educational, social and cultural background. She is using an ethnographic approach in her research exploring the school lives of disaffected children during their Year 6/Year 7 transition. The children are all pupils in inner city schools within the same 'family' of schools. All the schools have high levels of poverty among their students.

Discuss with a colleague what differences there might be in the cultural and social understandings and practices of the researcher and researched described above then consider and make notes on how this might influence the study:

- at the planning stage;
- in deciding what to observe and what to ask;
- in undertaking the observations;
- in analysing the data.

Key points

- Ethnography has roots in anthropology and sociology and draws on both.
- Ethnography explores the culture and social worlds of particular groups through a process of in-depth observation.
- In education ethnography can be used to explore phenomena as diverse as power relations, policy impact and organisational culture.
- Ethnography requires the researcher to be the key research method, immersed in the setting under investigation.
- Ethnography emphasises the use of observation, interview and field-notes in the observation of social phenomena.

Websites ⌐

http://www.bera.ac.uk/educational-ethnography/ This web page gives an account of the history and current use of ethnography in educational research and provides links to other useful resources.
http://www.youtube.com/watch?v=vZnbZ792X_A&noredirect=1 Although couched in marketing terms, this YouTube video gives a short and accessible introduction to netnography.

References and further reading 📖

Angrosino, M. and Mays de Perez, K. (2000) 'Rethinking observation from method to context', in N. Denzin and Y. Lincoln (eds), *Handbook of Qualitative Research*. 2nd edn. London: Sage.

Atkins, L. (2009) *Invisible Students, Impossible Dreams: Experiencing Vocational Education 14–19*. Stoke-on-Trent: Trentham Books.

Colley, H., James, D., Tedder, M. and Diment, K. (2003) 'Learning as becoming in vocational education and training: class, gender and the role of vocational habitus', *Journal of Vocational Education and Training*, 55(4): 471–97.

Denscombe, M. (1998) *The Good Research Guide*. Buckingham: Open University Press.

Fontana, A. and Frey, J. (2000) 'The interview: from structured questions to negotiated text', in N. Denzin and Y. Lincoln (eds), *Handbook of Qualitative Research*. 2nd edn. London: Sage.

Hammersley, M. and Atkinson, P. (2007) *Ethnography: Principles in Practice*. 3rd edn. London: Routledge.

Humphreys, L. (1970) *Tearoom Trade: Impersonal Sex in Public Places*. London: Gerald Duckworth and Co.

Kozinets, R. (2006) 'Click to connect: netnography and tribal advertising', *Journal of Advertising Research*, 46(3): 279–88.

Kozinets, R. (2010) *Netnography: Doing Ethnographic Research Online*. London: Sage.

Madriz, E. (2000) 'Focus groups in feminist research', in N. Denzin and Y. Lincoln (eds), *Handbook of Qualitative Research*. 2nd edn. London: Sage.

Oxford University Press (OUP) (2003) *Compact Oxford English Dictionary*. (ed. C. Soanes.) Oxford: Oxford University Press.

Pole, C. and Morrison, M. (2003) *Ethnography for Education*. Maidenhead: Open University Press.

Stenhouse, L. (1985) *An Introduction to Curriculum Research and Development*. London: Heinemann.

Troman, G., Jeffrey, B., Walford, G. and Gordon, T. (2006) Editorial, *Ethnography and Education*, 1(1): 1–2.

Vidich, A. and Lyman, S. (2000) 'Qualitative methods: their history in sociology and anthropology', in N. Denzin and Y. Lincoln (eds), *Handbook of Qualitative Research*. 2nd edn. London: Sage.

Walford, G. (2007) *Educational Ethnography*. London: TLRP. Available at: http://www.bera.ac.uk/educational-ethnography/ (accessed 22 November 2011).

Wellington, J. (2000) *Educational Research: Contemporary Issues and Practical Approaches*. London: Continuum.

Yin, R.K. (2003) *Case Study Research Design and Methods*. 3rd edn. London: Sage.

CHAPTER 9

DISCOURSE ANALYSIS AND POLICY ANALYSIS

Summary

This chapter highlights the ways in which the impact of policy and policy discourse on educational provision and practice have been substantial and unrelenting over the past two decades. It discusses the principles of discourse analysis and demonstrates how this can provide a useful tool in analysing national, local and institutional policy documents and discourses, and in exploring the convergence or divergence of policy and practice in all sectors of education.

Key words used in this chapter are: *discourse, rhetoric, policy, ideology, polemic, metaphor, policy analysis, textual analysis, power relationship.*

What do we mean by 'discourse'?

The word *discourse* has a number of applications. In this chapter we shall be discussing three of them. First, we can take 'discourse' to mean the *expression of a point of view* which is taken for granted and not questioned. We are not going to use the word 'argument' here, because very often a discourse is communicated not by clear argument, but by less obvious means such as a careful choice of emotive words, or a careful selection of facts which leaves out the ones that do not 'fit' the point of view which the discourse seeks to perpetuate. When we perform a discourse analysis on a speech or a piece of writing, we are simply unpicking it in order to identify the discourse – the point of view that it is taking for granted and encouraging us to take for granted, too – and to analyse exactly what devices or 'tricks' it is using to do that. There are a number of discourses around education – beliefs or understandings about education which we take for granted and accept uncritically as a given or a norm. This would include the idea, for example, that a school education for children is a good thing, both for children and for society. And yet is there any reason why we shouldn't question this belief, as Ivan Illich does in his book, *Deschooling Society* (2011)? Government White Papers provide ideal material on which to practise discourse analysis, written as they are with a political motive to persuade. They often make use of emotive language and may make creative or selective use of research data which appear to support their argument.

The persuasive language in which such material is usually written is known as rhetoric. The rhetorician chooses words carefully to persuade others to share their point of view. The uses and abuses of rhetoric can be illustrated by the following story. In 1995 the then Conservative Secretary of State for Education, Gillian Shephard, was reported in the *Guardian* newspaper as having sent a memo to her cabinet colleagues advising them on the vocabulary they should use when speaking about the government's education policy. She was quoted as saying: 'We must emphasise words that people find attractive, such as standards, discipline, and choice' (Gillian Shephard, quoted in the *Guardian*, 15 September 1995: 6). (In fact, an unfortunate newspaper misprint resulted in the list of 'attractive' words appearing as, 'standards, discipline and *chaos*', which is another matter entirely but adds some humour to the story.) The point to note here is that the emphasis is on *words*; and people are to be won over by *words [they] find attractive*. The presentation of the policy can be seen here assuming more importance than its substance. The politicians are being advised to include certain words in their discourse, rather than receiving advice on how to convey statements of policy purpose or intent. This is one of the characteristics of rhetoric; that it dislocates words from context and sometimes distances them from their original sense.

Let's take that third 'attractive' word, for example: *choice*. If we look back at the White Papers which encapsulate the education policy of the 1990s, we see the word *choice* repeatedly emphasised. The impression given is that changes to education policy meant that parents were being presented with more choice about the education of their children and the type of school they could attend. However, it has been persuasively argued (for example Ball, 1994) that there exists a fundamental contradiction around that word, *choice*, and that those – and subsequent – policy developments served instead to restrict the choice of learners and parents by placing the power of choice with the schools. This was because some schools were being given more power to select their intake, both at 11 and 16. This ability to select meant good results and a high position in the league tables, so that these became the schools for which there was most parental demand for places. Inevitably it became the 'best' schools, not the parents, who were able to pick and choose. *Choice*, then, may be an attractive word but it is also a slippery one and that makes it very useful for the purpose of rhetoric when it is words rather than arguments which are intended to carry the day. You may remember Humpty Dumpty's conversation with Lewis Carroll's Alice in which he claims that: 'A word means just what I choose it to mean.' (Carroll, 1871). He could as easily be talking here of the rhetoric of political persuasion. And, of course, when words become dislocated from their original meaning the result could indeed be *chaos*.

There is one more term we need to discuss in this context, and that is *ideology*. An ideology is an uncritically held belief. We often hear about religious ideology or political ideology; but any belief system which we hold to be 'common sense' and take for granted without analysis or question – such as that education should be compulsory, or that there should be a power relationship between teacher and pupils, or that children with wealthy parents should have access to educational advantage – falls into this category. Our ideology is made apparent through our discourse, as, for example, a particular political ideology is expressed in the discourse of government White Papers. So, if discourse is an expression of ideology, then rhetoric is the vocabulary, the sentence structure, the figurative language we carefully choose in order to make our discourse more persuasive. The ideology behind the government discourse about *choice* in the 1990s was a belief that market forces should be applied to education provision to create a situation in which schools must compete with one another. According to market ideology, competition would bring about a raising of standards. *Standards*, you will remember, was another one of those 'attractive' words.

It is important to note here that the term *discourse analysis* is used in a very specific and non-negotiable sense by some social science researchers who work closely within a philosophical framework informed by postmodernist theorists such as Michel Foucault (1926–84). The application of discourse analysis as we describe it in this chapter for the purpose of small-scale educational research might, from their point of view, be more accurately described as *textual analysis.* In a chapter whose focus is on words and their sometimes contested meanings, some difference over definition of terms is fitting and perhaps inevitable.

Discourse as verbal interaction

We will also be using the word 'discourse' in this chapter in its other sense: that of *communication or verbal interactions* in general. If we were analysing common or typical patterns of spoken interaction between teachers and pupils, for example, we might refer to these as 'classroom discourses' (Woods, 2006).

Policy analysis

This chapter will also explore *policy analysis* as a method of research. This is an approach in which the researcher analyses national, local or institutional policy, particularly in terms of its actual or potential impact on a sector, institution or group of learners. If we take the government policy of encouraging schools to transform themselves into academies, for example, we might see a researcher exploring the process and consequences of such a change of status for the pupils, the staff and for other schools in the area. Unlike discourse analysis, policy analysis does not focus primarily on what lies behind the language or rhetoric in which policy is couched, but on policy itself, its congruence (or otherwise) with previous policy trends and whether it achieves, or has potential to achieve, its stated aims.

Summary so far

We are looking, therefore, at three different types of analysis in this chapter. They are:

1. Discourse analysis, focusing on policy and rhetoric (and alternatively referred to as textual analysis).
2. Discourse analysis focusing on communication and interaction in education settings.
3. Policy analysis.

We shall go on now to take each of these in turn and look at how a researcher might approach them in a real-life setting.

Vignette 1: discourse analysis

Stevie, a deputy head in a secondary school, is interested in the public perception of teachers and wants to look at how past and present education policy may have shaped the way teachers are seen by parents and others. She is also interested in how it may have shaped, and be continuing to shape, relationships between teachers, schools and parents. In order to explore these matters further she decides to analyse the language and arguments used in a number of key education White Papers from the 1990s to the present. In doing so she identifies a number of discourses around the idea of parental choice, parents and consumers and education as a commodity, as well as what appears to be a questioning of teachers' professional expertise and openness. Stevie begins to wonder about the impact of these discourses on how teachers and managers in schools see themselves, their professional role and the relationship between parents and school. And so she decides to follow up the initial discourse analysis by interviewing a sample of teachers and encouraging them to talk to her about these things. In analysing the interview transcripts she pays close attention to the language her participants use, just as she does in analysing the discourse of the White Papers.

We'll look first at how Stevie writes up her discourse analysis of the education White Papers of the 1990s. Here is a short extract from her M.Phil thesis. Read it through carefully and then consider the questions raised in the discussion that follows.

The White Paper I shall consider in this section takes one of Gillian Shephard's 'attractive' words as part of its title: *Choice and Diversity* (DES 1992). It reiterates themes familiar from the White Papers discussed in the previous section. Early in the document *needs, choice,* and the devaluing of the expertise of teachers are knitted together in two sentences, the first of which also provides an example of an unsubstantiated statement:

> 'Parents know best the *needs* of their children – certainly better than educational theorists, or administrators, better even than our *mostly* excellent teachers … The Government is therefore firmly wedded to parental *choice* and involvement.' (DES, 1992, paras 1.6–1.7, [My italics])

In the course of its 64 pages further generalised and unsubstantiated claims are made. These include, for example, that pupils who play

(Continues)

(Continued)

truant will be unhappy, unfulfilled and turn to a life of crime (DES, 1992, para 1.25); that regular attendance at schools leads individuals to be well-balanced and less likely to become criminals; that a good school ethos is dependent upon deep parental involvement. These are presented as undisputed 'facts', and thus render invisible or 'unthinkable' alternative understandings of how things are: that some criminals are well educated, for example, such as MPs who make fraudulent expenses claims; or that some schools provide an excellent education for pupils despite parental apathy; or that some parents' involvement in school matters may be counter-productive, violent, or in other ways undesirable. The discourse here is that parents know best when it comes to their child's education and that therefore, following logically from this, teachers don't. This is an example of the 'discourse of derision' which, according to Ball (1994), served to undermine the teaching profession in the 1990s, and the consequences of which, some would argue, continue to be seen today.

The discourse of this White Paper is firmly rooted in the ideology of the marketplace, sometimes to a startling extent. It speaks, for example, of local authorities 'rationalising their respective stocks of schools'. It casts the parent as consumer, telling them that they have 'rights' which this Government policy will win for them. These rights include, of course, *choice, quality, accountable* teachers and clear information about what is going on in schools. This last point is an effective rhetorical device, in that it plants the unlikely suggestion that things are going on in schools in the 1990s which are *not* currently being disclosed to parents. By inference it demonises schools and teachers as being somehow shady or untrustworthy or having things to hide. In terms of rhetoric, this is a very clever piece of rabble rousing. Because *of course* parents should know what is going on in schools. Who would want to argue with that? The fact that *there is nothing going on which they don't already know about* becomes lost in this clever manipulation of words. For example, this Paper tells us that parents:

> 'have a right to that information. The government is determined that they shall have it, and that it shall be given in a straight-forward and simple way – characteristic of an open society – rather than in jargon-laden, inward-looking and technical language suitable only for the professional.' (DES, 1992, para. 1.36)

There are several things going on in this passage. Firstly there is the presentation of government in avuncular role, securing our rights for us like a kindly uncle. Secondly there is the presentation of the 'professional' – presumably a teacher or educationalist – as a secretive and elitist enemy against whom the government must take up the struggle on our behalf. Thirdly there is an example of what a psychoanalyst might call 'projection': attributing one's own shortcomings to another. Hence we are told that it is the educationalists who are fogging the issue through the cunning use of words. To cap it all, this section of the Paper is entitled, 'School Inspection and the *Demystification* of Education' [my italics].

Discussion

What this extract shows us is a detailed analysis of the discourse of one White Paper. There are several things we should note about it in terms of how Stevie presents her work.

1. It quotes the key passages that it discusses. This is important if the reader is to follow the argument which focuses closely on specific words and statements.
2. It provides exact references to the words or passages it refers to. You will see that these are paragraph references rather than page references. This is good practice, but only possible with documents which are written in report format using numbered paragraphs and sub-paragraphs. It is particularly useful now that such documents are widely accessed via the internet rather than in hard copy.
3. The quoted passages are set out in such a way as to clearly distinguish them from Stevie's main text. They are indented and contained in quotation marks. Some researchers might choose to use a smaller or different font as an additional distinguishing feature.

Moving now from presentation to content, here are some questions for you to consider:

- Does Stevie make a convincing argument?
- What reasons would you give to support your answer?
- Are the meanings of *ideology, discourse* and *rhetoric* clear and distinct in the context of her argument?
- Are there any points at which she seems to use rhetoric herself?
- From this extract we can assume that the White Paper is written as a

polemic; that is, it presents a one-sided argument for the purpose of persuasion. While we might agree that this is part of a White Paper's function, should the researcher's *analysis* of this discourse slip into polemic? In your view, does Stevie's do this?

Building critical research skills: activity

Online applications such as Wordle can be used to support the analysis of textual documents. The image in Figure 9.1 shows the outcome of the Executive Summary of the White Paper 14–19 *Education and Skills* (DfES, 2005) inserted into Wordle or similar software. This can provide a starting point for thinking about analysis as it will give a rough indication of word frequency – the most frequently occurring words are given greatest prominence in the word cloud.

Task 1: Using the word cloud illustrated in Figure 9.1, identify three key words arising in the document. Then choose one of those to analyse in greater depth: look for it in the original document (available at: http://webarchive.nationalarchives.gov.uk/20050301193000/dfes.gov.uk/publications/14–19educationandskills/). If this policy is not relevant to your setting, then identify and use a national policy document which is and use that instead. You can paste it into Wordle at: www.wordle.net. As well as identifying the word frequency, it is important to identify how each key word is used and what other words it is most frequently linked with. For example, you could pose the following questions as you are reading:

- Does this statement make sweeping claims?
- What assumptions (about education, individuals or groups) underpin it?
- Is it supported by evidence?
- Does it imply judgements, marginalisation or homogenisation of particular groups? (Remember Stevie's reference to what Ball (1994) calls the 'discourse of derision' about teachers.)

Make notes of your findings and discuss them with colleagues or other members of your learning group. Have they drawn similar or different conclusions from the same document?

Task 2: Now perform the same activity using a different, but related policy document. For example, if you have used the *14–16 Education and Skills* White Paper you could also look at the Leitch Review of Skills (2006). Once you have repeated the activity, consider whether there are any areas of convergence or divergence. Quite often, different points of policy can be in tension with one another.

Figure 9.1 Analysing text in Wordle

Reflective activity

What conclusions have you drawn from your analysis about:

1. The words or ideas which are being emphasised in these documents?
2. The intention or purpose of the documents?
3. The ideas or arguments which these documents ignore or render invisible?

Analysis of individuals' discourse

As we know, Stevie, having made a discourse analysis of the White Papers, went on to interview teachers as the next step in her research. She applied the same analytical approach to the interview transcripts. Below you will find an extract from one transcribed interview, followed by a draft of Stevie's analysis. Read them through carefully and consider the questions which follow:

Transcript of interview with Teacher 1

Stevie So how would you describe the public perception of teachers?

Teacher I sometimes think they have a very poor perception of us. And personally I think the media are to blame. It's like they're at war with the profession. We're portrayed as layabouts who get too many holidays and have an easy life. TV drama shows teachers behaving unprofessionally. There's even a comedy show – can't remember which one – which has a running gag about how people only go into teaching as a last resort – you know – for

(Continues)

(Continued)

losers. I don't think they realise – schools can be a real battleground. It takes guts, sometimes, to come in day after day. And the papers blame us for kids' bad behaviour, when we all know bad behaviour's nearly always the parents' fault. And when we try to do something about unacceptable behaviour, the paper headlines scream blue murder and accuse us of bullying or unfair exclusion or failing the kids we're supposed to teach. It's like we're the enemy. Everything we do is turned around and used as ammunition against us. If kids do well, the papers say it's because standards are being lowered. If kids do badly, they shoot us down for failing them. Whatever the big education story of the day, teachers are always in the firing line. We're never portrayed as the heroes. Sorry. But I feel really strongly about this.

Stevie   That's OK. I can see you do. That's fine. But my next question is about government policy on education. To what extent, if any, do you think that's shaped the public perception of teachers?

Teacher Well, frankly, in my view, over the past quarter century or so – that's most of my teaching career – I've seen teachers increasingly disempowered. We used to have some say over what was taught and how. That is, we used to be regarded as professionals who could be entrusted with decision-making about how, why and what pupils learn. That's all gone. The National Curriculum sets it all out for us now. There's no room for inspiration or creativity in the planning of lessons. We just receive our orders now and have to carry them out to the letter, and our professional judgement doesn't come into it any more. For example, if we think the kids are being over-tested and that's affecting their motivation – too bad. Nothing we can do about it. If it's all become teaching to the test so that kids are bored and the less able ones feel like failures – nothing we can do about that either. But when kids are unmotivated and bored, who's blamed? The politicians and policy-makers sitting safely behind the lines? No. It's us, the teachers, being offered up like cannon fodder ...

Stevie   Sorry. Sorry to interrupt. But are you saying ...

Teacher I'm saying that the current public perception of teachers is almost entirely as a result of misguided policies which have presented teachers with an impossible task, disempowered them and left them in the firing line. There are a lot of dedicated and inspiring people in this profession, but, in somebody's famous words, we're lions led by donkeys.

Stevie   So how, in your view, does this affect the relationship between teachers and parents?

Teacher   Well, sadly, it often turns what should be a collaborative partnership working for the best interests of the child into a running battle, where the parents take up a defensive position and won't back up the school on matters of discipline. Or they get aggressive and accuse us of this, that and the other. And what are the kids to make of that? If they see that their parents don't respect us and don't back us up, they're not going to respect us either, are they? That's what the politicians and media have done. They've waged a war on teachers and now they're seeing the results of it: unmanageable kids, social disorder, violence on the streets. We keep on keeping on, but I fear it's a losing battle.

Analysis of Teacher 1's discourse

There are two main discourses apparent in this teacher's responses. The first could be summarised as '*The media and politicians have undermined and disempowered teachers*'. The second, and less obvious, is a discourse around professionalism and the purpose of schools. I shall begin with an analysis of this latter discourse, as it provides a context and explanation for the first. It is an account of teaching as a noble profession whose members demonstrate courage and tenacity ('It takes guts, sometimes, to come in day after day') and possess admirable qualities ('dedicated and inspiring'; 'professional judgement'). It paints a picture of how schools might be if teachers were treated as 'professionals who could be entrusted with decision making about how, why and what pupils learn'. For example, there would be 'inspiration or creativity in the planning of lessons' rather than 'teaching to the test' and over-testing. It also makes two important claims about the purpose of schooling. The first of these is explicit. It is that schools and parents together should form 'a collaborative partnership working for the best interests of the child'. The second is implicit and seems to be a claim about the ideal role of teachers and schools in creating social order and providing a moral compass. Since teachers are disempowered to the

(Continues)

(Continued)

point where they cannot serve this function, this discourse suggests, we see the result in 'unmanageable kids, social disorder, violence on the streets'. We might summarise this strand of his discourse then, as '*If teachers were respected and allowed to follow their professional judgement, schools would be able to provide a more positive experience for pupils with the result that social disorder and violence would be reduced.*'

The other discourse apparent here is the one we have identified as '*The media and politicians have undermined and disempowered teachers*'. In combination, these two discourses are making the claim that unmotivated learners and incidences of public disorder are a direct result of the demonisation of teachers by means of politics and the media. The claims about the disempowerment and undermining of teachers are sufficiently apparent in this teacher's discourse to need no further elaboration here. However, what is particularly noticeable in the delivery of this discourse is the number of metaphors of war and conflict:

- *at war with the profession*
- *schools can be a real battleground*
- *we're the enemy*
- *they shoot us down*
- *We're never portrayed as the heroes*
- *We just receive our orders now*
- *The politicians and policy-makers sitting safely behind the lines*
- *the teachers, being offered up like cannon fodder*
- *left them in the firing line*
- *a running battle*
- *They've waged a war on teachers*
- *we're lions led by donkeys.*

(This last is a reference to British soldiers of the First World War attributed to Max Hoffman (1869–1927) and quoted by Alan Clark in his work, *The Donkeys* (1961)).

What are we to make of this recurring allusion to war? According to Lakoff and Johnson (1980) the metaphors we use are an indicator of the way we construe the world. The discourse of this teacher, littered with references to battle, is perhaps indicative of the level of conflict he perceives between teachers and those who would disempower them; or of the extent to which teaching has become an embattled profession. Certainly his choice of words and imagery adds emphasis to his discourse, but does it do more than that? Could it be seen as an indication that he is speaking from the heart – in other words, that he is voicing genuinely held views rather than telling me, the interviewer, what he thinks I might like to hear? This would be the Freudian conclusion, perhaps – that he is unconsciously drawing on a vocabulary and imagery which express his feelings, and may not even be aware that he is doing so. For the purpose of this paper I can only draw attention to this bombardment of metaphors, about which it is impossible to draw any reliable conclusions.

The *teachers know best* and the *demonised teachers* themes in this interviewee's responses are identified here as discourses because they are presented to the interviewer as unexamined and unsubstantiated matters of 'common sense'. This is not to say, however, that there is no truth to them. Differently presented, with reference to sources and examples, and with substantiated instances of correlation or other empirical evidence critically examined, these matters could be termed arguments, and as such would demand an answer.

Reflective activity

- To what extent do you agree with this analysis?
- What methods does Stevie use to support her argument?
- How reliable is her analysis in your view, and why?
- Is the interviewee's discourse open to any alternative interpretation?
- What might be the pitfalls in using an analysis of discourse as research data, and why?

Stevie points here to the significance of metaphors in the analysis of discourse. This can be a useful approach to take although, as she points out, we have to be careful not to fall into amateur attempts at psychoanalysis. But if we consider, for example, the now widespread use of the word 'deliver' to describe what teachers do (they *deliver* lessons; they *deliver* the curriculum), we can see how this semantic development could be taken as supporting evidence for the interviewee's claim ('The National Curriculum sets it all out for us now. There's no room for inspiration or creativity in the planning of lessons') that teachers lack the autonomy they once had to apply their own professional expertise to lesson content and teaching, and now simply hand on a curriculum in which they have no voice. Thus the term 'deliver' has become part of the wider educational discourse which we all use for the most part uncritically, so that its implications for the role of teachers go largely unnoticed.

Something you may have noticed in reading through the interview transcript are the instances in which Stevie, as interviewer, controls the pace and direction of the teacher's responses. There is a *power relationship* here. The teacher apologises to Stevie for the strength of his response, and she tells him, 'That's OK'. She gives him permission to speak his mind. A little later, however, she interrupts to get him back on track. She does this politely ('Sorry to interrupt. But are you saying …') but she wants clarification and so stops him. In this relationship the control – the *power* – is with the interviewer. If Stevie were interviewing her head teacher, however, the situation might be reversed. In the context of education certain power relationships are taken for granted, and it is this aspect of discourse which we shall look at now.

Vignette 2: analysis of classroom discourse

Most of us share certain assumptions about the patterns of communication that are appropriate in schools and other educational institutions. For example, we accept that the teacher will, or should, exert control over who speaks and when; and we share a general agreement over what is acceptable or unacceptable for students or teachers to say or write, both in terms of language and topic. These general agreements or set of assumptions typify the discourse of education, within which predictable power relations operate. We can see it at work in the following classroom interaction. Read it through and consider the questions which follow.

Teacher Let's make a start then. Matthew? Let's make a start, and you'll need to make some notes, so … Yes, Dina? Dina is it? Have I got that right?

Dina Erm, yes. Erm, are you going to be giving us a handout? Because …

Teacher Yes, I'll be giving a handout at the end. Listen, everybody. I'll be giving a handout at the end, but it's still important that you take notes. Why is it important that you take notes? Thanda?

Thanda Because we remember stuff better if we've taken notes and erm, and erm we erm …

Teacher And we listen more carefully to what's being said, don't we. So it's important to take notes, and that's why it's essential that you develop your note-taking skills. Now, how many of you have actually been taught how to take notes? Put your hand up if you've had some sort of formal input on note-taking. Three. Three of you out of what, 25. That's not good, is it? So that's why I'll be giving you some prompts about the key bits that you need to note down. Darryl?

Darryl What?

Teacher Darryl, you've just walked in five minutes late. So …

Darryl Sorry. It was …

Teacher OK. Sit down then and let's get on.

Reflective activity

- In which sector of education do you think this class is taking place?
- How are the power relationships within this extract of dialogue made apparent?
- Which small extracts might you choose to quote if you wished to illustrate these power relations at work?

Building critical research skills: activity

In fact, this example of classroom interaction is taking place in higher education. The students are all graduates on a teacher training programme. (If you find this surprising, read the extract through again and notice how the teacher is encouraging the class to think about note-taking and punctuality from a teacher's point of view.)

Analyse the *pattern of communication* in the classroom extract. For example, you might begin like this:

1. Teacher gathers attention of class.
2. Learner asks question (puts hand up?).
3. Teacher answers.
4. .... etc.

Reflective activity

- Consider the extent to which this *pattern* could apply in any sector of education, with any age group.
- We might refer to this as a typical discourse of education, based upon an unquestioned power relationship between teacher and learner. Our acceptance of this discourse as the common sense notion of 'education' renders invisible or 'un-thinkable' other ways in which education might be accomplished. You could consider here, for example, Freire's notion of educator and educatee collaborating in a process from which both are learning.
- How might an analysis of the discourse of education (as for example, in the task you have just completed) be useful as a method of research? You might like to consider this in the context of exploring classroom interaction, teaching style or learner behaviour.

Vignette 3: policy analysis

In following Stevie's research earlier in this chapter we explored discourse analysis by focusing on her scrutiny of language and how it was used. You may have noticed, however, that in the wider context her research also encompassed several aspects of policy analysis. That is, she was examining a series of White Papers and identifying the common policy themes; and she was following up by exploring the impact of this policy trajectory in a sample of schools. We're going to turn our attention now to another researcher, Jean-Luc, whose focus is specifically on policy analysis. His research does not include a particular attention to vocabulary or rhetoric. His concern rather is to explore how education policy in his own country – a democratic republic in Africa – has been influenced by the rule of successive colonial powers; the extent to which such policy trajectories have continued since the country gained its independence; and the impact of policy on schools and learners.

Below you will find an extract from the introduction to his MA dissertation. Read it through carefully and consider:

- its strengths and weaknesses as an analysis of policy trajectory and impact;
- the ways in which his approach differs from Stevie's in terms of content and style.

Education policy in the Republic of XXXX

Introduction

In the pre-colonial era from the mid-nineteenth century until 1894 there was no central policy for schooling or further education. The schools that existed were set up mainly by Baptist missionaries and were established mainly in the more accessible coastal regions. The curriculum was what we would now consider a primary school curriculum, focusing on reading, writing and arithmetic, with the addition of Bible study. All teaching, reading and writing was in English. The education provision, therefore, acted as a vehicle for instilling European ideas and values, including Christianity. In other words, it was ideologically driven and, although naturally there are no 'policy documents' as such from this pre-colonial, pre-republic era, a discourse implicit in such educational provision as existed was that to be educated was synonymous with adopting European language, values and beliefs. It was an imposed system rather than one based on identifying and meeting the specific needs, cultural, occupational and practical, of the population. As I shall go on to argue, the *imposition* of education policy and practice by those with power is not peculiar to nineteenth-century missionary projects, nor indeed to what is now the Republic of XXXX. I shall refer to this aspect of power relations as 'education without consultation'.

Between 1894 and 1963, the country was annexed first by Italy, then by Germany, and finally by Britain. Under Italian rule, civil unrest meant that little was accomplished in terms of setting up formal systems of education. The policy appears to have been to withhold education beyond a basic, missionary school level for fear that a higher level of learning might equip sections of the populace to question their subjugation and argue for their rights. With the advent of the German occupation in 1906, however, education provision was rapidly expanded. German educationalists were tasked with devising a five-year curriculum to be taught in Government Schools which were rapidly established in the capital and across most of the country. Instruction was in German and again included Christian religious study. In 1910 a law was passed establishing as policy that German was to be the *only* language of instruction used in schools, and severely restricting the use of the population's mother tongue to specific and limited interactions. Here again we see the underlying ideology that can be simplified as: European = Good; African = Bad. This law became known as the Law

(Continues)

(Continued)

of Language. However, it also established the policy that the elementary level of education was to be made compulsory for all, and to this end it provided for funding to the original mission schools, contingent upon them agreeing to support and expand the acquisition of German language and culture.

We see here, in what at first sight appears to be an enlightened policy of education for all, that education is being appropriated for political ends; that is, for the expansion of the ruling power's influence and values. It is a clear example of how power relations within the discourse of education can be hidden behind our common sense understanding of 'what is'. We can see it clearly enough here, because the government in question is a foreign colonial power. But this serves to remind us that it is possible for any government to further its own ideals and values through its policies on education; ideals and values which become apparent when we apply a critical analysis to the discourses which underlie the policy statements.

Building critical research skills: activity

Task 1: Review a recent policy relevant to your sector of education as set out in White Papers over the past five years. (You can find all recent education White Papers on the Internet.) Do you notice any internal contradictions or inconsistencies? Is there a consistent and identifiable policy direction? If so, what underlying discourses are driving it?

Task 2: Take one policy which is of particular relevance or interest to you, or which has had a noticeable impact on your institution or your professional practice, and evaluate the extent to which it is consistent with (a) the other policy developments you have identified; and (b) the internal policies or preferred practices within your own institution.

Reflective activity

Reflect on the potential or actual consequences of the policy you identified in Task 2 for your own institution.

1. How is the policy implemented?
2. How does it impact on individual staff and students?
3. Are there any unintended or negative outcomes as a result of the policy?
4. What discourse or discourses are apparent in this policy?

Conclusion

In this chapter we have looked at four of the ways in which discourse analysis can be useful to us in carrying out qualitative research. In summary, these are:

- the analysis of political discourse found in the language of White Papers on education, which allows us to identify and explore underlying ideologies;
- the analysis of the language used by individuals in their discourses, through which we might identify their uncritically held beliefs and values;
- the analysis of classroom interactions, through which we can explore the discourse of education and its underlying power relations;
- the analysis of education policies, their origins, trajectories, impact, and underlying discourses.

Key points

- Definitions of discourse.
- The principles of discourse analysis.
- Educational discourse.
- The impact of policy and policy analysis.
- Rhetoric, discourse and ideology; and how these render some questions invisible.

References and further reading 📖

Ball, S.J. (1994) *Education Reform: A Critical and Post-structural Approach.* Buckingham: Open University Press.

Bridges, D., Smeyers, P. and Smith, R. (2009) *Evidence Based Education Policy: What Evidence: What Basis: Whose Policy?* London: Wiley-Blackwell.

Carroll, L. (1871) *Alice Through the Looking Glass, and What Alice Found There.* London: Macmillan.

Clark, A. *The Donkeys. A History of the British Expeditionary Force in 1915.* London: Hutchinson.

DES (1992) *Choice and Diversity.* London: HMSO.

DfES (2005) *14–19 Education and Skills.* Cm 6476. London: HMSO.

Freire, P. (1996) *Pedagogy of the Oppressed.* 2nd revd edn. Harmondsworth: Penguin.

Illich, I. (2011) *Deschooling Society,* New edn. London: Marion Bryars.

Lakoff, G. and Johnson, M. (1980) *Metaphors we Live By.* Chicago, IL, and London: Chicago University Press.

Leitch, S. (2006) *Prosperity For All in the Global Economy: World Class Skills.* London: HM Treasury.

Ozga, J. (1999) *Policy Research in Educational Settings.* London: Oxford University Press.

Woods, N. (2006) *Describing Discourses.* London: Hodder Arnold.

CHAPTER 10

TEXT AND IMAGE IN QUALITATIVE RESEARCH

LYDIA SPENCELEY

Summary

This chapter investigates the relationship between research and images. In doing so it examines the evolving relationships between image and text, the image maker and the image, the viewer and the image and it also investigates the connections between context and interpretation in meaning making. It also discusses the difficulties of using images as a research tool and explores the possibilities which they present when used in conjunction with other research tools as part of a unified strategy.

Key words used in this chapter are: *image, meaning, interpretation, viewer, context, symbols and signs, semiotics, hermeneutic.*

Introduction

One of the more complex areas to research in the field of education is that of an individual's or groups' perception or understanding of a topic or issue.

Questions may be asked, and other research techniques used in in order to gain information from groups or individuals but do their answers reflect their true feelings and understandings or are they influenced and mediated by external factors such as the language used by the researcher (who is often also the teacher) and power relations which exist between the researcher and the respondent? Is there a way in which these factors might be bypassed in order to allow the researcher to access responses generated by feelings and emotions rather than answers controlled by the conscious mind structured by society?

In this chapter we will attempt to find a way to access the affective domain and in so doing will advocate the use of images as research tools, but first it is essential that we think about what we know about images and their current uses as research tools.

Building critical research skills: thinking about images

Activity 1
This short activity is designed to focus your mind and self-identify what you know and understand to be the types of data collection methods associated with qualitative research.

Give yourself 2 minutes to identify as many ways of gathering data for qualitative research as you can.

Think about the methods that came most readily to your mind and the method you used to note them. How many of the methods you have noted rely primarily on data collected through the medium of words, verbal or written? Did images as a research method appear in your notes and if so, whereabouts did they appear; towards the beginning of your thought process or towards the end? How did you record your thoughts; as words, as a chart, as a list, as a mind-map, a spidergram or as a drawing? *Why?*

Activity 2
Another short activity; another set of answers to help you to focus your mind.

Allow yourself 1 minute to identify areas in which images are used in qualitative research.

Think about the answers you have given; are images used as primary or secondary sources of information? What types of images were they; were they graphs and charts or images and pictures? Were they used to support findings derived from other research methods or as findings in their own right? When you thought about images was there an accompanying text to interpret and explain the information that they contain? *Why?*

The *Concise Oxford Dictionary* (Oxford, 1998: 677) defines 'image' variously as being 'a representation of the external form … a mental representation … and idea or conception'. Since the earliest times mankind has used images to express what can be seen, thought or understood using whatever media were available. Pre-literate man recorded the world in the cave paintings at Altamira and Lascaux using simple tools and pigments, modern children frequently draw to express that which they do not possess the language to express, while post-modern man records the world using digital representation and the electronic media of the Internet. Whatever the medium used to record images there appears to be a consistent need within the human psyche to use images as a form of self-expression. So, why are images so infrequently seen as a method for data collection?

Perhaps part of the answer lies in the last paragraph; research is frequently perceived to be an activity which is primarily a linguistic rather than a visual process (Collier and Collier, 1986). The world in which we research places great emphasis on 'hard evidence', data which is used to support inference drawn from research in the form of records, documents or statistics based on the apparently 'scientific' methods of investigation associated with the quantitative paradigm. Education in all its forms is consistently judged on its ability to produce particular types of data-driven evidence of improved recruitment, retention and achievement and of the degree of 'value-added' to learners' lives through the process of education. Despite the increasing ocular-centrism of modern life, in which images are increasingly available through mass media, images continue to be associated with pre-literate people and children and are seen as lacking in sophistication; almost anyone can make an image of some sort, but not everyone can write.

The education system itself is complicit in promulgating this notion, relying on text and language as primary means of communicating standardised interpretations of facts and information. Children are taught to read at an early age but through the education system they are simultaneously taught to value text over images, to express themselves using the signs and symbols of written language rather than those which come more naturally to them in the form of drawing or images. As the growing child embraces what Bourdieu (1988) describes as the 'consecrated knowledge' of language and literacy, the 'gold stars' and accolades issued by schools for written work replace the heretical and unregulated self-knowledge expressed in the drawings which once decorated the refrigerator within the home, and image making is relegated to the weekly art class.

Given the pre-eminence of text as a form of investigation why then should the use of images be discussed as a form of enquiry for research purposes? Many writers (including Chaplin, 1994; Rorty, 1989) have argued that language itself both constructs and maintains the dominant hegemony of a society by its ability to define and delineate the thoughts and perceptions of its users through the imposition of all-pervasive 'regimes of truth' (Foucault, 1979). The ability of language, which is shaped by the society which we inhabit, to define our mental processes affects the way in which we learn to perceive and understand the world, a concept perhaps best illustrated in Orwell's description of the power of language to construct and manipulate thought in his novel *1984*. Images, however, need not be mediated by language; they are available to all who view them and, according to Benjamin (1985 cited in Emmison and Smith (2000)), they are able to access space in the mind which is informed not by the conscious, but by the unconscious, provoking reactions in the individual which are triggered by unreconstructed feelings and emotions. In this way Weber and Mitchell (1995: 34) argue that images offer an opportunity to access: 'That which is not easily put into words, the ineffable, the elusive, the not-yet-thought-through, the subconscious.' By escaping from the straitjacket erected by language, images can facilitate our entry into the world of the affective domain of learning (Bloom, 1956).

Entering the world of the affective

Vignette 1: reading images

Lizzie, who works in the teacher education department of a further education college, is interested in understanding the emotional responses of beginning-teachers to working in the lifelong learning sector. In her role as a tutor she has talked to an established and tightly knit group of adult learners who are now approaching the end of the first year of their Cert. Ed/PGCE awards. All the group members are relatively new to teaching within the sector and have come into teaching as a second career, and in her discussions with them she has found that in addition to their being confused by some of the new challenges that have been 'thrown at them by management', as one of her learners put it over the year, they remain particularly concerned by two factors which she feels are significant:

- the difference between the type of learners they thought they would be working with (adults) and those they are actually working with (predominantly 14–19);
- the difference between their expectations of their learners' motivation to learn and the reality of the classroom situation and how they react on a personal level to this perceived dissonance.

Although her learners are open to discussion (and moans and groans!) about the disparity between their preconceived perceptions of their learners in terms of age, motivation, interest, behaviour, and so on, and the reality of working with learners in the classroom, she has found that they are reluctant to discuss the feelings generated by the situation in which they have found themselves. From listening to learners in class discussions and individual tutorials she has begun to identify some core themes, but recognises many of the learners are finding it difficult to verbalise their responses to their situation and also that they are reluctant to enter into either group or individual discussions to investigate the reasons for their reactions. She suspects that this may be due to a fear of expressing negatively perceived feelings of frustration, confusion or anxiety and is concerned that this may be increasing the feelings of low self-esteem and inadequacy as teachers to which some learners have privately admitted.

Figure 10.1 Brick wall

Figure 10.2 Bin liner

Lizzie decides that a different approach is necessary. The majority of the group are happy to enter into discussions about a focused topic which is related to their knowledge and understanding of teaching, and she decides to introduce images in order to help learners to spotlight their thoughts and feelings. She asks the groups to bring images, which they feel represent the difficulties they face in their current teaching practice, to class, and then work with others in small groups to develop collages which are subsequently discussed within the supportive framework of small groups of critical friends (who have agreed to adhere to strict ground-rules in respect of confidentiality and respect) in order to 'free up their memories, and create a piece of shared "business"' as Loizos (2000: 98) describes it, and identify areas of common concern which can then be discussed as general topics by the class.

In the course of the discussions held by one of the small groups, two images which one of the group members had taken on a mobile phone attracted particular attention. Look at the images in Figure 10.1 and Figure 10.2 and write down your immediate thoughts on what they might mean to the person who took them before reading the explanation given by the image-taker, then consider the points raised in the discussion that follows.

When I took these it was a really bad weekend anyway, it had been a bad week at work and I was really fed up; the brick wall was, how I felt about teaching and how I wasn't getting on very well with it. But it was also, because I was also working part-time as an adult adviser and all the community provision was being threatened with being withdrawn, so it was like people were asking me about courses because part of my job was to help people decide what course to do, but ... everyone's jobs were under threat and that.

I think, like there's lots of reasons really, I think one big thing was time. I mean I was only teaching two classes a week and it just seemed to take up all my time. I was setting up a new course, so I think in retrospect that was part of it, it was taking so long because I was doing all the materials from scratch. I just thought 'I don't know how I would ever do this full-time', so I think that was one of the main reasons was that I was taking loads of work home and it was affecting my home life as well and I just wasn't happy really. I think as well, I don't like standing up and talking in front of a lot of people. I seemed to be taking such a lot of work home really and, I know teachers do take a lot of work home, but I wasn't really, you know I wasn't getting much sleep at night, you know working hard, I was so tired all the time.

I was thinking at the time, I keep beating myself up because I've made little mistakes, going home at weekends and feeling really crap about it. And really in the grand scheme of things I'm not a surgeon responsible for somebody's life, but I just felt that I'd got a real responsibility to the people I was teaching and I think, when they got upset about their learning or not understanding something, I really take it on my shoulders more than I should do. That was kind of what that was all about, I felt that if I was a teacher I needed to be perfect and I don't think you can be.

The bin liner, I thought it was perfect because I daren't show you the rubbish in there. I felt I was having to put the rest of my life on hold really, for the teaching, and other people, other teachers, around me seemed to cope alright. Although they were really busy they didn't seem to be affected as much but, I suppose they weren't training as well. It's a bit silly looking back but I had an evaluation back after the unit that I taught, and there were a couple of people, and they were saying that they wanted a print out of everything I did on the power point as a handout so they could write notes and things, and in an ideal world it's nice but when I did that they got wasted and chucked in the bin and it just felt like all I was doing was being chucked back at me and I was wasting my time.

I don't think I ever want to work teaching full time, I might do it part-time. I mean I'm doing some training in a couple of weeks so, that's just two short sessions with somebody else so that might be OK – we'll see.

In the small group discussion of the images shown above Lizzie noted that Jay's colleagues understood the picture of the brick wall, with several of them noting that they had been 'banging their head against a similar one' when working with learners. The other image, effectively a black space, was one that the discussion showed that they initially assumed to be simply the result of a camera malfunction rather than an attempt at self-expression and consequently dismissed it.

The image of the wall was one which they could interpret because they had some understanding of the image itself and by being familiar with the abrasive texture and apparent solidity which the image represented they could use this information to infer meaning. When interpreting, or 'reading', the image of the bin liner the group initially lacked a frame of reference through which to construct an interpretation of the image and it was not until they heard Jay's explanation that they realised its significance in depicting the depth and nature of his concerns about teaching and were able to compare these with their own experience and emotional response to teaching.

Look at the impressions you noted earlier on the possible meaning of the images to the person who offered them to the group. Did your interpretation of the images match Jay's or the group's or did you construct an entirely different meaning? *Why?*

Discussion

Ball and Smith (1992: 18) note: 'It is people and not a camera who take pictures ... [but images themselves] ... are not unambiguous records of reality'. As is shown in the example above, images are by their very nature representations developed by specific individuals, or groups of individuals, and are located within a defined historical and temporal context. The images themselves do not change (unless they are artificially altered) and unlike words they present the same information without differential emphasis, simply offering a set of symbols to be decoded and given meaning by the observer. Images are viewed by others through the lens of personal experience and it is quite possible that individuals (particularly those who do not share common understandings) see the same image but ascribe to it an entirely different set of meanings, thus, as Prosser (2000: 117, in Simons and Usher (2000)) notes, 'one person's representation may be another's misrepresentation'.

Ball and Smith (1992: 18) argue that 'different interpretations of the image do not exhaust the significance that can be attributed to them' by individuals and this is a key factor which has to be considered when working with images as research tools. On the surface an image may be purely representational, presenting information as data through the depiction of a family scene or a picture of a favourite landscape for example, but, as the group in the example above found, images also work at a deeper, more subliminal level, permeated with subtle meanings, associations and memories and they contain within them the personal metaphors and narratives of the creator which are not necessarily obvious or understood by the viewer.

Not only is meaning given to an image by the originator but images are also given meaning by the individual viewer who interprets the data presented in the image through the lens of their own experience. Each viewer, therefore, has a separate and discrete relationship to the 'text' of the image which is presented to them. The image itself is multi-layered, containing data which needs to be considered in terms of its historical, social, political and cultural contexts, but the interpretation of each aspect of the image, the 'data' it presents for analysis, is structured by the personal, cultural and social affiliations of the viewer. Meanings attributed to the image are, therefore, neither fixed nor static entities, but are developmental, emerging out of the relationship of the viewer to the image (originator, passive viewer, historical viewer, and so on) through an active process of interpretation of the data presented within the image which takes place between the 'reader' (or viewer) and the 'text' (or image) (Atkinson, 1992). However, as meaning is derived from an individual, subjective and situated process of decoding and translation which is both transitory and ephemeral, it is also subsequently open to revision and reinterpretation as the reader's relationship to and interaction with the image changes, or their knowledge or understanding of the metaphors and data it presents alters. As such every image is open to a multiplicity of interpretations and 'meaning', becomes a concept which is both polysemic and therianthropic, an unstable entity which is difficult to research in isolation. Individuals interpret images in different ways according to their personal experience and understanding of them. It is important, therefore, to recognise that, as Pink (2001: 17) notes, although visual research methods 'particular attention to visual aspects of culture … [they] … cannot be used independently of other methods … nor can an exclusively visual approach to culture exist.'

Connecting images and words

Building critical research skills: activity 1

Select two or three images from different sources. Spend a few minutes looking at them and write down key words which describe the feelings which the images evoke in you. Ask colleagues to look at the same images individually and write down the feelings which the images evoke for them. Compare the lists:

- Are the lists similar?
- Are the same words used?
- Are there differences and if so, what are they and what do you feel they indicate?

Discussion

An image, as Collier and Collier (1986) note, can arouse immediate, power-ful, but uniquely subjective responses in an individual as images are interpreted at subconscious or unconscious levels within the confines of the lived experience of the viewer. As the meaning derived from the image is both exclusive to the individual and contextually specific it is not readily gen-eralisable and requires a mediating construct, such as language, in order to facilitate comparative readings of images.

The use of language as an intermediary is, however, something of a double-edged sword. Verbal appraisal of images subtly changes the relationship between the viewer and the image from one which is instinctive, reactive and largely passive, to one which is intellectual, thought-through and active. By moving the reader away from the intuitive, implicit knowledge derived from the direct observation of an image towards what is perceived by society to be a more accessible, objective and sophisticated form of communication, language facilitates the identification of divergence and convergence in meaning between individual interpretations of the same data-set. It can thus be argued that this active interpretation of data releases images from their limitation as objects which can only be interpreted individually and intu-itively, and instead enables them to become a basis for the more systematic production of knowledge. However, it also needs to be borne in mind that the reality within which we work and research is one which is socially con-structed and that language, Bourdieu (1990) argues, has the ability to structure thought by interposing forms of socially desirable 'misrecognition' between the reader and the image in order to hide that which society deems inappropriate or dangerous. Language is, therefore, able to control the 'uncertain signs' (Barthes, 1997) which may be contained within images which need to be co-ordinated and manipulated through explanation and familiarisation in order to maintain the prevailing social hegemony.

When comparing the list that you made with the lists that were made by your colleagues in the first part of the activity above you will find that there are differences in the words that were used to describe responses. The images were chosen by you in the context of your role as a researcher; you were aware that you were both analysing the images personally and also researching the response of others to the same images. Depending on the images that you selected you may find that there are significant differences in the range of words which have been included in the lists and there may be elements of strong similarity or dissonance between them. Whatever the results it is unlikely that all your respondents will have chosen the same words to express themselves. Initially they responded to the images in terms of their personal lived experience, but by asking them to express their feelings in words you introduced a context which required them to intellectually rationalise their immediate responses to the images. Nevertheless, through the use of another qualitatively based investigative tool, that of language, you now have achieved a means of accessing the individual interpretations of the data generated by the images while remaining within the confines of the hermeneutic tradition.

Building critical research skills: activity 2

As a group ask your colleagues to discuss the images and agree a list of words which they all agree describe the feelings which the images generate.
Compare this list with the previous lists:

- Are the lists similar?
- Are the same words used?
- Are there differences and if so, what are they and what do you feel they indicate?

Discussion

In the first part of the exercise your respondents were working as individuals responding to images in the context of their own lived experience. In the second activity your respondents were working as a group, using language as a mediator to compare their impressions of both the latent and manifest content of the images. When you compare the lists which were jointly prepared with those created individually in the previous activity you will find that there are differences, some words will have disappeared, others may have been grouped to illustrate themes. *Why?*

The informational text of the image itself and the shared experience of having interpreted the images has led to the development of an entirely new context in which the images are being 'audienced' ('the process by which a visual image has its meanings re-negotiated, or even rejected, by particular audiences watching in specific circumstances' – Rose, 2001: 25). The relationship of the viewer(s) to the images has changed and they have now become reference points for the discussion, deconstruction and analysis of both the overt and covert content they contain while also acting as a stimulus for the joint and several exploration of the emotional and mediated responses of individuals. The images have become a method of facilitating the sharing of individual perspectives and experiences in order to develop joint understandings and new, socially constructed meanings, which act to connect the image with the context in which it is read in a singular manner.

As is demonstrated by this activity and in the earlier vignette, when the context in which the image is read is changed, the meanings which are attributed to it are likely to be modified. The continually evolving relationship which exists between the viewer and the image cannot be disassociated from the context in which meaning-making is carried out and thus the triangular interaction between the three factors is one which must be taken into account when using images as research tools.

Building critical research skills: activity 3

Review your findings from the previous activities in the light of the points discussed above.

Vignette 2: using images in classroom research

Ellen is working with a group of adult learners who are investigating what it is to be a teacher as part of a module for a higher education qualification in teaching. She has taught this element of the course before but has never been entirely happy with the results when reading the assignments submitted by her learners at the end of the module. She feels that they do not engage with the issues at a deep level, preferring surface descriptions of generic stereotypes to exploring their personal opinions and feelings and the ways in which these might potentially influence teacher–learner relationships. After consulting her reflective journal she discovers that for the past couple of years she has taught this section as a discussion-based session following individual research by learners, but last year one of the learners presented an image of a 'gentleman of the road' as he described it as part of his feedback to the group and this sparked off a lot of interaction in the group.

Following the learners' lead, Ellen decided to explore the concept through images and initially divided the learners into groups, issuing them with pens, paper and crayons, before setting one group the challenge of drawing a primary school teacher and the other group of drawing a secondary school teacher. The groups were able to communicate in any way they chose but had to agree on the elements included in the drawings. Once the image had been drawn the groups were asked to write single words on the drawing describing the attributes they associated with the teachers they felt they had depicted. Two of the images are reproduced at Figure 10.3 and Figure 10.4.

Figure 10.3 Primary school teacher   Figure 10.4 Secondary school teacher

Ellen found that both the construction of the images and the subsequent formulating of captions resulted in some animated discussion between learners, who consistently verbally contextualised elements of the drawings in their personal experiences of schools and teachers in the unbidden oral narratives which accompanied their creations. In creating visual metaphors in the drawings they were finding triggers to rediscover memories that for many of them were passive and submerged but which had, nevertheless, shaped their views of the persona, qualities and generic traits associated with teaching (and teachers) in distinct contexts, for as Weber and Mitchell (1995: 34) note: 'What we have seen or known, thought or imagined, remembered or repressed, slips unbidden into our drawings, revealing unexplored ambiguities, contradictions and connections. Things which we have forgotten, that which we might censor from our speech and writing, often escapes into our drawings.'

In the next step in the exercise Ellen asked the learners to draw a representation of a teacher in the lifelong learning sector (LLS). When the groups had been working together to produce the previous set of drawings, Ellen had noticed that there was a high degree of consensus as to what should be included both visually and in caption form, but when undertaking this exercise she found that the learners appeared to be less certain of themselves and the drawings were made slowly and accompanied by much more debate and consultation. When discussing the images with the group afterwards, she found that the learners, even though all of them technically worked within the LLS, had found it difficult to define what it was to be a teacher in the LLS. Using the images as a focus for discussion Ellen slowly worked with the group to tease out the reasons for their uncertainty. Eventually most of the learners agreed that it was generated by the lack of shared experience which they could use as a lens for the exercise, as all had entered teaching after long periods in other professions and relatively few had any experience of being taught in the sector before they began to teach. Ellen also found that it took much longer to analyse the images than in the previous exercise, with discussion being centred around the underlying discourses which had influenced the development of the images rather than on the personal and narratively based discussion generated by the earlier images. *Why?*

Discussion

The images which were produced by the second exercise, which are shown at Figure 10.5 and Figure 10.6, were significantly more abstract in their composition than the first drawings, with fewer descriptors. The descriptors which are included are somewhat intangible and relate less to the personal attributes of teachers than those on the previous images and require significantly more explanation in order for viewers to understand their meaning.

The images were used to focus the discussion, but this time the emphasis was on the codes and signs contained within the content. In doing this the group was entering the realm of semiology or semiotics (the study of signs and symbols) which Rose (2001: 69) somewhat poetically describes as a means of 'laying bare the prejudices beneath the smooth surface of the beautiful'. If, as is argued by philosophers such as Foucault and Bourdieu, society is a social construction governed and shaped by its prevailing discourses then the images which are generated within that society will contain representations of the discourses. Semiotic analysis uses a case study technique to identify and interpret the signs within an image which denote the influence of the prevailing discourses. At a basic level, semiotic analysis identifies three types of signs which, it is argued, helps the viewer to interpret the relationship between the signifier (the sign) and the signified (the meaning of the sign):

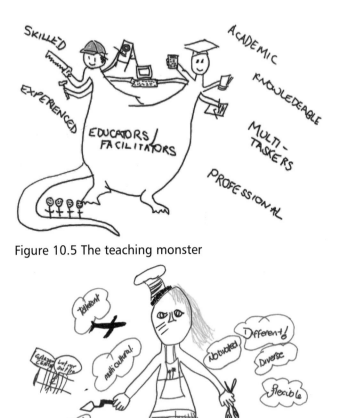

Figure 10.5 The teaching monster

Figure 10.6 All things to all men

1. *Iconic signs*: these represent that which is signified; so in the image above the drawing of the half man/half woman person is a representation of the teacher and the two-headed monster represents the two main strands of teaching in the LLS, vocational and academic.

2. *Indexical signs*: these represent the inherent (and often culturally specific) relationship between the sign and the meaning. In the image above, the tools being held by the half-man/half-woman indicate the importance of the vocational element of the teacher's role in the LLS and the computer linking the vocational and academic 'heads' of the monster denote the centrality of ILT to both elements.

3. *Symbolic signs*: these represent a conventional but sometimes arbitrary relationship between the signifier and the signified, thus the multiple arms in Figure 10.5, The Teaching Monster, symbolise the multiplicity of jobs the

teacher may have to carry out, whereas the apparent dead body, prisoner and plane in Figure 10.6, All Things to All Men, represent forensic science, teaching in prisons and travel and tourism respectively as subjects taught within the sector.

By reading the signs both jointly and severally the reader can begin to iden-tify some of the influential discourses which govern not only the relationship between the signs in the image but also those which underpin its production. In the man/woman drawing there are a number of inclusions which when read as a whole would seem to indicate the prominence of the vocational education discourse within the sector, that is, the dominance of tools and the relative lack of written material together with the inclusion of a booklet labelled 'NVQ'. The words which have been included on the drawing, 'tol-erance', 'diverse', 'flexible' and 'different', again draw attention to one of the meta-discourses governing the sector, that of inclusion. These discourses are echoed to some extent in the 'monster' drawing but others which are per-haps hinted at in the other half-man/half-woman drawing are more apparent, the need for flexible staff with a range of skills and capable of multi-tasking is highlighted through the many armed caricatures and this aspect is re-emphasised by the inclusion of the word 'facilitator' in addition to 'educator'. Interestingly, in this drawing more formal aspects of education, symbolised by the 'teacher' figure in the mortar board and gown, are included and appear to have been given an equal level of importance with the vocational aspect of the sector, something which is perhaps a reflection of the changing role of the sector in society in terms its projected role in facilitating access to higher education.

Semiotic analysis can potentially identify representations of the prevailing cultural influences which are not necessarily acknowledged by the author of the images. Bourdieu (1991: 129–33) points out that any image 'expresses, apart from the explicit intentions of the ... [image-maker the] ... schemes of perception, thought and appreciation, of a whole group', and the individual interpretation of the image by the viewer is not, therefore, necessarily generalisable. The reliance of meaning-making through interpretation on the temporally and culturally specific context of both the image maker and the viewer means that the validity, reliability and consistency of all and any interpretations of the data presented in an image can be brought into question. Nevertheless, as is shown in the vignette above, images are a useful focal point for discussions of both the familiar and the unknown or unrecognised. In themselves images do not necessarily provide agreed information, they simply present data for interpretation and it is only when combined with language in the form of discussions or interviews that their true value and significance are discovered.

Building critical research skills: activity 4

Select a favourite painting or drawing and identify the semiotic signals which it contains.

Ask colleagues to talk to you about the image and from this identify any semiotic influences.

- Are the lists similar?
- Where there are differences, what are they and what do you feel they indicate?

Review your findings in the light of the discussion above.

Conclusion

Although largely associated with a supporting role in research, for example, helping in the presentation of written findings by making them more accessible, images need to be taken seriously because not only are they not entirely reducible to their content they also have an effect on the viewer in thei own right. If, as the variously attributed saying states, 'the eyes are the windows to the soul' then images could perhaps best be described as being a portal into the affective, giving researchers a means of accessing the deep-seated and frequently ignored unconscious and subconscious reactions of the viewer. As has been discussed above, the reaction to images is individual and each viewer receives and interprets data from images subjectively, using their lived experience as a method of constructing meaning for the information presented. Naturally, as with any investigative strategy within the hermeneutic tradition of research, the very fact that the validity of the findings associated with it are open to question, means that many academics will dismiss it as a tool for enquiry, but its function as a tool for exploring the 'hard-to-reach' areas of the affective domain give it a unique place in the array of tools available to the researcher. As a tool used in isolation it presents difficulties to the user; it is difficult to identify precise meaning, interpretations are always subjective and not open to generalisation, data is difficult to analyse, and so on, but when used in conjunction with other methods such as discussion or interviews it facilitates access to values, beliefs and attitudes at the micro level and an insight into the relative strength of the different prevailing discourses at a macro level.

As Walker and Wiedel (1985: 206) note: 'To find a place for the visual is not ... to develop yet another specialised and precious research concern, but to broaden access to our work ... [as researchers].'

References and further reading 📖

Atkinson, P. (1992) *Understanding Ethnographic Texts*. London: Sage.

Ball, M.S. and Smith, G.H.W. (1992) *Analyzing Visual Data*. London: Sage.

Barthes, R. (1977) 'The Rhetoric of the Image,' in *Image, Music, Text*. London: Fontana.

Bloom, B.S. (1956) *Taxonomy of Educational Objectives, Handbook I: The Cognitive Domain*. New York: David McKay.

Bourdieu, P. (1988) *Homo Academicus*. Stanford, CA: Stanford University Press.

Bourdieu, P. (1990) *Photography: A Middlebrow Art*. London: Polity Press.

Bourdieu, P. (1991) 'Towards a sociology of photography', *Visual Anthropology Review*, 7(1): 129–33.

Chaplin, E. (1994) *Sociology and Visual Representation*. London: Routledge.

Collier, J. Jr and Collier, M. (1986) *Visual Anthropology – Photography as a Research Method*. Albuquerque, NM: University of New Mexico Press.

Emmison, M. and Smith, P. (2000) *Researching the Visual – Images, Objects, Contexts and Interactions in Social and Cultural Enquiry*. London: Sage.

Foucault, M. (1979) *Discipline and punishment: The birth of the prison*. New York: Vintage Books.

Loizos, P. (2000) 'Video, film and photographs as research documents', in M.W. Bauer and G. Gaskell (eds), *Qualitative Researching with Text, Image and Sound*. London: Sage.

Oxford (1998) *The Concise Oxford Dictionary*. 9th edn. Oxford: Oxford University Press.

Pink, S. (2001) *Doing Visual Ethnography*. London: Sage. A useful book which looks at the practicalities of using images as a research tool in addition to examining ethical issues.

Prosser, J. (ed.) (1998) *Image-based Research – A Sourcebook for Qualitative Researchers*. London: Falmer Press. A good general source of information from a range of contributors.

Rorty, R. (1989) *Contingency, Irony and Solidarity*. Cambridge: Cambridge University Press.

Rose, G. (2001) *Visual Methodologies – An Introduction to the Interpretation of Visual Materials*. London: Sage. A wide ranging text which discusses some of the main methods associated with research using images.

Schratz, M. (ed.) *Qualitative Voices in Educational Research*. London: Falmer. Contains some useful information on images in research among some interesting approaches to qualitative research in general.

Simons, H. and Usher, R. (2000) *Situated Ethics in Educational Research*. London: RoutledgeFalmer.

Walker, R. and Wiedel, J. (1985) 'Using photographs in a discipline of words', in R.G. Burgess (ed.), *Field Methods in the Study of Education*. London: Falmer Press.

Weber, S. and Mitchell, C. (1995) *'That's Funny, You Don't Look Like a Teacher'. Interrogating Images and Identity in Popular Culture*. London: Falmer Press. An interesting and insightful examination of the use of images for research in a compulsory education setting.

Worth, S. and Adair, J. (1972) *Through Navajo Eyes*. Bloomington, IN: University Press. Somewhat dated now but worth reading as one of the foundation stones of ethnographic methodology.

CHAPTER 11

ANALYSING AND REPORTING QUALITATIVE DATA

Summary

In this chapter we look at some of the difficulties and ambiguities we may encounter when we set out to interpret and analyse our data; and we discuss how these can be acknowledged and addressed. We look, too, at the issues which arise whenever we begin the process of selecting data for presentation. To do this, we compare the researcher's role in the first instance to that of a detective faced with an abundance of information who must embark on the demanding task of drawing likely conclusions about relevance and meaning. The chapter goes on to examine a range of approaches which can be used for the analysis of qualitative data gathered by interview and other means. This discussion is based largely around the interview transcripts from Chapter 5 with which the reader should already be familiar. The chapter closes with the discussion of an extract from a research assignment.

Key words used in this chapter are: *subjectivity, bias, interpretation, presentation, evidence, selection.*

Looking for evidence

Imagine this scene from a typical whodunnit of the golden age of detective fiction. A detective is called to a grand country house where the chauffeur has been found dead in the stables. During the first day of his enquiry the detective is able to assemble a range of information. Some of these are 'facts', in the sense that they are demonstrably 'true'; such as that the chauffeur has died as the result of a bullet to the brain. However, the detective has also collected information of another kind. For example, the housekeeper has told him that the chauffeur was planning to run away with the younger daughter of the house. Now, while the cause of his death is a fact verifiable by medical examination, the intentions of the dead man are less easy to ascertain, and perhaps impossible to prove. The younger daughter adamantly denies the housekeeper's story. The detective can find no letters or keepsakes that would support the theory of a secret liaison; and no other members of the household have given any hint that such a relationship was going on.

Clearly, the detective finds himself facing a difficulty. If the housekeeper's tale is true, the detective has been presented with a possible motive for the man's death. The girl's father, owner of the grand house and a member of the landed gentry, would almost certainly be violently opposed to such an unsuitable match, perhaps to the point where he was prepared to kill to prevent it happening. Or it might be that the older sister, feeling overlooked and left on the shelf, or possibly even a little in love with the chauffeur herself, killed the man in a fit of jealousy. Or perhaps the younger daughter had another suitor – a rival to the chauffeur – who decided to get rid of the opposition once and for all. These are all possible lines of enquiry which the detective could pursue. On the other hand, if the housekeeper's story is simply supposition or a piece of malicious gossip, the detective is back to square one, with no idea at all of what the motive might be for the man's death.

He now has a dilemma, of course, which is whether to raise with other members of the household the question of a liaison between the chauffeur and the younger daughter. We can see how tempting this might be for him. Corroboration would lend weight to his emerging theory and would begin to justify a logical and satisfactory interpretation of events. Remember, however, that no one except the housekeeper has made any mention of such a possibility. There is no 'weight' to this evidence. No corroborative evidence has been offered. Indeed, it could be argued that the 'weight' of evidence indicates that the housekeeper's account is mistaken since no such affair is mentioned by anyone else. And if the detective, in the manner of a researcher using a grounded theory approach (Glaser and Strauss, 1967), tests this line of enquiry by returning to his other informants and raising it with them, doesn't he risk planting the idea in their minds? Might the butler, for example, think to himself, 'Hmmm. Well, now he mentions it, that chauffeur was a very handsome fellow, and I did see her speaking to him once'. In other words, by testing in this way the trustworthiness of the information he has received from the housekeeper, the detective risks contaminating all the evidence subsequently collected.

The detective here is, in a very real sense, a qualitative researcher. He has his data. It amounts to a collection of apparently unrelated information: a man dead of a headshot; date and time; observations of participants' reactions; and interview responses from family and staff; none of which throw any light on a probable motive. And then there is the housekeeper's testimony – a clue – which offers the possibility of a workable theory, a logical explanation. But unless it can be tested and corroborated, it cannot be counted as evidence. No arrest can be made; the case cannot be considered solved. Happily, the researcher is more fortunate than the policeman, because we are not obliged to come up with a cut and dried 'solution'. We can present possibilities and theories and we can argue for or against them, and – as long as our processes are transparent, our approach ethical and our methods grounded in good practice – we will be considered to have done our job successfully.

Let's pause for a moment here and consider some of the terminology we've used in telling this story. You'll have noticed that some of the words are set in inverted commas: 'facts' and 'true' and 'weight of evidence' and 'solution'. This is to remind us that these words and concepts must be handled with extreme caution when writing and speaking about research. To say that something is a 'fact' or is 'true' or that you have found the 'solution' is to claim that it is known with absolute certainty. But there are surprisingly few things about which this claim can be accurately made! Philosophers will tell you that belief is a necessary condition for knowledge. In other words, you can't be said to *know* something unless you *believe* it. However, we have to be careful here, because this is *not* the same as saying that to believe something is to know it. The great analytical psychologist, C.G. Jung once famously said, when asked whether he believed in God, 'I don't believe. I know'. As researchers, analysing our qualitative data, we may come to believe that we have found a definitive answer or outcome. But, unless there is certainty, we shouldn't claim it as a 'fact' or the 'truth'. This doesn't invalidate our research. Indeed, it is probable that we have not set out to prove anything, but rather to shed light on an issue (illuminative research) or to explore it (exploratory research).

Philosophers will also tell you that a thing must be *true* before it can be counted as *knowledge*. And here we have what is perhaps the biggest stumbling block for qualitative researchers. If we are not looking for what is 'true', then in what sense are we adding to the sum of knowledge? Hammersley (2008) argues that qualitative researchers have failed to answer satisfactorily the criticisms of quantitative researchers, including the accusation that qualitative research often fails to produce findings which are generalisable (that is, applicable or 'true' outside the specific context in which the research was conducted), and the accusation that their explanations of cause and effect often cannot be conclusively proven. The response of qualitative researchers to that first criticism, particularly in the field of education, might be to say that we are often not looking for generalisable findings, but are exploring specific issues within specific schools or colleges. The second criticism is more difficult to answer. In action research, for example, if we change our classroom seating arrangements and produce a measurable improvement in pupil performance, we might believe that this is a straightforward case of cause and effect, but we must not lose sight of the possibility that the improved performance was entirely coincidental, or due to a change in the weather, or to our own more optimistic manner, or the subject of the lessons, or the absence of a trouble-maker … and so on.

As qualitative researchers we often have to base our arguments on 'weight of evidence' rather than conclusive proof or incontrovertible evidence. To return to a legal analogy, our role may sometimes resemble that of the judge or magistrate more closely than that of the positivist researcher. But 'weight of evidence' is not the same thing as 'interesting evidence' or 'evidence which confirms my own theory or hunch'. When following leads in our qualitative data we need to look for recurring themes – ideas, images, answers which crop up repeatedly and from more than one source. This is what we mean by 'weight of evidence', and we'll be returning to look at this in more detail in the second half of this chapter.

We began with a detective story. Let's compare our detective's situation now with that of an educational researcher in a school.

Vignette 1: the researcher's dilemma

English GCSE results have been disappointing for the previous Year 11, well below the cohort's predicted grades, and Marina is tasked with finding an explanation which will enable the school to achieve improved predictive accuracy for the current Year 11. The researcher interviews the Year 11 tutor and all members of the English department. She can't interview the Head of English because he has left for a post overseas and his replacement won't be starting until the beginning of the spring term. So far, Marina's data consists of the predicted results, the actual results, some examples of coursework (where the standard appears to be consistent with the prediction), and transcripts of interviews with staff. None of this sheds any light on the problem, except for one comment by a member of the English team who has suggested that the predicted grades for the cohort in question were misleadingly optimistic and that the coursework may have been reworked by the previous department head to bring it in line with those predictions. He suggests that the candidates' overall final grades reflected their poor performance in the examinations, and were in fact a more accurate measure of their attainment.

As well as contemplating the serious ethical implications of exploring this theory, Marina now also has the dilemma of whether or not to sound out other members of the team for corroboration. If they have not raised this possibility with her already, will she be contaminating subsequent data by putting this idea into their minds – an idea for which she has no supporting evidence? Should she rather accept that the available data (with the exception of this unsubstantiated suggestion from one member of the English team) can yield up no explanation for the anomalous results? Indeed, when presenting her findings, should she mention this piece of data at all? Will this response from one participant assume significance despite its lack of 'weight' if the researcher feels under pressure to come up with an answer? We must hope not. But this is a methodological and ethical dilemma which you may find it useful to discuss with colleagues or fellow students.

Both stories we've looked at so far in this chapter show us, among other things, that when interrogating and analysing data, there may be the temptation to clutch at evidence that will give us clear or convenient answers, or answers which are consistent with our own espoused theories. We shall explore this point further when we come to analyse some interview transcripts later in the chapter.

Data, evidence and 'proof'

One point that these two stories do demonstrate very clearly is that *data* are not the same thing as *evidence*. We've seen that the word 'evidence' is used to describe pieces of information which support a theory, argument or hypothesis, and we have already questioned whether we can be justified in formulating a theory based on a suggestion from only one respondent and unsupported by the rest of our data. In order for it to be counted as a convincing piece of evidence there must be further data which support this same interpretation of events. And, indeed, assuming additional data were found, *evidence* is not the same thing as *proof* or 'truth', and we must be careful not to present it as if it were. Instead, we might use one of the following forms of words:

- 'The evidence suggests that ...'
- 'From the evidence it could be argued that ...'
- 'The evidence points to the possibility/probability/likelihood that ...'

As we have seen, 'proof' and 'truth' are problematic concepts, and particularly so in qualitative research; and this is where our detective's role will differ most markedly from that of Marina, our researcher. He will be expected to provide proof against which there can be 'no reasonable doubt'. Unlike the qualitative researcher, who can offer her research findings as 'illuminating' or 'exploratory', the detective must present his theory as 'the truth' by supporting it with incontrovertible evidence. Our detective investigating the chauffeur's death cannot yet do this.

Evidence is the data we select in order to support our argument
- We talk about 'interrogating' our data.
- We do this in order to identify whether there is a case to argue.
- We then select for presentation the data relevant to our argument.
- When we present data in this way we call it 'evidence'.

Some readers will perhaps be familiar with the real-life case of the Road Hill House murder of 1865 recently re-told in Kate Summerscale's best-selling book, *The Suspicions of Inspector Whicher* (2009). On this occasion the eponymous detective was sent from London to investigate the unsolved murder of a young boy which had horrified and fascinated Victorian England. He meticulously gathered extensive *data* from which he eventually formulated a theory as to the identity of the child's murderer. However, because of the lack of conclusive *evidence*, Inspector Whicher was unable to convince the authorities or to make his accusation stick. Years later, a confession by the murderer proved his theory to have been absolutely correct; but too late, alas, to save the detective's career and reputation. The title the author chose for her account of this case is telling. A 'suspicion' is only a theory. Unless supported by sufficient evidence it cannot be expected to convince others or add to the sum of our understanding.

So far we've looked at situations where the data does not offer sufficient evidence for us to arrive at a convincing argument or theory. But difficulties in formulating a theory or argument can arise also when our data appears to present us with a wealth of evidence – if that evidence is conflicting. So let's go back now to Marina, the researcher investigating the disappointing GCSE grades, and look at an alternative version of that story.

Vignette 2: the researcher's dilemma – an alternative story

Tasked with investigating why a Year 11 cohort in GCSE fell well below their predicted grades in GCSE English Language, Marina sends a questionnaire to all staff in the school, which she follows up with interviews. She also analyses documentary evidence and sits in on classes and staff meetings. The questionnaires allow respondents to remain anonymous. She notices that three factors are mentioned several times on the completed questionnaires in response to the open question: 'Last year's GCSE English results were disappointing. Why do you think this might be?'

Summarised, these are:

- This Year 11 was the first cohort to be affected by reduced literacy provision further down the school.
- The school took a decision to drop GCSE English Literature from the available options for this cohort, which may have meant that they were reading less.
- The intense level of support which pupils received for their English coursework produced work which raised unrealistic expectations of their exam performance.

In the follow-up interviews none of the staff mention the first two factors, and only one mentions the third, adding his comments about the previous Head of English, as we saw previously.

The researcher's dilemma is now a rather different one. Instead of having very little data, she now has several possible lines of enquiry. But this data is only found in the questionnaire responses; with one exception, it doesn't emerge again from the interviews. This is perhaps less surprising than it might at first seem. Her respondents may consider themselves safe enough behind the anonymity of the questionnaires to offer theories which imply a criticism of school policy, but feel too exposed in a face-to-face interview to reiterate them. What is Marina to make of this?

Building critical research skills: activity

Consider the following questions and make a note of your answers. You may do this alone, or you might find it useful to discuss the questions with colleagues or fellow students.

- When she realised that the interviewees were not going to volunteer any of the theories that had emerged in the questionnaires, should Marina have raised these possibilities herself and asked for the interviewee's view? How would you justify your answer to someone who took the opposite view?
- Should Marina conclude that the third theory – the one about the previous Head of English – carries the most 'weight' because it is the only piece of data found in both questionnaires and interview responses? Again, think carefully about how you would justify your answer to someone who took the opposite view.
- Assuming we decide that the data is weighted evenly and the researcher can discover no conflicting evidence to contradict any of three theories offered, how would she go about presenting her findings? You might like to plan this out in note form so that you can compare your version with Marina's, which you will find at the end of this chapter.

Assembling the evidence: selecting data for presentation

When we have conducted our research and come to write it up, we have to make important decisions about the choice of data which we will present in order to support our argument. It would be very unusual to include entire interview transcripts and whole sets of completed questionnaires – although it is always important to be able to say where this data can be located and that it is securely archived in order to preserve confidentiality where appropriate. It is, however, common practice to present a summary of the data as an appendix to the report or paper or assignment. This might be a questionnaire or an interview schedule with responses summarised against each question. But for the purposes of presenting your academic argument you will need to select examples of your data to use as evidence.

There are potential difficulties here of course. An obvious one is that it is possible for two researchers to construct different arguments from the same body of data if they choose only to present that evidence which supports their point of view. This partial selection may happen because of a researcher's unconscious bias; but it is also possible – though we hope unlikely – that an unscrupulous researcher might knowingly pick out data to support a particular discourse to which they are committed. Our GCSE researcher, for example, might be a firm believer in the liberal model of education and deplore what she perceives as a dumbing down of the curriculum. The questionnaire responses about the school dropping English Literature from the GCSE options would provide valuable ammunition for her, and so she may be tempted to present this bit of data and not any of the rest. For this reason it is essential that our selection of data for presentation should be *transparent.* That is to say, we must always explain and justify how we went about making our choice.

What are the dangers in selecting evidence?

- We may select as evidence only the data which supports our own argument, even if the *weight* of evidence contradicts it.
- We may ignore and not mention data which contradicts our argument.
- If we already have a hypothesis the danger of bias in selection is greater.
- Therefore our analysis and our criteria for selection must be transparent.

Vignette 3

In Chapter 5 we met Bashir, the MPhil student who was researching head teachers' attitudes towards vocational qualifications, and in particular the status they attribute to them in relation to general academic qualifications such as A levels. We followed him through the process of planning, designing and conducting his interviews, and we observed one of his interviews in progress. Bashir has now formulated the theory, based on the five interviews he has completed so far, that vocational qualifications are regarded by most secondary heads as second best.

Building critical research skills: activity

Imagine, now, that he asks you, as a colleague, if you would like to read through his latest interview transcript (below) so that you can see for yourself. What evidence can you find in it to support his emerging theory?

Interview 1

BP   Can you tell me a little bit about your sixth form provision here at X School?

Head   Yes, we provide two progression routes here from GCSE. First, there is the A-level strand, which constitutes most of our post-16 provision. And then there is the vocational pathway which is a smaller and more recent strand, which is to say that it recruits at present a smaller number of students than the traditional academic sixth form. But numbers are growing, year on year, so that it may eventually match, in numbers terms, the A-level cohort.

BP   Why do you think recruitment is expanding so rapidly on the vocational course?

Head   Well, several reasons, really. I mean, these are the youngsters who in the past would have left school with a GCSE or two and gone into employment or to the further education college – that sort of thing. And, of course, there aren't the jobs now, and the FE college is some distance away and public transport around here is expensive and infrequent. So really staying on at school has become the preferred option.

BP   But what I mean is, why is it the vocational sixth form that's expanding, rather than the A level sixth form?

Head   Oh well, you're talking now as if there were two different, separate sixth forms, and that's not the case. It's one sixth form – we're very clear about that. There's one sixth form common room, and one set of rules and one collective assembly. So I don't want you to get the idea that this is some sort of sheep and goats set up. It's not. Not at all. But the vocational numbers are expanding because these are the youngsters, as I said, who wouldn't traditionally have stayed on. They're not suited for A-level study and they're not qualified for it – in the sense that they don't have a firm foundation of good GCSE grades. And given the choice, they wouldn't opt for A-levels in any case.

BP   So they're given the choice?

Head   No. What I'm saying is that if they *were* given the choice they probably wouldn't want to do A levels. It's not an academic future that they're after. They sights are fixed on employment in the much shorter term.

> *BP* But these vocational qualifications can be used for entry to higher education, can't they?
>
> *Head* Well yes, of course. That is to say, you know, that er, that er many universities consider them now and they are part of the points system for entry, of course. But I think it would be fair to say that most of our sixth formers who are aiming to progress to higher education will do so through the A level route.
>
> *BP* So how many of the vocational students apply for university entrance – let's say, last year.
>
> *Head* Well, none of them last year. Because, you see, that's not what they're aiming for.
>
> *BP* And this year?
>
> *Head* None. But I don't think you're hearing what I'm saying here. Progression to higher education isn't part of the purpose of our vocational stream post-16.
>
> *BP* So how would you describe its purpose? In a nutshell.
>
> *Head* The purpose is in line with government policy, which is to prepare young people for the world of work and for their role in contributing to the country's economy.
>
> *BP* OK. So I'd like to ask you one more question, if I may. And that's about how you select which route – A level or vocation – each student will take when they enter the sixth form.
>
> *Head* Well, that's very straightforward. They self-select. That's to say, if they don't have good sound GCSE results – five A to C grades including maths and English, we don't accept them into the A level stream.
>
> *BP* So they don't have choice.
>
> *Head* No. And nor should they.
>
> *BP* And what if a student with good GCSEs wants to take the vocational option?
>
> *Head* I think you said a couple of questions ago that that was the last one. So we'll finish there, if you don't mind.

Interpreting the evidence

Did you find the evidence you were looking for? Perhaps you identified some or all of the following phrases as supporting Bashir's emerging theory:

- 'these are the youngsters who in the past would have left school with a GCSE or two and gone into employment or to the further education college – that sort of thing.'
- 'Progression to higher education isn't part of the purpose of our vocational stream post-16.'
- 'most of our sixth formers who are aiming to progress to higher education will do so through the A-level route.'
- 'they don't have a firm foundation of good GCSE grades.'

But let's just look at these again. Do any of these quoted statements really demonstrate that this head teacher holds vocational qualifications in lower esteem than A levels? Couldn't they equally be taken to suggest that she sees the two post-16 routes as having quite different and distinct purposes? Such a view does not necessarily imply a value judgement. Perhaps the interviewer does not agree with this view; but it is difficult to regard any of the head's statements as conclusive evidence of her views about the qualifications' relative status. Indeed, it's possible that questions of value and status may be projected on to the head teacher's discourse by the interviewer himself as a result of his own view, for example, that progression to higher education is more desirable than direct entry to the world of work.

Let's assume for a moment that you decide to play devil's advocate and to argue with Bashir that, from your reading of the transcript, you can't see that vocational qualifications are held in lower esteem than A levels by that head. Read the transcript through again, this time looking for evidence to support this counter argument.

Perhaps the evidence you found included some of the following:

- 'It's one sixth form – we're very clear about that.'
- 'There's one sixth form common room, and one set of rules and one collective assembly'.
- 'The purpose is in line with government policy, which is to prepare young people for the world of work.'

This illustrates nicely the necessity for transparency, because a major difficulty when we come to analyse qualitative data is that *we are more likely to see something we are looking for than something we're not expecting to find*. When Bashir comes to select data for presentation he would achieve a greater degree of transparency if he applied and explained the following criteria.

Is the data I've selected for presentation:

- illuminative? (Does it throw light on the research question?)
- indicative? (Does it indicate something significant to the research?)
- representative? (Is it typical of the data as a whole?)
- illustrative? (Does it illustrate accurately the overall picture the data presents?

Remember, these are useful terms to employ when it comes to writing about the decision process you have followed in selecting qualitative data for presentation.

Let's have a look now at the transcript of Bashir's interview with a second head teacher, where he works roughly from the same interview schedule.

Interview 2

BP   Can you tell me a little bit about your sixth form provision here at X School?

Head   In terms of numbers, do you mean? Or what?

BP   In terms of the provision. What does the school offer in terms of qualifications post-16?

Head   I see. Well, we have a wide range of AS and A level subjects, including modern and classical languages, a full range of sciences, humanities and arts, and soft subjects such as drama, art, music. And alongside those we have vocational qualifications in the areas of sport management, travel and tourism and erm another one, something to do with social care. And those, the vocational subjects, are offered at both level 2 and 3, so there's something for pupils who didn't do well at GCSE but don't want to re-sit them. You know, they've lost interest in all that, but they'll engage with subjects they've not done before, subjects they consider to be more to do with the adult world I suppose you could say.

BP   And how well do these subjects recruit? All of them. In terms of numbers.

(Continues)

(Continued)

Head   We had a problem a couple of years ago of falling rolls in the sixth form. At that time it was just a normal sixth form, of course, catering for the more able pupils and offering only A levels. But numbers were falling and we faced a position where we were having to think about dropping some A levels from the curriculum and even perhaps making cuts in staffing. But then our curriculum deputy came up with the idea of building up numbers by setting up a suitable provision for pupils whom we wouldn't normally have encouraged to stay on at school. And the vocational curriculum was ideal for this purpose. So this is what we did, and of course it saved our proper sixth form from cuts and curriculum shrinkage. So we have nice buoyant numbers now overall post-16. The majority are pupils we would never have envisaged retaining in the sixth form, but they and their vocational programme have allowed our high-quality A level provision to continue.

BP   So do pupils have a choice over which route they take in the sixth form?

Head   There's a wide range of AS and A levels, as I said, yes.

BP   No. I mean are pupils able to choose whether to go the A level or the vocational route?

Head   I don't quite understand the question.

BP   Well, could a pupil on entering the sixth form here say, 'I'd like to do AS levels'. Or 'I'd like to do a vocational course'.

Head   No, that's not how it works. It wouldn't work that way. Pupils have to have the necessary qualifications to enter the AS and A2 programme. They have to have grade 1 or 2 at GCSE in the subjects they wish to study. Which is only common sense really. So the more academically able pupils enter the sixth form – by which I mean the AS/A level programme. And the rest we put on the vocational programme – I was going to say 'of their choice', but we have to exercise a bit of caution there because some of them we know are going to be trouble.

BP   So what proportion of pupils at this school use their vocational qualifications to progress to higher education?

Head   Oh, I think there was someone this year who got a place on a sports science course somewhere or other. But normally, if a pupil is aiming for university we steer them towards the sixth form proper.

Discussion

You will have noticed on reading this through that we do in this instance seem to have some evidence here to support Bashir's emerging theory about vocational qualifications being held in low esteem. We might quote some or all of the following extracts of the head teacher's discourse to support this argument:

- 'the vocational curriculum was ideal for this purpose … it saved our proper sixth form'
- 'the more academically able pupils enter the sixth form – by which I mean the AS/A level programme. And the rest we put on the vocational programme'
- 'on the vocational programme …. some of them we know are going to be trouble.'

The reference to the 'proper sixth form' is a bit of a giveaway! However, we must still exercise caution. First, we need to remember that this is one head teacher speaking. We cannot make claims about head teachers in general based solely on his or her expressed views. To generalise from the particular or make broad claims based on small evidence is the methodological equivalent of attempting to balance an elephant on a pea.

Secondly, as with the previous transcript, it is possible to extrapolate short passages from the head's discourse which appear to present a positive, or at least equitable, view of vocational qualifications. For example:

- 'And alongside those [A levels] we have vocational qualifications'
- 'the vocational subjects, are offered at both level 2 and 3, so there's something for pupils who didn't do well at GCSE but don't want to re-sit them.'
- 'they'll engage with subjects they've not done before, subjects they consider to be more to do with the adult world'.

Readings and misreadings

So, if we now apply the selection criteria we listed earlier in the chapter, to what extent can we say that each of these six comments, quoted from the second interview transcript, is:

- illuminative?
- indicative?
- representative?
- illustrative?

To apply these criteria effectively we have first to look at the head teacher's discourse as a whole. What is the overall impression we get of this interviewee's views? What arguments are being put forward? What sort of language is being used to describe the two cohorts of pupils and the two progression routes? Looking at the data as a whole and reflecting on it are essential first steps in analysis. Diving in and plucking quotes out of context is a practice best left to unscrupulous journalists. However, although like Inspector Whicher researchers may arrive at an answer through intuitive interpretation of the data as a whole, they will be unable to carry the argument if they don't or can't present convincing evidence to support their case. So we start with the whole picture and then proceed to the detail.

Selecting and presenting data

Read/listen/watch

|

Reflect

|

Select

|

Explain your rationale for this selection

|

Present

Wellington (2000: 135–9) helpfully breaks the process of dealing with data down into six broad stages:

1. *Immersion,* or what Wellington calls 'getting an overall sense or feel for the data' (2000: 135).
2. *Reflection.*
3. *Analysis,* or the breaking down of the data into its component parts.
4. *Synthesis,* or the search for patterns, common themes, arguments or ideas.
5. *Location and relation,* or identifying how these fit with other current research.
6. *Presentation,* which in Wellington's list also includes *selection.*

The common themes, ideas or arguments identified in stage 4 of this process are known as *categories.* If we apply this to Bashir's two transcripts which we looked at earlier we would come up with a synthesis which looks something like Table 11.1. And so on. Further interview transcripts can be similarly scrutinised for data which falls into these categories.

Table 11.1 Interview themes

Categories which interviews with heads 1 and 2 have in common
• Selection post-16: vocational or academic route • Vocational qualifications not used for progression to HE • Good GCSEs a requirement for progression to A levels

We can see this process, too, in the example of Marina's GCSE research. In analysing questionnaire responses she identified three recurring ideas (Table 11.2). However, when she came to analyse her interview transcripts, as you will remember, she found no common themes. The categories identified from the questionnaires were not replicated in the interviews and it was not possible to make any meaningful synthesis of the interviews as a whole. This is sometimes the case, and it is important that we accept it and write it into our research report, rather than persevering with the analysis to the point at which we begin to read things into the data which are not really there. If there are patterns, they will, under careful scrutiny, become evident. If there are not – well, that too is a legitimate and interesting finding in itself.

Table 11.2 Questionnaire themes

Why did Year 11 fail to meet predicted English grades? Categories identified in open responses to questionnaire
• This Year 11 first to be affected by reduced literacy provision further down the school • GCSE English Literature dropped from available options. So this cohort maybe doing less reading. Impact on performance? • High level of support for their English coursework. Raised unrealistic expectations?

Minimising subjectivity and bias in the analysis and presentation of data

We have largely used interview transcripts as examples in this chapter. But, of course, the principles and processes that we've discussed apply equally to other sources of qualitative data, such as questionnaire responses, observations, focus groups, documentation, pictures, and so on. Whatever data we are working with, we must remember that, as researchers, it is our role to communicate it as accurately as possible to our audience or readership. If we are analysing and presenting the discourses, views, ideas, memories or stories of others, as we so often find ourselves doing in the field of education, we must ensure that these do not, by a process of being mediated through our own preconceptions and opinions, become distorted and contaminated. We must ensure that the authentic voice of our participants is, as far as possible, retained. We are the go-between whose role is to convey (and make sense of) the data gathered from our participants for a wider audience. Think of the researcher as a window through which the data must pass to reach an interested readership. If the window is of stained glass – that is, if we allow our own views and ideas to contaminate our data – they will emerge subtly altered, coloured by our own prejudices and agendas. As far as it is possible, therefore, we must aim to offer a clear glass window so that the data to be disseminated is as little changed as possible by our mediation and so that our participants retain their authentic voice.

Technology can be a helpful tool in this process. The use of applications such as Wordle, for example, will allow us to identify categories – key words and recurring themes – with a degree of objectivity which would otherwise be impossible. Close attention to the language used in partici- pants' responses can also be a useful way of gaining some distance from the content. For example, a category analysis of figurative language, such as we discussed in Chapter 9, could help us to more objectively evaluate the value judgements underlying a participant's discourse. A well-crafted literature review (see Chapter 4) will also provide us with a framework on which to base our analysis, if we use its themes as headings under which to present our data.

We must also ensure that we minimise subjectivity and bias in the *presen- tation* of our data. We have already discussed the need for transparency in our choice of data for presentation, and we have seen that there is a useful research vocabulary we can draw upon to guide and justify our selection. This will help ensure that the data we present to the reader is not partial or carefully edited to prove a point. We've all heard the joke about the review quoted in metre-high letters outside the theatre which says: 'This show is ... incredible', when what the review said in full was: 'This show is terrible. It's incredible that anyone would waste their money on a ticket.' As researchers, our choice of what to quote should be guided by a transparent, honest and ethical approach towards our data.

An example report of qualitative data from an MA assignment

It's now time for Marina to write up her research. As well as giving it to the head teacher, she will be submitting it as an assignment towards her MA in

Education. Here is an extract from her 'Findings' section. Read it through carefully and then consider the questions which follow.

The open question in the questionnaire asked: 'In your view, what factors might have contributed to last year's Y11 failure to meet their predicted English grades?' This was completed on all 15 returned questionnaires, and included three recurring suggestions which can be summarised as:

- This Y11 cohort was the first to be affected by reduced literacy provision further down the school (5 responses)
- GCSE English Literature had been dropped from the available options. So this cohort may have been doing less reading, which could have had an impact on their performance (3 responses)
- A high level of support for their English coursework could have raised unrealistic expectations (4 responses)

The responses quoted below are representative and illustrative of the questionnaire findings as a whole:

'English language skills are developed through reading. This cohort had less incentive to read because for the first time the KS4 curriculum didn't include literature. This was a management decision.'

'This last Year 11 hasn't had the same degree of literacy support as in previous years.'

'It wasn't that the exam results were too low. It was the coursework marks that were too high. They had too much help with it, in my view. Those coursework marks raised expectations too high.'

However, with one exception, follow-up interviews raised none of these points, which may suggest that participants were reluctant to engage in face-to-face discussion which could be seen as critical of school policy. Indeed, no common themes emerged from the interviews.

Documentary evidence confirms that this was the first cohort affected by changes to literacy provision to sit their GCSEs, and that for the first time English Literature had not been offered as an option in KS4. The issue of support for coursework is less easy to verify.

Reflective activity

1. Has Marina been transparent in her selection and presentation of data? If so, how has she achieved this? If not, what could she have done differently?
2. Has she presented her evidence with an appropriate level of objectivity? If so, how has she managed this? If not, how could she have worded her findings differently?
3. Look at how she has handled the issue of coursework. Has she, in your view, given it the right degree of emphasis? Should she have made more of it? Should she have included it in her findings at all? Explain your answer.
4. Is there anything in the way Marina has written up her findings here that you would find useful in presenting your own work? For example, look at her use of language ('may suggest ...' '... less easy to verify') and the explicit numbers attached to responses.
5. She writes that 'no common themes emerged from the interviews'. Does her reporting of this detract from or add to the professional quality of her work?
6. She summarises the themes from the questionnaire responses and then quotes some examples. Why do you think she does this? What does it add to her report?

Key points

In this chapter we have looked at the following:

- What we mean by 'facts' and 'truth'.
- Concepts of knowledge and belief.
- The distinction between proof and the weight of evidence.
- The need for transparency in the selection and presentation of data.
- The need for objectivity in interpreting evidence.
- How to avoid only seeing what we expect to find.
- Useful stages in the analysis of data.
- Minimising subjectivity and bias.
- Allowing participants their authentic voice.
- Writing up your findings.

References and further reading 📖

Glaser, B.G. and Strauss, A.L. (1967) *The Discovery of Grounded Theory: Strategies for Qualitative Research.* Chicago, IL: Aldine.

Hammersley, M. (2008) *Questioning Qualitative Enquiry.* London: Sage.

Summerscale, K. (2009) *The Suspicions of Mr Whicher.* London: Bloomsbury.

Wellington, J. (2000) *Educational Research: Contemporary Issues and Practical Approaches.* London: Continuum.

CHAPTER 12

DISSEMINATING YOUR RESEARCH

Summary

In this chapter we discuss ways in which the outcomes of your research can be made available to a wider audience in order, for example, to share suggestions for good practice with colleagues or with other institutions; or to engage in debate on questions which are of interest to the profession or academic community. In order to explore this, we draw on the real-life experiences of teachers-as-researchers as they present their own accounts of the processes and purposes of dissemination. The chapter picks up the point made in Chapter 1 about the purposes of research, and argues that it should not be regarded simply as a means to an end – an exercise undertaken to gain a higher qualification for example – but as an activity which helps define what it means to be a professional educator.

Key words in this chapter: *dissemination, presentation, publication, debate, peer review, conference, impact, audience, readership, tone, style, content.*

Dissemination: why and how?

In several of the previous chapters we have discussed the *purposes* of research. It may be that your primary purpose in undertaking a piece of small-scale qualitative research in education is to meet the requirements for a professional qualification or for a higher degree. In many of the vignettes we've seen so far, the researchers have had this purpose uppermost in their minds. But, if your research is worthwhile to you and its results have an impact on your professional practice or understanding, then it is likely that it will also be of significance and interest to others. The research process doesn't end, therefore, at the point where your assignment, project or dissertation receives a pass or distinction. This is the point where it enters the next phase: the sharing or dissemination of your work.

There are many ways in which this can be done, both formally and informally, through writing and the spoken word, with colleagues inside your institution or with a wider audience outside it, with practitioners or with academics and researchers. Your audience or readership and the medium through which you present your work will determine both your selection of content and the style, tone or 'voice' in which you communicate.

> ### Reflective activity 🔳
>
> In Table 12.1 and Table 12.2, we've listed some ways in which you might disseminate your research findings. Read through them and consider:
>
> - which method/s might be most appropriate for the dissemination of your own work;
> - which methods you would feel most comfortable with;
> - which methods you would like to try, but for which you would need further advice and support;
> - whether there are other ways in which you could share your work which are not listed here.

Real-life accounts

We're going to look now at how five researchers went about sharing the outcomes of their research. The accounts are presented in their own words, and each vignette is followed by a series of comments and questions which are designed to support your reflection on what you have read. Some of the accounts are by 'early career researchers' who have undertaken their research project as part of their professional development, towards gaining a Master's degree, for example. Others have carried out their research as an integral part of their professional responsibilities. You will notice, as you read their accounts, the variety of ways in which they have disseminated their work, and the range of purposes which led them to do so. Look out for methods of dissemination other than those listed in Tables 12.1 and 12.2.

Table 12.1 Disseminating your research through the spoken word

Informal	Formal
Discussion with colleagues within your own work environment	Addressing formal meetings or in-house staff development days
Discussion with your research participants	Presenting at practitioner conferences or workshops
Addressing meetings of colleagues between institutions	Presenting at research conferences
Speaking informally to managers and other key stakeholders	Presenting your findings to policy-making committees and bodies
Networking	Interview with press
Other?	Other?

Table 12.2 Disseminating your work through the written word

Informal	Formal
Written summary of findings for colleagues or team	Writing an account for the press (e.g. a press release)
Written summary of findings for participants	Writing a piece for a professional journal or magazine
Email contact with other colleagues or researchers	Writing a formal report for your head teacher, board of governors, etc
Blogs and Tweets	Writing a research paper for an academic journal
Other?	Other?

Vignette 1: disseminating research findings about staff coaching

> The subject of my MA module research was the evaluation of a staff coaching programme in a state comprehensive school. There were two main conclusions of the research; firstly, that it was really a mentoring programme, as it was perceived by participants to have been a very nurturing and reflective process, rather than being directive, and secondly, that voluntary participation, choice in pairings and the separation of this scheme from the Performance Management process were deemed to
> (Continues)

(Continued)

have been vital to the success of the programme. I carried out the research using semi-structured participant questionnaires before and after the coaching process.

It was important to me that the research was not just for academic purposes and to further my own ambitions, but that it should also have a positive impact in the school where I work; after all it was a genuine evaluation of the programme and the good will of both the school management and of the participants were vital in terms of the success of the coaching programme itself, as well as in the production of data for my research. I therefore provided all participants with a summary of my findings and believe this was important as it led to many further informal conversations with participants, whose feedback up to that point had been anonymous, but who were now encouraged and reassured by the findings and wanted to elaborate on the responses they had provided and further emphasise the positive outcomes that they had experienced of the programme.

In addition I provided a summary to the coaching programme coordinator who was a member of the Senior Leadership Team and for him, this feedback was invaluable in setting up the subsequent cycle of coaching within the school as he understood how important the voluntary nature of participation had been in the success of the scheme thus ensuring this was maintained in the second cycle. The school has since appointed a new head teacher, who has also shown an interest in the outcomes of the research and in how coaching or mentoring could be expanded further as a method of in-house staff development.

Additionally, at the time of the research the school was a Training School and was being supported and monitored by a consultant from the Training and Development Agency for Schools, who was very interested in the findings of this project. He cited this at one of the East Midlands regional meetings for Training Schools as an example of good practice in terms of action research and as evidence of the positive impact of coaching in schools.

Finally, I presented my work at one of the research seminars held by the University Education Faculty where I studied for my Masters. This seminar programme allows MA and PhD students to present their research and gives other students the opportunity to develop their own skills as they can critically evaluate the work and ask questions about the methods, methodology and conclusions. This ultimately led to my work being published in the University's *Research into Teaching* journal.

Caroline Tomlinson, Rushcliffe School, Nottingham (2011)

Discussion

This researcher gives us a very clear account of the dissemination of her work in terms of *what, why* and *how.*

- She begins by presenting the two main conclusions drawn from her research. In other words, she tells us the important part first. This would be essential in, for example, a press release. It provides us with a context in which to read the rest of her account.
- She then makes a statement about purpose. She tells us that the research was designed to *have a positive impact in the school,* and was not only about gaining a qualification or career progression.
- We're then given a clear account of the methods and process of dissemination, both within the school and to the wider professional and academic community.

Notice the range of ways this researcher has used to share her findings, both formally and informally, both spoken and written. And notice, too, how she reaches a wider and wider audience/readership as the dissemination process snowballs. If you would like to read her research paper it can be accessed as follows:

Tomlinson, C. (2011) 'Coaching or mentoring? How successful was the introduction of a coaching programme in a Nottinghamshire School in terms of achieving institutional goals and participants pairings?', *Research into Teaching,* 1(3): 50–65.

Vignette 2: disseminating research findings about graffiti

My thesis (Cassar 2007a) investigated a number of girls' writings as they occurred in the form of graffiti in a post-secondary school in Malta. These writings were written on the doors inside the female students' lavatories. As a teacher working in this school for many years, I was able to collect ethnographic data. The subject matter of the absolute majority of the graffiti dealt with sexualities and romantic relationships issues. Although nearly all of them were anonymous, some mobile phone numbers were written, so that presumably students could be contacted for further advice regarding their 'romantic problems'.

(Continues)

(Continued)

The graffiti were considered deviant and against the rules of the institution. As a teacher I held a certain position of power and I had the 'duty' to report anyone who vandalised the school's property. Although it was difficult to identify who the graffitists were, an inquiry could have been carried out by means of the mobile phone numbers, which some of them wrote. At the same time, I also wanted to respect the girls' voices, as I believed in their search for sexual knowledge. It was therefore difficult for me to compromise my dual, contradictory roles: to legitimize the girls' valid concerns, which I felt could be a form of empowerment for them, through their shared knowledge and at the same time respect the institution, of which I formed a part. At times, this situation caused me a sense of 'splitting' regarding my positionality (Haraway 1991). During the research process and through the dissemination of the findings my primary concern was to ensure that the graffiti writers were protected from harm.

In the absence of sexuality and relationships education in postsecondary education curricula in Malta, this study sought to challenge the silences surrounding this topic. The dissemination of the data, is considered a valid factor, which could contribute towards this aim. The graffiti were discussed in academic conferences in Paris (2007), Brussels (2008), Malta (2009), London (2010), Amsterdam (2011) and Geneva (2011). Different themes emanating from them were explored every time. In 2008, the study was also disseminated during a seminar for teachers, who worked in the same institution where the research was carried out. Some teachers were utterly surprised by their contents, as they had not been aware of them. Two published articles came into being (Cassar 2007b, 2009). The education supplement of a local newspaper devoted an article about the study (*The Sunday Times of Malta*, 2010, p. 69). In 2011 the Ministry of Education, Employment and the Family in Malta set up a new National Curriculum Framework (https://www.meef.gov.mt/Page.aspx?pid=543) and together with my colleagues at the university I submitted my comments and recommendations as regards the provision of sexuality education in schools. The study about the graffiti provided many valuable insights. Perhaps the next step involving the dissemination of the data should concern the protagonists of the study; the graffiti writers, who by now have moved on with their life. They could be made aware about the study through Facebook or other social networks. It would be fascinating to know how they regard my study and even more fascinating to get to know who they are.

References

Cassar, J. (2007a) 'Public and private spaces in adolescent girls' lives: school graffiti, sexualities and romantic relationships', unpublished Ed.D thesis, The University of Sheffield.

Cassar, J. (2007b) 'Unveiling desires: adolescents' hidden graffiti about sexualities and romantic relationships in schooled settings', *The International Journal of the Humanities*, 5(4): 179–83.

Cassar, J. (2009) 'Being a lesbian is no sin: religion, sexuality and education in the lives of female students', *Mediterranean Journal of Educational Studies*, 14(1): 45–67.

Haraway, D.J. (1991) 'Situated knowledges: the science question in feminism and the privilege of partial perspective', in D. Haraway (ed.). *Simians, Cyborgs, and Women: The Reinvention of Nature*. New York: Routledge. pp. 183–201.

Ministry of Education, Employment and the Family (2011) *National Curriculum Framework* (https://www.meef.gov.mt/Page.aspx?pid=543)

The Sunday Times of Malta (2010), 'The writing's on the wall', p. 69.

Joanne Cassar, University of Malta (2011)

Discussion

This account is very different from the first in a number of ways. The researcher tells us that her study 'seeks to challenge the silences' surrounding sexuality and sex education, and that 'the study about the graffiti provided many valuable insights'. There is an emphasis here on the researcher's *positionality* and the degree of role-conflict which the research entailed.

Reflective activity

- As you read it through, were you able to identify: (a) a research question? (b) a summary of the findings or insights?
- Were you able to identify the several ways in which the research was disseminated, and the scope and scale of that dissemination?

It is likely that you answered 'No' to the first question. The researcher has, however, provided you with a way to access this information by listing full references to her work at the end of her account. Notice, too, that she considers the participants (she refers to them as *protagonists*) of her study as a possible future audience for dissemination.

Vignette 3: disseminating research findings about pupil attitudes to collective worship

My MA research developed from a Statutory Inspection of Anglican Schools (SIAS) report for a Voluntary Aided (VA) High School which highlighted a lack of compliance with circular 1/94. This is the legal requirement to deliver a daily act of collective worship in all schools, which must be *wholly or mainly of a broadly Christian character*. In response to this report, the Standing Advisory Council for Religious Education (SACRE) Blackpool (2006) commissioned a small scale survey of 50 pupils from Year 10 and Year 6 classes across the borough to ascertain their views of Religious Education. The feedback highlighted a negative attitude held by the pupils and the lack of distinction for some, between Religious Education and Assembly (Collective Worship). I subsequently undertook group interviews with pupils on how they would want to engage with Collective Worship and also made observations of Collective Worship which supported the findings of SIAS (Sage, 2007; 2009).

Evaluative questioning identified that pupils felt disempowered in the High School setting as opposed to being encouraged to contribute to and lead 'Assemblies' in their primary phase of education. Pupils also voiced a negative 'vibe' which they considered a proportion of staff radiated. This, they considered, devalued and disrespected such times of 'Assembly'.

The difficulty for me was a reluctance by teachers to listen to pupil voices or to use resources which, although Christian in character, were not written for secondary phase Church of England Schools. Some resources were deemed by teachers to be too 'old fashioned' to be of use. The materials, developed in 1989, were previously deemed good practice but fell short of the National Society guidance (1994) and were focused on teacher delivery. However, this latter concern around resources being 'old-fashioned' was not expressed by the pupils and I wanted to respect their voice.

This led me to identify a need for pupil focused and led resources to be written with a view to enabling and encouraging both Staff and pupils to rediscover the value of acts of Collective Worship in the school and ensure compliance in this area. The existing 'Assembly' resource was used to form a starting point in the writing of secondary phase materials for the VA High School pupils. I believed that by bypassing teacher input and empowering pupils they would design and deliver acts of Collective Worship which were relevant, pupil centred and Anglican in identity.

The Collective Worship materials were collated and written to maximise the visual impact of the folders; retro in content, colour coded and divided into sections. The 6 sections encompassed stories linked to the Christian values agenda, the Christian saints and calendar, famous people and dates, Bible stories, prayers, important events, music advice and some examples of PowerPoint presentations. Sections on how to get started, planning and tips on delivery technique, evaluation documents, were included with a view to inspection criteria. All materials were developed as a response to the initial research with pupils in Blackpool. (Sage 2007; SACRE Blackpool 2006).

The resource was disseminated through teachers and advisors conferences (Rydal (2007), Lancaster (2008), Preston (2010) Leicester (2010)), which had local, national and international delegates from Church of England schools and Diocese Boards of Education and is now used nationally.

I was able to measure the impact of the resource on school ethos and distinctiveness in my own diocese via the inspection process and I have monitored the changing attitudes of staff and the reaction of pupils through observation of acts of Collective Worship via internal and external agencies and pupil written and oral feedback.

The dissemination of the materials was also directly affected by the faith commitment of the teachers (Sage 2009). Some teachers from Anglican Secondary phase across Britain replicated the scepticism found in the original High School. This has led me to create trial materials from the folder and personally launch the resource in schools setting and subsequently enabled me to continue to reflect and research the effectiveness of the resource materials disseminated from the conferences, and to empower pupils in their personal search for the sacred.

References

Barton, D., Brown, A. and Brown, E. (1994) *'Open the Door'*. ODES Ltd and The National Society.

Copley, T. (1989) *Worship, Worries & Winners: Worship in the Secondary School after the 1988 Act*. National Society/Church House Publishing.

SACRE Blackpool (2006) *The Student Voice in Religious Education*.

Sage, H. (2007) 'Student voice and collective worship', unpublished research paper, University of Cumbria.

(Continues)

(Continued)

Sage, H. (2009) 'Corporate and collective worship: personal dilemmas in a North West Church High School', unpublished research paper, University of Cumbria.

Department for Education (2011) 'Non-statutory guidance on Collective Worship', http://www.education.gov.uk/a0064979/collective-worship.

National Society Inspections (SIAS) http://www.churchofengland.org/education/national-society/inspecting-our-schools.aspx.

Helen Sage, Board of Education, Diocese of Blackburn (2011)

Discussion

This account is different again. Like the other two we have a clear statement of *purpose*. We know why the research was carried out. But here it was conducted as an integral part of the researcher's professional role. It is concerned with *pupil voice*, and therefore dissemination is more than ever an essential element of the research process. Without dissemination there can be little *impact*, and *impact* was a key purpose here. Note that the researcher is able to tell us exactly how that impact was monitored and evaluated:

> I was able to measure the impact of the resource on school ethos and distinctiveness in my own diocese via the inspection process and I have monitored the changing attitudes of staff and the reaction of pupils through observation of acts of Collective Worship via internal and external agencies and pupil written and oral feedback.

This highlights the role of research in bringing about change. How we measure that change in terms of scale and impact will differ from context to context and will be largely dependent on our own role and opportunities for access. But what we can be certain of is that without dissemination our research is unlikely to change anything outside our own individual professional practice.

Reflective activity

Before we leave this account, look again at the two following points made by the researcher in her account, and consider the part they play in *situating the researcher* within the research she is disseminating.

1. 'The difficulty for me was a reluctance by teachers to listen to pupil voices ...'
2. 'I believed that by bypassing teacher input and empowering pupils they would design and deliver acts of Collective Worship which were relevant, pupil centred and Anglican in identity.'

Vignette 4: writing research for different audiences

I first went to a conference a year after I had begun my PhD: my supervisor and I agreed that it was important that I presented aspects of my findings, as work in progress, as soon as practicable. Presenting conference papers at the *Higher Education Close-Up* conference in 2006 and the *British Educational Research Association* (BERA) conference in 2007 gave me the opportunity to seek feedback from more experienced researchers. I received useful comments regarding my research methodologies, my use of theory and the ways in which my research questions were formed.

In 2008 I again attended the annual BERA conference, delivering a paper called: *'I don't spend hours writing lesson plans because I don't get paid to do that': problematising the validity and reliability of portfolio-based assessment in FE teacher-training*. Only a few people came to the session. It was scheduled for a Saturday morning, the last session of the conference – a graveyard slot at best. But the people who were there again provided me with much useful advice. At the session was Susan Wallace, whom I had already met as we had both written textbooks for the same publisher. She was in the process of editing a book for teacher-training students in the post-compulsory education and training (PCET) sector that was going to consist of chapters that each provided a critical analysis of a single topic. She asked if I would rewrite my paper so that it would fit in to this volume. I agreed, and at the same time as I was rewriting my research for a textbook, I revised the original paper with the intention of submitting it for publication in a journal.

Textbooks and refereed journals represent two distinct genres of academic discourse: the language register, authorial voice and style of each

(Continues)

(Continued)

is quite different from the other, and this reflects the different reader-ship or audience that they are intended for. What I thought would be a simple, and relatively quick, task of revising my initial conference paper for the textbook turned into a more extensive reorganising and rewriting of the material. At the same time, I was revising the paper for publication in a journal: I had received positive feedback from the three peer reviewers, but this was nonetheless accompanied by recommendations for further work prior to publication.

The opportunity to turn some of my research into a chapter for a textbook meant that my findings could be made available to two groups of readers. For the PGCE students, the chapter would provide them with a worked example of research relevant to their teaching practice, providing them with material to reflect on and write about. For the academic audience, the article would provide a critique of a dominant mode of assessment practice in the HE sector that necessitated further inquiry.

References

Tummons, J. (2010) 'Are lesson plans important?', in S. Wallace (ed.), *The Lifelong Learning Sector Reflective Reader*. Exeter: Learning Matters.
Tummons, J. (2010) 'The assessment of lesson plans in teacher education: a case study in assessment validity and reliability', *Assessment and Evaluation in Higher Education*, 35(7): 847–57.

Jonathan Tummons, Teesside University (2011)

Discussion

This researcher provides us with an extremely useful, first-hand explanation of how and why we need to tailor our accounts of our research to meet the needs of different readerships or audiences. His story also illustrates the 'snowball' effect that we noted in relation to the first vignette: once you begin to get your work 'out there', further opportunities for dissemination tend to present themselves. The two written pieces he references above can be read side by side as an excellent example of how *the same research* can be presented for a readership of practitioners, with an emphasis on practical and professional issues, and for an academic readership, with an emphasis on conceptual frameworks, methodological approaches and relationship with other research in the field. In presenting your work to a specific audience or readership there will also be decisions to be made over lexis (the words you select to use) and syntax (the way your sentences are structured), as well as overall structure, tone and content.

Vignette 5: disseminating research findings about support for students with Asperger's syndrome

When it comes to disseminating your research findings, I would say the first step is believing that what you have discovered is worth sharing. I had conducted a small scale piece of research on the support for students with Asperger's Syndrome studying at Nottingham Trent University as part of my MA in Education. This involved interviewing students and staff about their experiences; identifying common themes, good practice and areas of particular difficulty; linking these findings to literature and other research on the subject and making some recommendations.

I passed. I was happy. And that would have been that, if I had not mentioned I'd done the work to a colleague. They had previously organised a training session on supporting students with Asperger's syndrome in higher education; in fact, I had attended that session and it had stimulated me to do the research in the first place. They were interested in what I'd found out. I was genuinely surprised and indeed flattered when they asked me to do a 20 minute input 'slot' on their next training session on this area, sharing my findings.

In retrospect, of course they would be interested. They had helped me with my research for one thing and I was providing some up to date research in their area. In conducting any piece of research, it is highly likely you will have involved colleagues and other professionals in the process – what better way to say thank you than sharing what could well be useful material to them. Have the confidence to go back to those that helped you – and this could even include learners, perhaps – and show them the results of their support and guidance!

I would add that when sharing your findings, do remember what might be relevant to your audience. The first time I did my 20 minute input, I was keen to tell the group of fellow academics about the

(Continues)

(Continued)

'process'. What they actually wanted was to get to the point, with key findings and some recommendations for good practice. They didn't want nor need to know how I'd conducted a questionnaire! Think about what your audience will find useful.

This process helped me grow in confidence but actually getting my research published in an education journal would not have happened without encouragement from my PGCHE tutor. The effect of someone whose opinion you value saying, 'this is good – let's get it out there!', is incredibly uplifting and like public speaking, the first time is always the hardest. Seeing your work in print can really inspire you to do further research, so don't be afraid of talking to people that have been published and ask about how they got their first 'break'. Every Professor started with a single article.

Paul Drury, Senior Lecturer in Special and Inclusive Education, Nottingham Trent University (2011)

Discussion

This account helps illustrate perfectly the point made in Vignette 4 above about writing for different audiences. This researcher is addressing us as colleagues and fellow practitioners. His tone is informal and yet remains entirely appropriate, his style is accessible and his account is clear and informative. By contrast, one or two of the vignettes we've read in this chapter address us primarily as fellow academics. Their style and tone is more formal. And indeed, we are – most of us – both practitioners *and* academic researchers. This book represents one place where those two roles meet. Therefore the range of styles we've seen, from formal to less so, are appropriate in this context.

This vignette provides us with an ideal note on which to end this section of the chapter. It underlines the importance of selecting material appropriate to your audience, and adapting to their needs. It reminds us that participants need to be thanked and that sharing research outcomes with them is one way of doing this. It speaks to us about the importance of confidence and encouragement, and the inspiration derived from seeing your work in print. Above all, it tells us that the 'first step is believing that what you have discovered is worth sharing'.

Building critical research skills: activity

For each of these five researchers who have been kind enough to share their experiences with us, this chapter has provided an additional opportunity to disseminate their research. Each writes about it in a slightly different way, with different emphases and, perhaps, different agendas. The way in which we present our research – what we say and what we don't say; our formal or friendly tone; our humour or lack of it; how we position ourselves within that research – all these things will be partly determined by our audience or readership, but also by how we see ourselves and our contribution in relation to others. With this in mind, you may find it useful to reflect on what you have learnt from reading these vignettes about ways of bringing your research alive for others and engaging and holding their interest. Leaving aside the research topics for a moment, did some of these accounts engage your interest more than others? And, if so, why, and how was this achieved? Was it because it connected with a particular interest of your own, or was it something more than this? If we believe that our research has the potential to influence practice or policy in a positive way, whether institutionally or beyond, we need to give careful consideration to the manner of our presentation as well as the content.

Key points

When disseminating the results of our research we need to remember that:

- The degree of formality in style and tone should be appropriate to the context. A verbal presentation to close colleagues and a written paper for a peer refereed journal will be likely to employ different sets of language and communication skills.
- Your audience or readership will want the following key information *as a minimum*:
  - What was your research exploring and why?
  - What were your findings?
  - What did you/will you do with them?
- If you are disseminating to other researchers, you will, in addition, need to fully explain and discuss your method and methodology.
- If you are writing a paper for a professional journal or presenting at a professional conference, your emphasis is likely to be upon implications for practice. If you are writing for an academic research journal or presenting at an academic conference, you will be required to give a convincing account of your methodological approach.
- Getting your work 'out there' will usually lead to further opportunities for dissemination. You just need to take that first step.

Further reading

Thody, A. (2006) *Writing and Presenting Research*. Sage Study Skills Series. London: Sage.

CONCLUSION

Summary

This final chapter draws together the content of the preceding chapters, placing emphasis on the key themes of the book: the interdependence of teaching and research, educational research for positive change and the importance of undertaking research which is ethical, moral, systematic and rigorous and clearly situated within a credible theoretical framework.

Qualitative research in education

As we have tried to make clear in this book, qualitative research in education is a wide-ranging and complex process. Qualitative research is a 'generative form of inquiry' (Peshkin, 1993) which draws on both interpretivist and critical paradigms (Denzin and Lincoln, 2000: x). Thus, qualitative enquiry is not a thing in itself, but rather a description of a broad field of research which encompasses diverse approaches and theoretical understandings, some of which are complementary and some of which are contrasting, but all of which seek to understand rather than prove or measure. This means that, for example, you could not do a piece of research which was both case study and action research, which are contrasting and very different approaches; however, as we demonstrate in the chapters discussing those approaches, you might undertake research which fell into either of those categories and which also drew on ethnographic methodology in terms of using particular methods to observe people and phenomena.

However, as we have also illustrated throughout this book, irrespective of the approach taken and however clear and well-considered your theoretical framework, undertaking a qualitative enquiry presents many potential pitfalls and is not something to be done lightly. That said, if we are committed to the values associated with education, such as the importance of the pursuit of knowledge, respect and social justice, it is incumbent on us to work for positive change in a critical and thoughtful manner. Such change cannot take place without first understanding the phenomenon, situation or context, and subsequently exploring what might lead to improvements: thus, research and education are interdependent. A commitment to professional and ethical practice means that our research has to be – and has to be seen to be – both ethical and moral. Also from an ethical and moral perspective, we are concerned with developing understandings that might lead to positive change, so research must have a positive purpose. Finally, as well as being moral and ethical, our research must be rigorous and systematic: it is highly unethical to predicate understandings or change on research which is open to question.

Ethical and moral issues in qualitative research

Coming to terms with these complexities, together with developing an understanding of the literature in your field and the notion of a conceptual or theoretical framework, can be challenging, particularly if you are a novice researcher. It is important to be clear that, while undertaking qualitative research in an educational context can present you with many 'big' questions or issues, there are rarely any 'right' answers to these. This is particularly the case where ethical issues are posed: as we have illustrated throughout this book, these can be significant. In these situations, as we have tried to make clear, your responsibility as a researcher is to consider the situation or issue impartially, and make sure that your research practice, as you continue, is moral. Sikes and Goodson (2003: 47–8) provide a summary of what they believe moral research practice to be. They suggest that moral practice is grounded in the researcher's life trajectory and seldom originates in contemporary marketised models of education which are concerned with profit rather than issues of social justice. Further, they go on to argue that adhering to a code of ethics 'reduces moral concerns to the procedural: a convenient form of moral reductionism' and that moral research should be conducted with 'regard for the specific conditions and circumstances of each particular research context'. Reflecting on these arguments can help when you are faced with ethical or methodological problems or dilemmas, and also presents challenges. These arguments make it clear, for example, that actions such as promising anonymity to research participants do not, in themselves, guarantee ethical and moral practice. They also imply, as we have argued elsewhere in this book, that it is necessary to think about our own moral and ethical values and how they influence both our research and our professional practice.

While we have made broad arguments around the need for moral and ethical research, we have, perhaps, emphasised two particular ethical issues which are particularly relevant to educational research: those of human relationships, including power relationships, and the thorny issue of informed consent. We have also discussed ways in which these issues might be addressed, primarily through the consideration and acknowledgement of the researcher's positionality.

Relationships and power relationships

Human relationship issues are a significant consideration in educational research, where they are often entangled with or developed from, professional relationships with children, students and colleagues. As we have discussed, they can be influenced by your role as an insider/outsider researcher, by the nature of the approach you are undertaking to your research and often by the sometimes unexpected outcomes of your research which can lead you into a position where the role of researcher may come into conflict with the job you are employed to do, or leave you with competing loyalties as you uncover different pictures to those that are accepted as reality by the organisation and the people within it. Such issues can impact on existing and future professional relationships. For example, people may trust you less as a researcher than they did as a fellow professional. The potential for challenges and conflicts of this nature highlights the necessity to be conscious of the way in which different relationships and perceptions of the research process might influence the outcomes of individual studies, perhaps in terms of trust and/or conflict. This is of particular concern where power issues also form part of the relationship complexities within the research and, given the hierarchical nature of education systems and structures, power relations will invariably form part of the relationship issues you will need to consider as part of your study.

As we have suggested, the power in the researcher–participant relationship is inevitably with the researcher, who often inhabits a very different social and political context to that of the participants and in turn this can increase the oppression of the participants through specific gendered or class-based interpretations of the research process and data. This is particularly the case where other participants in the research are from traditionally oppressed groups, such as women, those with disabilities or people from specific ethnic groups with a history of oppression. Undertaking research which is moral and ethical therefore, and acknowledging these issues, might involve a rethinking of the relationship with the participants in the research, and consideration of ways in which more collaborative and empowering relationships could be engendered which would act to minimise any constraints arising from perceived or actual power dynamics.

Positionality

Achieving a more participative and empowering approach, which can be argued to be both moral and ethical, involves the acknowledgement of positionality, giving consideration to how that may influence the design of the study, the collection and interpretation of data and relationships with other participants in the research. Sikes and Goodson (2003: 48) suggest the use of interior reflexivity, arguing that this is a better 'anchor for moral practice' than any external guidelines and this is a useful approach to take as you attempt to understand and clarify the relationship between your own values, assumptions and experiences and your research practice. During this process, the researcher attempts to question their own assumptions and behaviour at each point in the process, in order to achieve a degree of 'reflexivity, or 'introspection and self-examination' (Wellington, 2000: 200), something which forms another recurring theme in this book. Griffiths (1998: 96–7) also advocates that the researcher demonstrates reflexivity about their own position and interests, and reflexivity about their own understanding and values, arguing that this approach is designed to emphasise to researchers the need to take responsibility for their own practices. However, she does sound a note of caution in her suggestion that researchers need clarity about what types of responsibility they are, in fact, able to exercise, either as an individual or a group, pointing out that 'No one is responsible for everything'.

Informed consent

Taking responsibility for one's own research practices, as Griffiths suggests, is, as we have seen, a complex and challenging process which demands not only that we examine our own values, beliefs and prejudices, but also that we give detailed, rather than merely instrumental, consideration to a whole range of ethical issues and challenges. Key among these is that of informed consent, which forms another recurring theme in this book.

Within any study it is necessary to consider the ethical implications of requesting 'informed' consent from an audience which may consist largely of student participants (of varying ages and abilities) who will be unaware of the human relationship issues arising from educational research, particularly where these are ethnographic in nature. This lack of familiarity is also likely to be the case where, for example, parents or guardians give consent for their children or for vulnerable adults to participate in a study. These participants (or parents/guardians) will, by definition therefore, be giving consent but not informed consent. While this may satisfy some ethical guidelines, in terms of conducting educational research as moral practice it is merely an instrumentalist approach which is 'a convenient form of methodological reductionism' (Sikes and Goodson, 2003: 48). We have suggested that the best way to address this dilemma is by taking a situated, reflexive approach, while bearing in mind that 'taking account of my own position does not change reality' (Patai, 1994: 67).

Interdependence of teaching and research

The centrality of values to both teaching and research is one of the many ways in which the two practices are related. Other similarities are concerns with knowledge and with learning and with the role of the professional as both a teacher and a researcher. As we have argued throughout this book, research is central to the concept of teaching as a profession which regulates, monitors and improves itself. In this context, the 'professional' in education undertakes research which is moral in both its execution and in its outcomes and which provides a critical and analytical exploration of phenomena, culture, policies and practices, thus informing ongoing knowledge generation and development of practice. In other words, research is *part* of our professional practice as teachers, rather than an addition to it.

Stenhouse (1975: 143), in his call for a research-based model of teaching, argued that the teacher could be a restricted or extended professional: part of being an extended professional involved concerns around linking theory and practice; in other words, undertaking research and contributing to making those links. More recently, the notion of a *researching professional* was proposed by Wellington and Sikes (2006: 725) in the context of people undertaking professional doctorates. In the context of this understanding, a researching professional also implies an extended professional, as the individual works to extend their own knowledge, and form new understandings and develop new practice in education through the medium of their own research, and may be applied to anyone undertaking any form of practitioner research.

These notions of the researching professional engaged in ongoing systematic enquiry which responds to the challenges and questions faced by education professionals on a daily basis illustrate the interdependence of teaching and research as part of a complex and mutually dependent set of relationships. The focus of the research activity undertaken is, inevitably, disparate, reflecting the different settings professionals work in – formal and informal, from nurseries to universities and including alternative educational provision such as that offered by professions, prisons or charities – and their particular interests and concerns which may be as disparate as issues related to identities, sexualities, gender, motivation, inclusion, teacher education or social justice, but ultimately the research will inform or contribute to the development of professional practice. This diversity is reflected in the experiences of our contributors to Chapter 12. However, the interdependence of teaching and research is perhaps most obvious in the chapter on action research. In Chapter 12, the day-to-day practice of the professional becomes both the research focus and part of its process in an ongoing attempt to make positive change and, in this way, practice is enhanced, as in Helen Sage's study around the perceptions of the value of collective worship in Anglican schools, which began as a short-term project several years ago. Acting on the outcomes, she has engaged in long-term and ongoing action research to develop and implement new resources for this area, now widely used and impacting on practice on a daily basis.

In contrast to this ongoing cycle of change and evaluation, the ethnographer is immersed in a particular setting, perhaps as an insider researcher, and seeking to explore and understand social and cultural issues and lived experiences. Taken at face value, one might ask 'How does this impact on professional practice?' However, the ethnographer is undertaking a research process argued by Hammersley and Atkinson (2007: 209) to have an immediate goal of the 'production of knowledge'. The production of knowledge and new understandings change us as individuals, and where we change, our practice as education professionals – and sometimes the practice of others – can also change and develop. This is clearly demonstrated in Chapter 12. Joanne Casser's study on the emerging sexualities of young women, which, apart from instigating academic debate around the issue, has enabled her to contribute to a consultation on the provision of sexuality education in schools in Malta, thus influencing the curriculum in a very specific way and contributing to a research-based curriculum.

Other aims of ethnography (Hammersley and Atkinson cite political aims, for example) are perceived by them to be less important. However, in the longer term, political aims such as social change can have significant outcomes and again, Casser's study is illustrative of this, as she influences changing practice in a sensitive area within a traditional society. Similarly, Jonathan Tummons's research (also in Chapter 12) exploring 'taken-for-granted' aspects of teacher education in the context of assessment and reflective practice has generated debate – some of it contentious! – and now informs practice in the critical area of teacher education, demonstrating how the practitioner who undertakes ethnographic or case study research develops deeper understandings of phenomena or situations impacting on the educational setting, thus setting the scene for pedagogic developments and further study.

Undertaking research which is systematic and rigorous

We have referred to 'sloppy' research in a number of chapters (see Chapter 6 on case study for an example of this; also Chapter 8 on ethnography and Chapter 7 on action research) and emphasised throughout the importance of undertaking research which is systematic and rigorous and positioned within a clear theoretical framework. Unless your research is systematic and rigorous, it will always be open to question and criticism as being potentially unreliable. It will also mean that any changes to practice based on it, are not truly evidence based, and this raises a whole host of ethical issues. All too often initiatives in education are introduced based on little research, questionable research or even no research at all. It only takes a few people to be influenced by such initiatives and they become common practice and taken for granted across education. A good example of this is the use of learning styles questionnaires, still much in evidence in education, at least in the UK, despite most of them having been heavily discredited in a study by Coffield et al. as long ago as 2004 as well as being subject to more recent critique (for example, see Wheeler, 2011). If such approaches have dictated a particular teaching approach for a particular group or individual, based on faulty evidence, this implies that they could have been taught in a style or way which is not going to enable those students to reach their potential in that classroom: in effect, they have been harmed. Similarly, if you change practice based on sloppy, rather than systematic and rigorous research, then you too run the risk of causing harm to your students. By implementing change based on work which is 'systematic, credible, verifiable, justifiable, useful, valuable and trustworthy' (Wellington, 2000: 14) it is far more likely that you will be successful in undertaking research which contributes to real understandings and positive change in education.

Theoretical framework

A key criterion for undertaking research which is systematic, credible and so on, is, as we have argued, the use of a clear theoretical framework for the conceptualisation of the research process and data analysis. As we have acknowledged, this can be a daunting prospect. However, the use of a set of (coherent and credible) ideas or theories will facilitate both the practical aspects of your study (as in which type of approach to use, which methods and how to implement them) as well as the theoretical in terms of undertaking processes such as data analysis and interpretation. To use an analogy familiar to most teachers and drawn from reflective practice, it is merely using a particular 'lens' to view your research. Similarly, the theoretical framework might be viewed as a map providing direction through a study, or as a thread which gives coherence to each part of the research, from the question, through the literature review, method and methodology, data analysis and conclusions. Irrespective of the analogy which best explains the meaning of theoretical (sometimes called conceptual) framework, and of the complexity or otherwise of the ideas you use, a theoretical framework is an essential component of a credible and coherent research study.

Working within such a framework is a process which will also help you to construct meaning and thus develop knowledge as your research progresses. As we have seen, it has been argued that the main purpose of ethnographic research at least is the 'production of knowledge' (Hammersley and Atkinson, 2007: 209) and we have illustrated throughout this book the multitude of ways in which the production of knowledge directly impacts on practice.

Educational research for positive change

By positive change, we do not necessarily mean the development of new and different teaching and learning strategies, for example. What we do mean is increased understandings of the situations, phenomena and people among which we find ourselves. In turn, these understandings inform our professional practice. The understandings generated in this way may be as diverse as establishing that a particular behaviour management strategy is more effective with a particular group of young children to gaining insights into the lives of older, disaffected students and coming to understand how and why they come to exert individual agency in a rejection of the conformist education culture. Irrespective of the nature of the area you have researched, you will make changes. Implementing a behaviour management strategy which you have demonstrated to be effective with your class is clearly a positive change. Others are more subtle. Gaining insights into students' lives, as in the second example, may lead you to reflect critically on your practice to ensure that you are responding to all your students as individuals, rather than as a homogenous 'disaffected' group. Treating people with more respect in this way enhances relationships and, ultimately, will improve the teaching and learning within that group: another example of positive change.

Finally ...

On our own research journeys we have both found qualitative research in education to be exciting and challenging – a real 'buzz' in our professional lives. It has provided us with new insights into everyday situations and occurrences, informed our practice and changed our thinking. We hope that you find your own journey similarly rewarding.

References 📖

Coffield, F., Moseley, D., Hall, E. and Ecclestone, K. (2004) *Learning Styles and Pedagogy in Post-16 Learning: A Systematic and Critical Review.* London: Learning and Skills Development Agency.

Denzin, N. and Lincoln, Y. (2000) 'Introduction: the discipline and practice of qualitative research', in N. Denzin and Y. Lincoln (eds), *Handbook of Qualitative Research.* 2nd edn. London: Sage.

Griffiths, M. (1998) *Educational Research for Social Justice Getting Off the Fence.* Buckingham: Open University Press.

Hammersley, M. and Atkinson, P. (2007) *Ethnography: Principles in Practice.* 3rd edn. London: Routledge.

Patai, D. (1994) 'When method becomes power', in A. Gitlin (ed.) *Power and Method: Political Activism and Educational Research.* London: Routledge.

Peshkin, A. (1993) 'The goodness of qualitative research', *Educational Researcher*, 22(2): 24–30.

Sikes, P. and Goodson, I. (2003) 'Living research: thoughts on educational research as moral practice', in P. Sikes, J. Nixon, and W. Carr (eds), *The Moral Foundations of Educational Research: Knowledge, Inquiry and Values.* Maidenhead: Open University Press.

Stenhouse, L. (1975) *An Introduction to Curriculum Design and Development*. London: Heinemann.

Wellington, J. and Sikes, P. (2006) 'A doctorate in a tight compartment: why students choose to do a professional doctorate and its impact on their personal & professional lives', *Studies in Higher Education*, 31(6): 723–34.

Wellington, J. (2000) *Educational Research. Contemporary Issues and Practical Approaches*. London: Continuum.

Wheeler, S. (2011) 'A convenient untruth'. Available at: http://steve-wheeler.blogspot.com/2011/11/convenient-untruth.html?utm_source=twitterfeed&utm_medium=twitter&utm_campaign=Feed%3A+blogspot%2FcYWZ+%28Learning+with+%27e%27s%29.

INDEX

Added to a page number 'f' denotes a figure and 't' denotes a table.